SECRETS OF SUCCESSFUL INVESTING

Also by Gordon Pape

INVESTMENT ADVICE

6 Steps to $1 Million

Retiring Wealthy in the 21st Century

*Gordon Pape's 2002 Buyer's Guide
to RRSPs*
(with David Tafler)

*Gordon Pape's 2001 Buyer's Guide
to RRIFs*
(with David Tafler)

*Gordon Pape's 2002 Buyer's Guide
to Mutual Funds*
(with Eric Kirzner)

Making Money in Mutual Funds

The Canadian Mortgage Book
(with Bruce MacDougall)

The Best of Pape's Notes

Head Start
(with Frank Jones)

Building Wealth in the '90s

Low-Risk Investing in the '90s

CONSUMER ADVICE

*Gordon Pape's International
Shopping Guide*
(with Deborah Pape)

HUMOUR

The $50,000 Stove Handle

FICTION
(with Tony Aspler)

Chain Reaction

The Scorpion Sanction

The Music Wars

NON-FICTION
(with Donna Gabeline and
Dane Lanken)

Montreal at the Crossroads

Also by Eric Kirzner

Global Investing the Templeton Way

The Beginner's Guide to Investing
(with Richard Croft)

Investments, Analysis, and Management

SECRETS OF SUCCESSFUL INVESTING

A WINNING PORTFOLIO FOR ALL SEASONS

Gordon Pape
Eric Kirzner

Prentice
Hall
Canada

A Pearson Company
Toronto

Canadian Cataloguing in Publication Data

Pape, Gordon 1936-
    Secrets of successful investing : a winning portfolio for all seasons

ISBN 0-13-062282-6

1. Investments. 2. Portfolio management. I. Kirzner, Eric, 1945–. II. Title.

HG4521.P346 2001   332.6   C2001-901236-5

ISBN 0-13-062282-6

Editorial Director, Trade Division: Andrea Crozier
Acquisitions Editor: Andrea Crozier
Managing Editor: Tracy Bordian
Copy Editor: Lisa Berland
Proofreader: Nick Gamble
Art Direction: Mary Opper
Cover Design: Gary Beelik
Author Photograph: Lorella Zanetti
Production Manager: Kathrine Pummell
Page Layout: B.J. Weckerle

1 2 3 4 5   FR   05 04 03 02 01

Printed and bound in Canada.

This publication contains the opinions and ideas of its author and is designed to provide useful advice in regard to the subject matter covered. The author and publisher are not engaged in rendering legal, accounting, or other professional services in this publication. This publication is not intended to provide a basis for action in particular circumstances without consideration by a competent professional. The author and publisher expressly disclaim any responsibility for any liability, loss, or risk, personal or otherwise, which is incurred as a consequence, directly or indirectly, of the use and application of any of the contents of this book.

ATTENTION: CORPORATIONS

Books are available at quantity discounts with bulk purchase for educational, business, or sales promotional use. For information, please email or write to: Pearson PTR Canada, Special Sales, PTR Division, 26 Prince Andrew Place, Don Mills, Ontario, M3C 2T8. E-mail ss.corp@pearsoned.com. Please supply: title of book, ISBN, quantity, how the book will be used, date needed.

Visit the Pearson PTR Canada Web site! Send us your comments, browse our catalogues, and more. **www.pearsonptr.ca**

A Pearson Company

*To our families,
with the hope of a peaceful
and secure future*

CONTENTS

PREFACE

Many people believe that there is some kind of magical formula for investing success. In reality, there isn't. The ingredients are the same as those required for success in anything else you undertake: knowledge, self-discipline, patience, and hard work.

This book is designed to provide you with the first of those four ingredients. Some might argue that it's the most important one, but we believe all are equally crucial to achieving your financial goals. Knowledge in and of itself is of little value. What is important is the practical application of that knowledge. We can provide the raw material, but you have to use it to the best effect.

We believe that everyone who applies the principles contained in this book will achieve investing success over the long term. We mean that literally: *everyone*. We say that with confidence because the advice in the pages that follow is time-tested and proven. It works. Many millionaires will attest to it.

You'll find a fair amount of numbers and formulae in these pages, but don't be put off by them. They are used to provide background for anyone who wants it. They should not be regarded as a barrier, because in fact you don't really need to know all these details. What you do need to know, and to use, are the fundamentals of portfolio-building. By the time you finish the last page, we believe you will have those.

Gordon Pape
Eric Kirzner

1

A STRATEGY FOR

ALL SEASONS

The week that followed the September 11, 2001, terrorist attacks on New York's World Trade Center and the Pentagon was one of the most traumatic that most investors now alive have ever experienced.

When the New York markets finally opened for business the following Monday, September 17, it was to a wave of sell orders that was almost unimaginable. By the time the week ended, the Dow Jones Industrial Average had suffered its worst five-day loss since the depths of the Great Depression in 1933.

Although virtually every investor was hurt, some, namely those with suitable and conservative asset mixes, fared much better than others. And therein lies one of the fundamental secrets of successful investing.

In our collective 68 years of writing, lecturing, and advising on financial topics, the investment principle that we both share and hold paramount is that of asset allocation—getting a suitable portfolio mix. Successful investing goes far beyond randomly choosing a few stocks or mutual funds and hoping for the best. You need to know which securities to select, why you're selecting them, and how to choose the combination. And you need to know how to structure your portfolio to guard against catastrophes and world-changing events. That's what this book is all about.

As recently as 30 years ago, investment choices were limited to what we now consider plain vanilla bonds, preferred shares, GICs, stocks, and mutual funds. Believe it or not, there were fewer than 100 mutual funds in Canada at that time. Even a dozen years ago there were fewer than 600. Today, there are more than 5,000 mutual funds (including all the many variations) available to the Canadian investor. As well, we've seen the creation of a host of new investment options, including exchange traded funds, income trust units (which we view as a cousin to the mutual fund), index-based securities (such as the S&P/TSE 60 iUnits that trade on the Toronto Stock Exchange), absolute return funds, hedge funds, stripped bonds, instalment receipts, clone funds, and other innovative products. Investors must now cope with an incredible range of securities, many of which are confusing and some of which will not be appropriate for most people.

As a result, many investors become so immersed in trying to decide which securities to buy that they lose sight of the plain and true fact that the key to success lies in the construction of a portfolio—not in the specific securities that go into it.

Your goal as an investor is not to select this or that security or mutual fund based on some measure of past performance. Your real goal is to build a portfolio that fits within your comfort zone, and that will meet such demanding tests as those that arise from a war, a stock market crash, or a depression. Understanding the principles of building that portfolio, and applying them rigorously, will lead to results that will meet and even exceed your long-term financial objectives. This book will provide all the tools you need to do exactly that.

Let's get down to some basics.

What Is a Personalized Portfolio?

A personalized portfolio is really the end result of an investment process. You begin with a get-to-know-yourself investment questionnaire, bringing you to an asset mix decision, which we view as the first layer of diversification within any portfolio.

When we talk about the asset mix, we are talking about the percentage of a portfolio represented by each class of investment. For example, a portfolio mix might look something like the following chart.

TYPICAL PORTFOLIO MIX

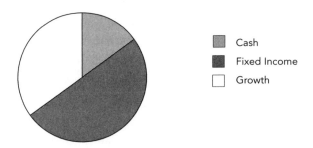

Cash
Fixed Income
Growth

There is a reason for using asset classes to describe your portfolio, and it's not because it's easier to say than: "I'm holding $40,000 of the Altamira Equity Fund, 500 shares of General Motors, $50,000 in government bonds, and $50,000 in GICs." We talk in terms of asset mix because we understand the importance that asset mix decisions play on the portfolio's overall return. Studies have shown that 85 to 90 percent of the variability of your return can be pegged to the asset mix decision. The remainder of your success depends on selecting one specific security over another (e.g., buying IBM rather than General Motors, or Microsoft rather than Nortel), and from market timing (shifting in and out of investments in response to economic changes).

In other words, by determining which percentage of your portfolio is committed to fixed-income assets, which percentage to equity assets, and which percentage to any other asset class, you have laid the basis for at least 85 percent of your total return.

Having established an asset mix, you then select individual securities or mutual funds using a process that brings four additional layers of diversification to the portfolio: geographic region, objectives, sector, and management style.

These additional layers of diversification add two major benefits to your portfolio: First, they help reduce the risk within the portfolio and second, they help make the portfolio more efficient. The litmus test for this process is really quite simple: Does the portfolio produce better than average returns with lower than average risk?

The Investing World Is Changing

What we are talking about here is a major change in the investing mindset from 20 years ago. Remember when the purchase of a mutual fund was, in itself, enough to provide diversification? It used to be that investors would look for ways to reduce their exposure to company-specific risks. Think of company-specific risk as those issues that are unique to a particular company.

An airline company, for example, is impacted by changes in of many types, from passenger loads (which fell dramatically immediately following the events of September 11) to the cost of jet fuel. Focusing on the latter point to illustrate, fuel costs are driven by changes in the price of oil. If oil prices rise, the cost of buying jet fuel rises, and the profit margins of the airline company get squeezed. When profit margins get squeezed, the value of the company's shares begins to decline. That's what we call company-specific risk.

With a well-diversified portfolio, you can reduce company-specific risk by purchasing a cross-section of companies within different industries. Keeping with our previous example, higher oil prices actually benefit oil companies. Due to our dependence on oil, there is not much elasticity in demand, so when prices rise—as long as they don't rise too much—consumers will complain, but they will still purchase the fuel, even though it is more expensive. For the oil company, profit margins expand and the stock price rises.

So here's a single issue, with very different outcomes for companies in very different industries. In theory, if you had shares of an oil company and an airline company in your portfolio, you would eliminate much of the risks associated with changes in the price of oil. Taking that theory to the next level, a portfolio of about 30 carefully chosen stocks in a cross-section of industries should reduce 95 percent of company-specific risks.

But who can afford to buy 30 Canadian companies? The cost for such a portfolio could be as high as $200,000. This is where mutual funds excel. A good-quality Canadian equity fund easily replaces a portfolio of 15 or 30 carefully chosen Canadian stocks. And, for added comfort, you get a professional portfolio manager to lead you down the right path at the right time in the business cycle (at least you hope so). But what a stock portfolio or a diversified equity mutual fund cannot do and shouldn't do is eliminate market risk.

Creating Mutual Fund Portfolios

Years ago, most people did not see market risk as a major concern and investors became complacent about their portfolios. The thinking was quite straightforward: Buy a good-quality, well-diversified mutual fund and relax.

October 1987 proved to be the first financial watershed for the baby boom generation. Before the stock market crash that year, few investors believed that market risk would ever have much of an impact on their pocketbooks. But when the Canadian stock market fell more than 20 percent in one day, so did most Canadian equity mutual funds. The plunge on Wall Street was even more dramatic. That event awakened many people to the role of diversification.

There were more shocks to follow, including the recession of the early 1990s, the Asian flu crisis of 1997, the bear market that began in the spring of 2000, and, of course, the attacks of September 11 and their aftermath.

On each occasion, investors took some time to lick their wounds but they eventually adapted and tried new approaches. Somewhere along this evolutionary investing track, the idea of building portfolios of mutual funds was born. What was the reasoning behind this approach? It's quite simple: Each fund eliminates company-specific risk, and the portfolio as a whole reduces market risk. (A portfolio can't eliminate risk entirely, mind you. But a portfolio of funds representing different asset classes and geographic areas does reduce some of the volatility attached to market risk.) It is important to keep in mind, however, that there is more to being a successful, in-control investor than simply being able to say you have pulled together a portfolio.

Yes, a portfolio of six to ten mutual funds may let you sleep comfortably at night. The challenge is to make sure each fund you choose is actually bringing some added value to the portfolio. It doesn't help much to have three funds that do exactly the same thing.

It also doesn't help if your advisor recommends a portfolio of funds but you really don't know what each fund has to offer. They may be the right choices but, without a frame of reference, you can't know for sure. This kind of uncertainty can make you question your advisor's motives. Was this or that fund recommended because your advisor earns a higher commission on it? Actually, the truth is probably more simple but in some ways more alarming. The plain fact is that some financial advisors aren't very adept at building portfolios, and the investor suffers as a result.

The Better Way

There is a better way to build portfolios, and that is to buy the best funds in each category, without regard to specific fund families. Rather than getting into the debate around index funds versus actively managed funds, pay attention to a rigorous portfolio-building process that brings together the best funds within a well-diversified format.

Will your portfolio be immune to the ebbs and flows of the business cycle? Not entirely. However, it will be as insulated as possible from economic shocks. You can rest assured that you did all you could to smooth out the fluctuations. But also important, you will have a framework for examining your advisor's recommendations. If both you and your advisor come to similar conclusions, that helps build mutual respect. Mutual respect brings with it confidence, the cornerstone of a long-term relationship.

So what's so new about this portfolio-building process? It's the realization that selecting the right portfolio involves a lot of science and some art as well. The science involves laying the foundation for making portfolio decisions; the art consists of mixing and matching within a portfolio to provide above-average, risk-adjusted performance.

Beyond Mutual Funds

There was a period in the early to mid-1990s when mutual funds were just about the only practical alternative for investors who didn't want to invest directly in the stock market. But that's all changed. Although mutual funds continue to be an important portfolio-building tool, there are many alternative products to use in constructing a portfolio that will meet your specific needs.

The bottom line is that, in today's market, we need to look beyond the base performance numbers and ask some pointed questions about the quality of the return, about the risk involved in attaining the return, and about the reasonableness of the passive alternative.

We're not suggesting you opt for the low-cost alternatives. Traditional mutual funds may be the right choice for you. But knowing that you have alternatives helps you assess a fund's quality and performance.

How This Book Will Help

We receive questions from investors every day, most of them by e-mail. The wide range of subject matters they cover makes it clear to us that many Canadians don't really understand the portfolio-building process, are confused about which securities to select, are skeptical of some of the advice they are getting, and aren't sure where to turn for answers.

We have tried to structure this book to deal with these concerns. We will provide a building-block approach to portfolio building, explain the critical elements that go into a proper plan, outline the pros and cons of various investment alternatives, discuss various important strategies, and offer some tax-management advice. Ultimately, we'll show you how take a disciplined, asset allocation–based approach to your investments.

In the process, we'll introduce you to some of the world's great investors, such as the legendary Sir John Templeton and Warren Buffett, and tell you some of their secrets. We've created a personality profile questionnaire that asks a series of questions to help establish the best asset mix for you (see chapter 6). Our questionnaire will guide you to an appropriate asset mix decision. There may be more detailed questionnaires out there, but in our experience this one has generally worked quite well. Whether you're a very conservative investor or a super-aggressive investor, you will find yourself in one of our investor profiles, which will point you to the right asset mix decision.

That's the essential starting point of your personal portfolio-building process, and it's the issue that lies at the very core of this book. But we don't stop there. You'll pick up some useful investment finance background material in chapters 4 and 5 and then learn in chapter 6 about the mental demons that affect your decision making and how to avoid them. Measuring how your portfolio is performing is the subject of chapter 7. We'll talk about the various strategies of investing in chapters 8 through 19 and then wrap up with a thorough review of some of the important and lesser-known investment vehicles such as absolute return funds and hedge funds, labour-sponsored funds, closed-end funds, royalty trusts, and unit trusts. And we'll give you a nice summary of all of the key points at the end.

By the time you've finished, you'll know all the secrets to a lifetime of successful investing. And you'll be able to ride out the inevitable shocks and strains that lie ahead, knowing that your money has been invested wisely and that your risk level is tolerable and manageable.

Wrapping Up

With a wide range of securities as well as over 5,000 mutual funds to select from, investors face a formidable array of choices. Many investors become so immersed in trying to decide which securities to buy that they lose sight of the plain and true fact that the key to success lies in the construction of portfolios. We are referring to getting the right asset mix—the proportion of safety, income, and growth securities in the portfolio.

Getting your asset allocation right is one of the fundamental keys to investing success. As much as 85 to 90 percent of your total return can depend on having the correct portfolio mix. The specific securities you select are of secondary importance.

2

SECRETS OF THE GREAT INVESTORS

Investment styles come and go. You may recall the heyday of the Altamira Equity Fund. Back in the 1980s and for the first half of the 1990s, the fund was managed by Frank Mersch, well known as a growth manager who followed a sector rotation style.

Simply stated, Mersch would make big bets on specific sectors of the economy. He would either be *really* right or *really* wrong. For a period of time he was *really* right, and money flowed into the fund at a record pace. Needless to say, other fund companies came out with their own version of the sector rotation style. However, the cycle turned and sector rotation fell out of favour. Today, very few managers practise that kind of management style. (We'll have more to say about this and other investment styles in chapter 11.)

The next hot trend was the "growth" explosion in the 1990s, with its focus on the "new economy." That period came to an end in March 2000 with the collapse of the high-tech and biotech markets.

But just as cream rises to the top, so does quality. And ultimately it is the old-fashioned, fundamentals-based investment approach as practised by the masters that predominates. And the style consistent with this is "value."

Fundamental Analysis Is the Base

The focus of value investing is on fundamental security analysis. Fundamental analysis presupposes that the information contained in financial statements, economic forecasts, and other publicly available documents provides valuable clues for assessing the intrinsic value of a security. The financial analyst estimates a firm's earnings and dividends, and then looks to see if his figures differ from the market consensus or are not currently incorporated in the market price of the security.

Value and growth investing have long represented two basic approaches to stock selection. Although definitions vary, the price/book value (P/B) and the price/earnings ratio (P/E) are often used to distinguish the two approaches. Benjamin Graham was one of the founders of modern fundamental analysis. His recommended yardstick for value investing was to focus on stocks trading at 33 percent below their tangible book value per share and 33 percent below net current asset value per share.

The great fund managers—the legends such as Warren Buffett, Sir John Templeton, and Peter Lynch—are all value-based managers.

What Do the Great Value Managers Do?

Ideally, a value manager will buy a stock for less than the break-up value of the company—the price it would fetch if all the individual components were sold. Usually, such companies have solid earnings, generally pay a dividend, and carry very little debt. Value managers buy these out-of-favour companies and wait for the rest of the market to discover what they have known all along.

Managers employing a value approach will focus on low price-to-book (P/B) and low price-to-earning (P/E) stocks. Often, these are small-cap companies. By contrast, investors looking for growth focus more on high-multiple stocks. These two styles represent interesting extremes. Value stocks are often of neglected or disliked companies that have had recent financial problems, while growth stocks are generally stocks of admired companies with strong track records. Value investing has proved to be the more intriguing and the more rewarding of the two styles in the past. A recent study reported a 3 percent per annum excess return of value stocks over growth stocks over a lengthy holding period, with the excess return a decreasing function of firm size (i.e., the small-cap value stocks had the largest excess returns).

What exactly is the value approach? The best way to describe it is to say you are buying assets, earnings, and dividends at a price below their perceived value. Call it bargain hunting, value searching, or what you will, an undervalued stock is trading for less than it is really worth. How does it get there? Academic researchers ascribe the basic premises underlying value investing to quirks (one study called these "mental demons") in investor behaviour, rather than to fundamental factors.

Behavioural studies have shown that the value world is a place where investors don't like to be! Stocks often become undervalued because they have poor track records, so people tend to be uncomfortable with them. The pattern of creating losses for investors has placed these stocks in the "fallen angel" category—a long history of losses creates distrust and distaste. The stock has disappointed investors enough times that they no longer trust it—and they shun it. Some call it a neglected stock theory—we call it the "despised stock theory."

Add to the "fallen angel" notion the observation that many "value" companies are small-capitalization firms with little public exposure, which means they are ignored by institutional investors (mutual funds, pension plans, insurance companies, etc.). This lack of mainstream retail and institutional investor demand means that the stock becomes undervalued and trades at a low P/E, low P/B, or a low price/dividend (high dividend yield.) This behavioural theory provides a plausible explanation for the finding that value stocks have tended to earn higher returns than growth stocks over the past two decades. Practitioners look at it another way.

Value investing is associated with a number of investment legends. We've mentioned Benjamin Graham, Warren Buffett, and Peter Lynch, but one of the greatest all-time exponents of the value style is Sir John Templeton. As Templeton said to one of this book's co-authors a number of years ago in an interview: "If you are building a house, developing a golf course, or running a doctor's office, you're not in a contest with anyone. But you can't buy a stock unless there's somebody willing to sell it. And because you can't buy unless somebody sells, it's likely that a year later, or five years later, *one of you will wish you hadn't done it.*" He went on to say, "Because it is a contest, and is therefore different from almost every other business activity on earth, you must not go with the majority. You can gain opportunities in investing only by doing something that the majority are against doing or something they don't know about." This parallels his oft-quoted admonition to "buy when others are despondently selling and then sell when others are actively buying." What Sir John was describing was value investing–picking stocks based on bargain levels–not growth. "You never achieve superior performance by buying what the crowd is buying."

The key principle of fundamental analysis is that you are searching for mispriced securities. An attempt is made to determine the true or intrinsic value of a security. Then the intrinsic value is compared with the security's current market price. If the market price exceeds intrinsic value, the security is overpriced. If the intrinsic price exceeds market price, the security is underpriced and a bargain. This can be expressed as a price or a yield–the result is the same.

Sir John Templeton on Value Investing

Let's examine value investing in greater depth with Sir John Templeton. In late summer 2000, Eric Kirzner made one of his periodic forays down to Nassau, Bahamas, to interview Sir John, the founder of the large and very successful Templeton family of mutual funds (now Franklin Templeton) and one of the very first portfolio fund managers to recognize the value of global investing. Although Sir John now devotes most of his time to his well-known and respected spiritual and philanthropic activities, he still retains his keen and insightful view of global investment developments.

What follows is a transcript from that interview. Anyone wishing to know the true secrets of successful investing should read it carefully.

EK: How are you feeling, Sir John? How you are spending your time today?

JT: As you know, I sold out all my activities, everything to do with business, when I was 80 years old, seven years ago, to the Franklin Group. Now I am busier and more enthusiastic and joyful than I ever was because some of the charity programs I am financing have become more beneficial.

I sold out to Franklin not because I lost interest in investment but because over the past 45 years, when I was helping people get better investment performance than they might otherwise, I found it made them happy temporarily, but it didn't make the million people in our funds happier in their home lives. And it didn't seem to be making the world a better place.

I kept asking myself for 30 years, was I in the right field? And is there something I can do to have a permanent benefit to humanity? So 30 years ago I started the first of my programs, patterning it after Alfred Nobel and how he awarded his prizes. The prizes created breakthroughs in physics, medicine, and chemistry and had an amazing effect on thousands of brilliant people doing research and hoping some day they would win a Nobel Prize. It's been a great stimulus to progress in all of the sciences. I thought at the time that giving a similar prize ("Templeton Prize") for spiritual progress would have a similar effect. I was learning that spiritual wealth was more important than monetary or physical wealth. Since the Nobel Foundation was giving five prizes, I decided to give one prize and deliberately make it larger than his prizes in order to say to the world that breakthroughs in spiritual revelation were more important. I thought the Templeton Prize would stimulate the same research as the Nobel Prizes the foundation was giving. We have been doing it for 29 years now but it has not had the effect that we had hoped for it in creating original spiritual thought. But I intend to continue.

EK: Back in 1997 you said to me that no one should have their investment assets in the country in which they lived. Do you still believe that?

JT: If your job and the success of your business depends on where you live, common sense and basic diversification means you should invest most of your assets somewhere else. If I was teaching college students, I would tell them to review their portfolios every year and make sure that at least half their assets were outside their own industry and their own nation. It's just not logical to think that all of the best investments are likely to be found in one location. If you look everywhere you will find lots of good opportunities.

EK: You, along with Benjamin Graham and Warren Buffett, are as closely associated with value-based investing as anyone in the world. Furthermore, you were one of the first to espouse global investing.

JT: I was one of the first to talk about global investing in the U.S. Over a century ago they started it in Switzerland.

EK: Value investing is not in vogue today. Do you still follow bargain hunting or value-based investing in your personal investing?

JT: Let's put it on tape. The investing world is rapidly changing. When I first became an investment counsellor in 1937, there were only 17 mutual funds on earth. And the total assets of all the mutual funds were less than one million dollars. Today, on a given day, funds still in my name can take in as much as a billion in a day. That is fantastic.

When I first started, I joined the New York Society of Security Analysts. There were only 20 members and it was the only such organization in the world. Today there are 32,000 chartered financial analysts. So methods of selecting stocks are more sophisticated and more diverse. But, and this is the key point, up to five years ago we thought that buying a share at a low price relative to earnings, assets, and dividends was the right way to do it. But beginning five years ago we had a psychological change where people stopped caring what the earnings or the dividends were. They only wanted to know whether it went up yesterday. We republished a 150-year-old book called *Popular Delusions and the Madness of Crowds*, about famous bubbles. I never imagined five years ago that people would get as wild as they are now.

I never imagined that people like Benjamin Graham and Warren Buffett and I would miss out. We are regarded as old fashioned. Why listen to anyone who is still looking at assets and dividends? Instead why not buy something that is going up more quickly?

The big question is—is this high-tech craze a bubble? I and almost everyone I know say this is a bubble—just like the South Seas or the Tulip Bulb craze. Or to make it more up to date, look at the railroad craze. When railroads came in 150 years ago, people said the world was never going to be the same—that people who put all their money in railroad shares were going to get wealthy. Well, the time to get out of railroad shares was 1855. Then we had electricity and the world was never going to be same—you can put electricity through wires and light your house without candles. Power plants were built everywhere—except that the best time to get out of electric stocks was 1910! And the same for automobiles—where the time to get out of automobile stocks was 1928. Along came the oil boom. People said God doesn't make oil very fast any more so prices are going through the roof, so you better buy oil shares. But the time to get out of oil shares was 40 years ago. Even the aviation industry—I remember in 1936 I could fly from New York to Dallas in only eight hours. People said the world would never be the same and it wasn't, but the time to get out of airline stocks was 1955. They've been poor investments since. And so on.

So now the only thing you have to do to get rich is to buy tech stocks, particularly Internet stocks, and the world is never going to be the same—everything is going to be different. But the prices have been pushed up to such levels now that I think there will be a burst. I believe it will be the biggest burst in world history. The biggest bubble up to now was the Japan bubble. After Japan opened stock markets again after the war, stocks were very cheap. We couldn't find bigger bargains anywhere in the world than Japan as early as 1962. And it just continued. We reached the stage where my mutual funds and private clients were 50 percent in Japan. But prices kept rising and they were no longer bargains. By 1985, I was totally out, albeit four and a half years too early. The bubble went on until 1989—the Nikkei Index went to 39,000. And then it fell to 13,000. And 10 years later it's only at 16,000. So that was the biggest financial bubble in world history until now. And when the tech bubble bursts, I think it will be at least as bad as Japan.

[*Author's note:* He was absolutely right. Anyone who heeded his advice and sold their technology shares would have been spared major financial loss.]

EK: What is your approach to trading? When do you sell?

JT: I would have given the same answer every day of the past! More than 50 years ago I discovered that the best time to sell something was when you found something else that had at least 50 percent better value. You estimate value of different assets. If you find a good value asset that is at least 50 percent better value than an existing asset, buy it and sell the one you own. If it isn't at least 50 percent better value, don't do anything! And that avoids all of the questions about market timing and issues like that! Allow yourself a wide margin. Some people switch when they find something with 10 percent better value. I don't do that. I look for 50 percent better value.

EK: You had a lot of success with an overweighting strategy to Japan in the 1970s and 1980s. If I'm not mistaken you have stayed out of the Tokyo market for close to a decade now. What signs are you looking for before returning to the world's second-largest market?

JT: I got out of Japan too soon. There's no magic to it. But after a lifetime of watching, I know that when any nation's market has fallen by 50 percent the lustre is gone and you are getting back to basic values instead of excitement.

EK: Last time I was here (1997), you liked Russia, Korea, India, Turkey, the Ukraine, and Brazil. Are these still some of your favourites?

JT: Eric, this is something you should put in your article. Up until two years ago—July 1998—I could always find some nation where stocks are still cheap. But in the last two years I haven't found one. I've got out of just about everywhere. I've had to change my whole method of investing and look elsewhere. There just isn't a nation today where stocks are cheap.

EK: In all of the times I've interviewed you, plus our phone conversations, that's the first time I ever heard you say anything like that.

JT: That's correct. And neither has Louis Rukeyser. He interviews me every January. And he was amazed in January when he asked me the same question as you. And I said buy bonds, buy bonds!

EK: That's a big change. In 1993 and 1997 you were opposed to putting any wealth into bonds. You said bonds should only be held as a temporary convenience.

JT: That has changed. For the first time in my life I cannot buy common shares at bargain prices. But that is temporary. What you do is buy bonds, and wait for the opportunity to buy stocks again. And to buy bargains when they are bargains—not now! I estimated that before the next century is over the Dow will rise above one million, but that is being modest.

EK: So the global bull market is over?

JT: That's a huge question. I've never been good at that. I got out of Japan four and a half years too soon, so my timing isn't the best. But I will say that it is either over or about to be over. And I'd say that chances are 50 percent that it is over already. And it could be 10 years before you see the Nasdaq where it was on the 14th of March (2000). While you are waiting, you can buy U.S. government 25-year bonds at 6 percent.

EK: Going forward, what do you consider to be a good representative rate of return for stocks in any given year?

JT: Seven percent. If you want to know where the market will be in 50 years, start in 1980 and project forward at 7 percent. Population increase has been steady but slow, inflation has been up and down but has averaged 3 percent and I expect that to continue, and productivity gains are accelerating. So when you add them all up, 7 percent for earnings and prices of shares is pretty good and that should hold on a world basis.

Look at what that gets you. Money doubles at 7 percent every 10 years. So go back to 1980 and project to 2050 and you have seven periods of 10 years. Then apply the math—2, 4, 8, 16, 32, 64, 128. So by 2050, the market will be 128 times higher than it was in 1980. In 1980, the Dow was below 1,000, so 128 times that is 128,000 relative to the 11,000 it's at today. It all depends on your starting point.

EK: I assume that you had a professional relationship with Warren Buffett over the years?

JT: No. I've read about him and he knows about me but we have never spoken. We were both students of Benjamin Graham long, long ago.

Remember, this interview took place in late summer 2000. To put the time frame in context, the technology sector had gone into a steep dive in the early spring but then had rallied during the summer, and many investors thought the worst was over and that a new bull market was under way. As it turned out, the summer rebound was only a bear market rally. After Labour Day 2000, the real plunge began, with some technology stocks losing 90 percent or more of their value, including our own Nortel Networks. Sir John predicted the collapse absolutely correctly, based on the fundamental assessment of the market he used through his career—the search for true value. It's a key lesson that every investor should always remember. Fads will always end, bubbles will always burst. True value will always remain.

Also note that he recommended a switch to bonds at that point. Anyone who took that advice would have done very well, and it points to another important investing secret that we will underline repeatedly in this book: the need for a balanced approach that includes both equity and fixed-income components.

The High Dividend Effect

One of the most overlooked ways to generate healthy returns in the market is to seek out high-yielding common shares of medium- to high-quality corporations, particularly if those companies are expected to raise their dividends over time.

This strategy is very popular with the "value" experts and is based on the so-called High Dividend Effect, a finding that higher-dividend common shares have a tendency over the long run to outperform those with lower yields or no dividends at all. Benjamin Graham showed that investors have earned higher returns by concentrating on stocks with above-average dividend yields rather than seeking out lower-yielding growth issues. Furthermore, global support for the Dividend Effect was provided in a 1991 research study, which showed that investing in global markets with the highest yields provided the highest risk-adjusted returns, implying that global investors can achieve larger returns by investing in foreign markets with above-average dividend yields.

What are the factors that create a favourable dividend yield to start with? There are a few different situations that can lead to this outcome.

One is the "Fallen Angel" phenomenon we have already mentioned, when a stock's price drops because the company (or even the entire industry) has fallen out of favour with investors. However, if the distressed company continues to pay its usual dividend, then the yield on the shares rises as a result. Such a situation can create a great investing opportunity. If the company's credit rating remains strong in spite of the price pullback, and other business factors are also stable, the stock should return to its former price and yield levels. That will generate a high total return for those who bought at the lows.

A second possibility is that a company with a long and solid track record of high percentage dividend payments may not be attractive to investors who are interested in growth rather than income. Of course, as you've seen, these investors are missing the point when they avoid such companies—but that's to your advantage!

High dividend-paying common shares have a useful position in most investment portfolios. They help the diversification process and they can significantly augment your returns as well.

In general, for high-yield selections we like companies that meet the following criteria:

1. They have dividend yields at least twice that of the average yield on the blue-chip Toronto 35 Index.

2. The recent P/E ratio is within 80 percent of the yield on AAA-rated bonds.

3. The return on equity (ROE) is 10 percent or higher. ROEs of less than 10 percent are generally indicative of mediocre or poor financial performance.

4. The firm's credit rating is BBB or better. The high-dividend strategy focuses on the high dividend yield effect. Avoid low-credit-rating companies that might carry a financial or default risk.

Wrapping Up

Value investing is the search for undervalued securities and is the style used by the legends in portfolio management. Their lessons are:

1. Look to buy assets, earnings, and dividends at a price below their perceived value.

2. Hold stocks of good companies that are currently out of favour.

3. Trade infrequently as delineated in the "buy good companies and hold them forever" approach—the motto of Warren Buffett.

To follow the "value" approach of the experts you don't have to buy individual securities. You can look for the top mutual fund managers (such as AIC's Michael Lee-Chin or Mackenzie's Peter Cundill) that employ the Benjamin Graham bargain-hunting approach. Lots of choices are available.

3

UNDERSTANDING
ASSET CLASSES

Whether you are a retail investor with a $20,000 portfolio or a high-net-worth individual with savings of $5 million, your ultimate investment objective should be the same: to determine the appropriate target mix for you among the various investment classes.

This objective is commonly called *strategic asset allocation*. Don't let the designation scare you—it is simply a term for asset mix. But it represents the most important of all the investment decisions. Securities and portfolios contain what is called *systematic risk* (economy-wide risk, such as changes in interest rates or a change in fiscal policy) and *unsystematic risk* (risk related to an individual security, such as winning or losing a new contract or a change in labour costs). The objective of an asset allocation strategy is to design portfolios that not only have relatively high expected returns but also have only moderate systematic risk and virtually no unsystematic risk.

Why Asset Mix Is So Important

Imagine a cake baked with four cups of flour and ten pounds of sugar. Even those with a sweet tooth would find that a little rich! Unfortunately, we often find investors willing to mix their assets with the same approach to taste as our imaginary baker.

We think in terms of four major financial asset classes: cash, fixed income, equities, and specialized (which includes real estate, absolute return assets, commodity-linked assets, and a host of others). Although these classifications are convenient and describable, they are in reality blurred since many security types in a class have characteristics that overlap with other classes. For example, corporate bonds are affected not only by changing interest rates but also by the changing financial position of the underlying company (and hence its perceived ability to pay principal and interest on its bond obligations). Stock prices, on the other hand, are influenced by other factors than just earnings and growth prospects. For example, interest rates affect stocks, both by changing interest rates on P/E multiples and by impacting the firm's earnings.

Nevertheless, asset classes have specific return/risk characteristics that are reflective of their investment nature. Think of the asset classes as the "ingredients" of your portfolio. Just as with our imaginary cake, choosing the right recipe quantities, or asset mix, is the most important decision you and your financial advisor will make.

Asset allocation allows for meaningful performance measurement. An asset allocation policy such as a 20/30/40/10 mix among cash/income/equity/specialized investments is transparent and allows for performance measurement. Without a clear policy, you cannot set goals and measure performance against them. Remember, a basic principle of finance is that "what gets measured gets managed."

Asset Mix Ingredients

To get the right asset mix you first have to know and understand the ingredients—cash, fixed income, and equities. Here they are.

Cash

First, we have cash—clearly the lowest-risk asset in a portfolio. Cash and cash equivalents are generally short-term debt securities that are highly liquid and marketable. Cash and equivalents are usually defined as securities maturing in a year or less. They are normally issued and traded in large denominations of $100,000 minimums, although job lots of Treasury bills ($5,000 mini-mum) and money market funds are available for retail investors. Some products, such as Treasury bills, are pure discount securities, i.e., they are sold at a discount to mature at par value. Others, such as Certificates of Deposit, are pure yield securities.

Cash investments are as close to a risk-free investment as you can get, since they have little or no credit risk and very little interest rate risk because they are short-term investments. Cash and cash equivalents are designed to provide nominal capital preservation and liquidity for portfolios. They are generally good short-term interest rate hedges since they keep pace with short-term interest rate changes.

CASH SECURITIES AND PRODUCTS

Canadian-dollar denominated: Treasury bills, Canada Savings Bonds, money market mutual funds, Bankers' Acceptances, Certificates of Deposit and Bearer Deposit Notes, commercial and finance paper, Eurodollar time deposits, repurchase agreements (repos), reverse repurchase agreements, global money market funds.

U.S.-dollar denominated: U.S. Treasury bills, U.S. dollar money market funds.

Other foreign currency denominated: foreign currency–denominated money market funds.

We usually use money market funds as cash assets within a portfolio. Money market funds simply invest in short-term government Treasury bills or corporate notes. The yield on such funds is equivalent to the yield on the short-term cash investments they make, minus the management expense ratio (MER)—which in Canada, typically ranges between 50 basis points (0.50 percent) and 100 basis points (1.00 percent) annually. The aim for money market funds is usually to maintain a fixed net asset value (NAV) per share, usually at $10 per unit (occasionally $1.00 per unit). However, the fixed NAV isn't guaranteed—under extremely unusual circumstances, such as a sudden and large spike in interest rates, a fund manager might be unable to maintain the NAV at $10. However, there have only been a few such isolated cases in Canada and never with a mainstream mutual fund.

Canada Savings Bonds fall into the cash category because they have a fixed face value and are redeemable at any time. However, we classify Canada Premium Bonds as fixed-income securities because they are only cashable once a year. That makes them similar to GICs, which can only be cashed at maturity.

Because cash has a fixed value as an investment, it provides a stabilizing influence on your total portfolio despite its relatively low yield.

Fixed-Income Investments

We think of the fixed-income asset class as income producing, generally less volatile than equity assets, and, at times, capable of producing better-than-average capital gains. Those capital gains are generated by changes in the level of interest rates. When rates are falling, as they were for much of the 1990s, bond prices—and the value of bond funds—rise, producing capital gains. On the other hand, when interest rates are rising, bond prices fall, along with the value of your bond fund. We saw this in 2000 when central banks pushed up rates in an effort to slow what was then seen as an overheated economy.

Think of this relationship as the bond price–interest rate teeter-totter. Interest rates are an important consideration when building a portfolio. Rising interest rates not only have a negative impact on bond prices, they can also push down the value of equities (and, of course, equity mutual funds).

Fixed-income assets are designed to provide nominal capital preservation and liquidity for portfolios and to generate periodic income cash flow for spending or reinvestment.

Fixed-income products range from the lowest-yield, highest-quality government bonds to very high-yield, low-quality securities such as junk bonds. Although there is a wide range of products in this category, they are all subject to the following general guidelines:

- The longer the term to maturity, the greater the interest rate sensitivity.
- The higher the quality, the greater the interest rate sensitivity.

- The lower the coupon, the greater the interest rate sensitivity.

- The longer the duration, the greater the interest rate sensitivity.

FIXED INCOME SECURITIES AND PRODUCTS

Government, provincial, municipal, and corporate bonds; stripped bonds; low-quality, high-yield corporate bonds; bond mutual funds; mortgages, mortgage-backed securities, mortgage mutual funds; foreign-currency denominated bonds, eurobonds, global bond funds; preferred shares, deferred preferred shares; income component of split shares; real return government bonds; guaranteed investment certificates; Canada Premium Bonds.

Equity Investments

When we think of equities, we think of assets that are designed for long-term growth, that tend to be more volatile, that usually lead the performance parade, and, generally speaking, that do not provide much in the way of income. If you own shares of an equity mutual fund, you own an equity asset. It's the same if you own shares of BCE, General Motors, or IBM, although, as we have seen, individual stocks expose the portfolio to company-specific risks. Equities are primarily designed for capital growth and only secondarily for dividend income.

Equity securities are usually subdivided into domestic and foreign, and further subdivided into small-, medium-, and large-capitalization investments. Small-capitalization companies are usually defined as those with market values under $100 million, and medium-capitalization companies are those with market values of $100 million to $500 million. The usual definition of large capitalization is companies with market values of $500 million or more. The large-cap category includes common shares in major companies and investment funds specializing in such stocks. Large-cap companies are generally less volatile than small- and medium-capitalization firms. Based on quoted market values, the companies that comprise the institutional investor–based TSE 100 Index have quoted market values of $500 million and up.

Equity investments also include index products whose value is tied to the performance of a specific market index. Sometimes they are distinguished by style as well, with *value* equities representing companies deemed to be under-valued based on their assets and current earnings, and *growth* equities being shares in companies that are expected to show above-average growth based on future earnings potential. The high-tech boom of the mid- to late-1990s represented one of the most dramatic growth-oriented investment periods in history. When the bubble burst in March 2000, the growth period came to at least a temporary end. See chapter 11 for more insight into the importance of investment style.

Index-linked products are designed to track market indexes. Index partici-pation units, such as "i60" traded on the Toronto Stock Exchange, generally track indexes more closely than indexed investment funds, which generally underperform their benchmark due to management expenses, cash drag (the time differential between new money being received and invested), and track-ing error.

GROWTH SECURITIES AND PRODUCTS

Common shares, equity mutual funds (Canadian, U.S., and global), sector funds, exchange traded index funds (such as the i60s pegged to the S&P/TSE 60 Index), index mutual funds, American Depositary Receipts (ADRs).

Specialized Assets

Specialized assets include securities that are hybrid products (i.e., have both debt and equity features) or that otherwise are not easily classified in a partic-ular category. The specialized category also includes securities that hedge against inflation. One key diversification principle is purchasing-power protection—holding assets that guard against unfavourable inflation rate movements. Gold and real estate are still considered the ultimate hedge assets. Gold was an inflation hedge asset in the 1970s at a time when unantic-ipated inflation and interest rate movements prevailed. Gold also acted as a deflation hedge in the 1930s when the Federal Reserve Board attempted to support the banking system by raising the price of gold from $20 an ounce to $35 an ounce. Although subject to sometimes severe short-term swings (as investors discovered in 1991), real estate has over the long run been a suitable inflation hedge as well. This category also includes hedge and absolute return funds that are designed to have zero or very low co-movement with cash, fixed-income, and equity securities.

These products are so varied that generalization is impossible. However, a common characteristic is that they have often have low correlation with the core fixed-income and equity portfolio.

SPECIALIZED SECURITIES AND PRODUCTS

Real estate, real estate investment trusts (REITs), royalty trusts, gold, inflation-linked products, commodity-linked bonds, convertible bonds, hedge funds, absolute return funds, hedge pooled funds, speculative pooled funds, structured notes, commodity funds

---

Derivatives

We should mention one additional category: derivatives. Although derivative securities aren't really an asset class in their own right, investors and fund managers can use them to enhance income, reduce portfolio risk, replicate security classes (synthetic investing), buy strategically, adjust portfolio tactics, and adjust portfolio dynamics. Derivatives are securities whose value is derived from the value of some other underlying asset, typically the current price of a common share. For example, a call option is a contract that allows the holder the right to buy a specified number of common shares of a company at a set price over a particular time period. We'll show you a valuable application of derivatives in chapter 22.

The Asset Mix

We introduced the concept of asset mix in chapter 1, where we told you that studies have shown that 85 to 90 percent of your overall return can be related directly to this basic decision. To be more specific, a well-known and oft-cited study published in 1986)[1] indicated that the actual asset allocation selection

---

[1]Gary P. Brinson, L. Randolph Hood, and Gilbert L. Beebower, "Determinants of Portfolio Performance," *Financial Analysts Journal*, July/August 1986, pp. 39–44.

accounted for 93.6 percent of the variation in returns on very large investment portfolios. Other studies have supported this finding, concluding that the asset allocation decision, rather than the security selection and market timing decisions, had the greatest impact on total portfolio return and the variability of that portfolio return. Another 5 to 10 percent comes from market timing (shifting in and out of investments in response to economic changes). The remainder of the performance result arises from the choice of one specific security over another.

Let's look at an illustration of how asset allocation works. Consider a hypothetical portfolio that has only two components: the BC Canadian Equity Fund and the AG Canadian Bond Fund. The first represents your equity assets, the second your fixed-income assets.

For the 10-year period ending December 31, 2001, assume the BC Canadian Equity Fund averaged 14.8 percent a year. A $10,000 investment made on January 1, 1991, would have been worth $39,757.48 a decade later.

The AG Canadian Bond fund also has a decent 10-year track record, returning 9.2 percent, compounded annually. A $10,000 investment in the AG Canadian Bond Fund made in 1991 would have grown to $24,111.62 by the end of December 2001.

Now we are going to mix and match these two assets in a homegrown portfolio. Think of it as our version of investment taste testing. We'll use the table below to examine a number of variations on this theme, giving you a closer look at the importance of asset mix decisions.

THE IMPORTANCE OF ASSET MIX

	BC CAN. EQUITY	AG CAN. BOND	COMPOUND RETURN	VALUE OF $10,000
Portfolio A	100%	0%	14.80%	$39,757.48
Portfolio B	80%	20%	13.68%	$36,628.31
Portfolio C	60%	40%	12.56%	$33,499.14
Portfolio D	50%	50%	12.00%	$31,934.55
Portfolio E	40%	60%	11.44%	$30,369.96
Portfolio F	20%	80%	10.32%	$27,240.79
Portfolio G	0%	100%	9.20%	$24,111.62

Forget for the moment that either fund would have produced decent risk-adjusted returns over the last 10 years. In this taste test we are simply looking at what happens when different weights are applied to each asset within the portfolio.

If, for example, you used Portfolio D–50 percent BC Canadian Equity and 50 percent AG Canadian Bond–you would have locked in a base return of 12 percent without ever having selected a single security. Your $10,000 investment in January 1991 would have almost tripled to $31,934.55 by the end of December 2001.

Perhaps rather than holding a 50/50 split between these two funds, you decided to practise some nimble trading, say by buying and selling the funds at different points in the business cycle. You might add value, assuming your timing was right on and your pocketbook could withstand the tax implications of switching in and out of funds. But just how much added value? One percent compounded annually? Two percent compounded annually? The question is whether it is worth the effort. If you simply shifted your asset mix up a couple of notches, from portfolio D to portfolio B, you would have added 168 basis points (1.68 percentage points) in compounded annual return. That one decision made 10 years ago would most likely have had as much impact on your end result as shifting in and out of funds along the way.

And there's more. The incremental return that comes from the right asset mix decision goes beyond year-over-year excess returns. That's because returns compound over time. The value of the $10,000 invested in portfolio B is worth 14.6 percent more than portfolio D at the end of the 10-year period. If those returns remained consistent over the next 10 years, portfolio B would be worth $138,080, compared with $108,101 for portfolio D. That's a difference of $29,979, which means that portfolio B would then be worth 27.7 percent more than portfolio D after 20 years.

The difference in performance is the direct result of one asset mix decision made at some point in the distant past. The point is, even modest changes in your asset mix can lead to significant changes over the life of your portfolio.

Why Mix and Match?

One other issue about asset mix needs to be addressed. From the table above, we see that the best of our hypothetical portfolios is the one that has 100 percent of the assets invested in the BC Canadian Equity Fund.

That's really not surprising. Over the long term, higher-risk equity assets tend to outperform fixed-income assets, which in turn tend to outperform risk-free cash assets. So here's the question: If the investor has a long time horizon and we know that over long periods higher-risk assets produce better returns than lower-risk assets, why not simply put all your eggs into the equity fund basket?

It's a valid question, and for those who can withstand the risk it could in fact be a justifiable approach. But we don't recommend it. The problem is that investors don't work that way. There's a reason for trying to ascertain how much volatility you can withstand in your portfolio. If a portfolio is too volatile, you may sell too soon, and you usually sell at the bottom of a cycle. If you leave the party too early, it doesn't help you to know that equity assets tend to outperform over the long haul–you won't be there to reap the rewards. We mix and match portfolios to help smooth out the volatility. Our considerable history in this business tells us that investors only stay for the long term when they are comfortable with the ride. So think of the asset mix decision as your opportunity to test drive a portfolio at a speed that will help you sleep at night. A very low-risk asset mix might include 20 percent equities, 50 percent bonds, and 30 percent cash. More speculative investors might choose a spicier mix–say 20 percent bonds, 70 percent equities and 10 percent specialized.

And don't forget that Canadian equity, Canadian bonds, and Canadian money market funds are only three potential ingredients in your portfolio. Your ideal portfolio might include U.S. and international equity funds, perhaps a global bond fund, and even, under the right conditions, some individual stocks. Think of portfolio building as a process, where we arrive at the portfolio based on an examination of our investment personality.

This approach has to be better than what many Canadian investors are doing, which is focusing on security and/or fund selection based on past performance, to the exclusion of all other considerations. The result is predictable: an asset mix that has been determined by default, not by design. This means that 85 percent of your return will be determined without your conscious control, which we believe is a recipe for disappointment.

Wrapping Up

The various asset classes include cash, Canadian and foreign fixed-income securities, Canadian and global equities, and derivatives. Getting a suitable mix among those classes is what the principle of diversification is all about. By diversifying among all of the asset classes you reduce the potential volatility of your portfolio while enhancing your long-term potential returns.

The asset allocation approach, in our opinion, is the right way to go about portfolio building. In order to build a suitably diversified portfolio, you have to understand the nature of the various asset classes and know how to combine them into an appropriate asset mix for your specific needs. You'll learn how to put this process into action in chapter 7.

4

PUTTING INVESTING PARADIGMS TO WORK FOR YOU

Investment finance has undergone a spectacular metamorphosis over the past 50 years. New paradigms of investing and decision making have emerged and are now widely used by analysts, investors, and their advisors. Our investment choices and the decisions we make are based on these new paradigms of investment finance.

Some of this information may seem rather complex at first glance. But as you read through this chapter, you'll develop a basic understanding of how these new paradigms work and how you can apply the secrets they contain to your personal investing strategies.

Paradigm #1: Modern Portfolio Theory

Harry Markowitz is the founder of modern asset allocation principles. Markowitz's 1952 work on portfolio theory established both the principles and the mathematics of portfolio diversification. In a nutshell, what Markowitz's Modern Portfolio Theory (MPT) showed was that investors who diversify achieve better long-term investment performance results than those who don't.

Markowitz's Nobel Prize–winning work provided new insight into why and how diversification works. This, in turn, led to a new understanding of how stocks are priced individually, as well as how they are priced relative to a market portfolio.

The fundamental principle of diversification was eventually converted into modern asset-allocation techniques—and you need to do the same if you are to be a successful investor. Every asset allocation pie chart turned out by financial institutions and by financial planners today owes its origin to MPT.

The Capital Asset Pricing Model

William Sharpe, John Lintner, and Jan Mossin extended Markowitz's work into a theory called the Capital Asset Pricing Model (CAPM), which provides a methodology for pricing risky assets. The CAPM measures the relationship between the rate of return on a risky security or a risky portfolio and that of a representative market index. A resulting single measure, called *beta*, estimates the asset's or the portfolio's return relative to the return on a market index.

A security or portfolio that moves proportionately and in lock-step with the market is said to have a beta of 1.0. If, for example, the rate of return on a market index such as the TSE 300 Composite Index is 8 percent, then a portfolio with a beta of 1.0 is also expected to return 8 percent. High beta securities and portfolios (betas greater than 1.0) are normally more volatile than the market index and are expected to provide higher returns than the market when the market rises and lower returns than the market when it falls. These are called aggressive securities or portfolios. For example, a security with a beta of 1.5 would be expected to return 12 percent when the market index rises by 8 percent and to fall by 12 percent when the market index falls by 8 percent. Low beta securities and portfolios (betas less than 1.0) are less volatile than the market and are expected to provide lower rates of returns than the market when the market rises and larger rates of return than the market when the market drops. These are called defensive securities.

Betas are calculated using past security and portfolio data and hence are simply estimates of future relationships. In fact, betas for individual securities are quite unstable over time, although portfolio betas do display reasonable consistency.

The CAPM caught on quickly with the investment community, and today analysts use beta estimates as a matter of course. Now beta is an everyday word in the investment world.

The primary purpose of diversifying a stock portfolio is to eliminate the unique risk associated with each individual security, leaving the overall portfolio subject only to the "systematic risk" associated with the market itself. In other words, given a properly diversified portfolio and a stable market, the risk of a loss due to weakness in one individual security should be offset by the potential for gains by other portfolio holdings. Only when the entire market declines should the systematic risk become apparent in the portfolio's performance. How well a portfolio performs relative to a target index—its incremental return—depends on how much of the risk in each individual asset gets reduced through diversification.

You will find an understanding of both diversification and betas essential in determining your investment policy. That's because asset-allocation strategies embody the theories underlying both. Diversification is designed to reduce or eliminate the unique risk associated with individual securities, while asset mix reduces exposure to interest-rate, exchange-rate, and inflation risks. Thus, truly efficient asset allocation means creating a diversified portfolio of securities that react differently to various market and economic events and do so to varying degrees.

Implications of Modern Portfolio Theory

If you adhere to Modern Portfolio Theory, you focus your efforts on getting the right strategic asset-allocation mix rather than concentrating on security selection and market timing. Your asset-allocation decisions will have a far greater impact on your total portfolio return and will also help reduce the variability of your portfolio relative to your target index.

Paradigm #2: Efficient Markets Theory

The term "random walk" was first used in *Nature* magazine in 1905 in a scientific context. It referred to the observation that, under a microscope, the movement of particles followed no discernible pattern. It may seem a bit of a stretch, but this concept was in fact the foundation for the theory of how security prices move.

A number of academic papers published in the 1950s and 1960s documented a seemingly random characteristic of common share price changes, reporting that stock price patterns may not be distinguishable from randomly generated patterns, consistent with the notion of a random walk.

Originally labelled the Random Walk Theory, the modern name is now the Efficient Markets Theory (EMT). The EMT reflects the thrust of a large number of studies, all of which provided strong evidence that current stock prices reflect both past information (such as a history of stock price changes) and currently available public information (such as a company's financial statements). A modified statement of the theory is that security prices reflect all information after a set of active investors expends resources to ensure this result.

The EMT contends that you cannot expect to earn excess profits by employing conventional analytic techniques using information available to all. For example, an EMT proponent would say you shouldn't expect that analyzing patterns in security price changes would allow you to identify undervalued securities. Therefore, if you believe the EMT hypothesis, you would not accept technical analysis as a valid stock selection approach.

The first set of EMT studies focused on stock price movements themselves. The studies indicated that security prices seemed to behave in a manner similar to a fair roulette wheel, where each outcome is independent of the past. (If a roulette wheel is fair, then knowledge of recent outcomes—notwithstanding the protestations of the "system players"—will not be of any value in predicting the results of the next spin of the wheel.) The analogy to stock prices is that the past has no influence on the future and therefore cannot be used to predict upcoming price movements.

Ultimately, the question is: Based on all available information, does the market price of a security represent its true investment (or "intrinsic") value? If you believe the market is efficient, then you must accept the EMT's implication that the price does represent the security's true value–i.e., that securities are properly priced and therefore do not have expected risk-adjusted excess returns. This means that you cannot expect to earn higher returns than are appropriate for the risk of the security. Any excess returns will be deemed to be mere serendipity, due strictly to unexpected and unpredictable events and not to security analysis. For example, an investor might analyze the shares of Barrick Gold Corporation and conclude that they are undervalued at $25. Efficient markets theorists would argue that the investor's expected return on Barrick Gold is no different from its long-run expected average of, say, 9 percent per annum. If in fact the investor realizes a return of 20 percent over the next year, it would be attributed to sheer luck and not to stock selection.

Forms of EMT

Of course, the concept of market efficiency isn't quite that simple. The EMT actually comes in three forms—weak, semi-strong, and strong.

The weak form of EMT holds that security prices fully reflect past information (such as historical security price movements and trading volume). It has been tested in numerous ways, ranging from simple filter tests to more complex statistical studies. Researchers consistently found the following:

- Past price changes in securities provided no clues as to future movements.

- The size and direction of future stock price changes could not be predicted from the size and direction of past movements.

Stated another way, weak-form studies repeatedly found that analysis of the past cannot provide a profitable trading strategy.

The semi-strong form deals with publicly available information (such as financial statements and economic forecasts) and whether security prices fully reflect this information. Studies indicate in general that security prices efficiently adjust to new information and events. In other words, superior security returns cannot be achieved through fundamental analysis alone.

The strong form states that security prices reflect all information, including monopolistically controlled and specialized data. In other words, the strong form is said to be incompatible with both insider-trading profits and excess returns earned by active fund managers.

Tests of the EMT over the past five decades have generally supported the weak and semi-strong forms, as well as the strong form with respect to mutual fund managers, but not with respect to insiders.

However, there is some contradictory evidence. In 1981, Yale economist Robert J. Shiller published some research detailing his exhaustive examination of security prices and dividend payments spanning the period 1871 through 1979. He found a strong divergence between the market price of the S&P 500 and the Dow and the present value of the two indexes. Since a security is supposed to equal the discounted present value of future dividends, he concluded that stock prices did not fully reflect information. Adding fuel to the non-efficiency camp are the so-called anomalies that have been uncovered since the late 1970s. These oddities provide both negative implications for the EMT and positive encouragement for investors who prefer to seek out active trading opportunities and to place individual stock bets. Probably the most important anomaly is the "Small-Firm Effect," which is based on findings that securities of smaller companies have higher returns than those of their larger counterparts. One mammoth study, spanning returns over nearly 60 years, found that small stocks outperformed the S&P 500 Index by about 5.8 percent per annum.

The "Small-Firm Effect" is probably also related to the so-called "Neglected-Stock Effect," which documents the higher-than-expected returns on stocks that lack popularity with large institutions or are not widely followed by investors. (Some institutional managers are not allowed to invest in smaller-cap stocks.) Part of this phenomenon is explained by risk—smaller firms are more volatile than their larger counterparts, and are therefore capable of producing higher returns.

Other important anomalies include the "Low P/E Multiple Effect," a finding that securities with low price-to-earnings (P/E) multiples tend to yield higher returns than expected; the "Day-of-the-Week Effect," which indicates that stock returns and prices on average are lowest on Mondays and highest on Fridays; and the "End-of-the-Year Effect," an apparent tendency for securities, particularly those of small firms, to, on average, yield lower returns in December and higher returns in January. The seasonal pattern has been linked to tax-loss selling and to "window dressing" by fund managers, who may be shedding small-cap stocks in December and buying them back in January. Small firms also outperform large firms in January, and the "End-of-Year Effect" may be an extension of the "Small-Firm Effect."

Some 45 of these trading and pricing anomalies have now been documented. These seeming exceptions to the EMT provide grist for the view that superior investment analysis and investigation can yield positive returns. However, even though these peculiarities are well supported, the associated abnormal returns are not typically high enough to allow an investor to develop a profitable trading strategy after factoring in commissions and other trading costs.

An important observation that puts support for efficient markets theory in perspective is that of selection bias. What would you do if you perfected a foolproof method of picking stocks? Would you publish it, or keep it to yourself? Unless you're looking for a Nobel Prize in economics, you'd probably keep it a secret. Assuming most other people would behave in the same way, the best stock-selection methods are probably not published. This, in turn, implies that studies that examine analytical performance may be focusing on inferior stock-selection models—i.e., that researchers are not granted access to the methods used by really superior stock pickers. This so-called selection bias may account, at least in part, for how surprisingly strong support for the random walk theory really is.

Implications of Efficient Markets Theory

If you believe the markets are efficient, then your only acceptable investment strategy is to adopt a passive approach. However, if you doubt the validity of the EMT, you may prefer to opt for an active strategy. Be aware, however, that rejecting the EMT is not, in itself, sufficient cause to abandon a passive strategy. Even if you can select a superior stock based on active research, it still takes a lot of work—and you must be able to repeat the process over and over in order to build a complete and effectively diversified portfolio that will consistently outperform your target index. Very few investors are capable of this.

Therefore, you may wish to emulate the technique used by many pension funds and money managers, which is to use a blended approach that involves index-based products in conjunction with actively selected securities and/or actively managed mutual funds.

Paradigm #3: The Gambler's Ruin Principle

One reason so few individuals succeed in active portfolio management is the "Gambler's Ruin Principle," which refers to the problem of selecting the right idea, but utilizing the wrong implementation strategy.

For example, the Mexico Bolsa as measured by the bellwether General IPC index recorded a dramatic rate of return of over 80 percent in the calendar year 1999. An investor who bought a well-diversified Mexican mutual fund or a Mexican index product, such as Mexico iShares, would have matched or come close to matching the Mexican index. However, an investor who selected weaker individual Mexican stocks or poorly performing mutual funds could have recorded a gain well below that on the index. Thus, even though you might have anticipated the Mexican rally, you would have under-performed someone using a passive (index) approach because you chose the wrong investment vehicles or selected the wrong mix of stocks (perhaps over-weighting in weak sectors).

Implications of Gambler's Ruin

The principle of Gambler's Ruin demonstrates the necessity to identify and clearly focus on a particular strategy. If you want to invest in Mexico because you have formulated positive views on the country's economic outlook, then you should buy a Mexican index product. However, if you want to invest in undervalued Mexican securities because you believe that will give you a comparative performance advantage, then you should focus on a strategy of selecting individual Mexican stocks.

Paradigm #4: Global Investing Really Works

Despite the various economic, currency, and political crises (such as the September 11 terrorist attack or the Asian Flu economic crisis of 1997) that afflict parts of the globe at any given time, a well-diversified global portfolio will outperform a strictly Canadian one in the long run, based on both return and volatility.

Bruno Solnik's classic article on global investing (published over 25 years ago) was right on the money. Solnik demonstrated that a high degree of the variance in stock indexes is due to the unique risk of each country and can therefore be diversified away in an international portfolio of securities. He concluded, "The gains from international diversification are substantial. In terms of variability of return, an international well-diversified portfolio would be one-tenth as risky as a typical security and half as risky as a well-diversified portfolio of U.S. stocks (with the same number of holdings)."[1]

What Solnik really showed us was that Markowitz's Modern Portfolio Theory was right—diversification is a good thing, and global diversification is even better!

Why does global investing work? The massive surge of technological advances is making the world smaller and blurring communication barriers. The Internet has created an information flow explosion that was absolutely unforeseen two decades ago. If you are skilled at using the Net you indeed have the world at your fingertips. You can participate in a global discussion group, pick up information about the best restaurants in Vienna, and get quotes on Hong Kong stocks with a single keyboard stroke. There is little doubt that in the future there will be direct trading access to virtually all world markets from your home video screen (or whatever replaces a screen) and through the next generation of Internet-type networks.

Yet despite the explosion of telecommunications and information and the increased mobility of capital, we still live in a fragmented, segmented real world. Economic and political systems vary widely and geographical barriers are still visible. Events in New Zealand are very different than they are in Nunavut.

Furthermore, financial markets are organized quite differently. While the Toronto Stock Exchange is primarily an order-driven auction market where participants interact with each other, the London Stock Exchange is primarily a quote-driven market where investors trade with dealers rather than with each other.

Segmented countries and markets create investment opportunities. Since different forces are at play, markets are constantly fluctuating and not neces-

---

[1]Solnik, Bruno H, "Why Not Diversify Internationally?" *Financial Analysts Journal*, July/August 1974; pp. 48–54. See also Solnik, Bruno H., and B. Noetzlin, "Optimal International Asset Allocation," *The Journal of Portfolio Management*, Fall 1982.

sarily in unison, since countries are at different economic and political stages. Global diversification will capture these effects. In addition to supporting portfolio diversification, a globally diversified portfolio will also mean superior returns, risk reduction, and enriched investment opportunities.

It's quality rather than quantity that matters. Simply adding more and more securities to your portfolio may be a waste of time and money. Past a specific point, just making the portfolio larger will result in diminishing returns. The secret is to find countries that are vastly different from Canada, with stock and bond markets that don't move in lock-step with Canadian markets. Markets that move this way are said to have low or even negative correlation with those of Canada.

Foreign Investing Means Opportunities

Canada may be one of the world's major industrialized countries, with well-developed capital markets, including the seventh largest stock exchange in the world, the Toronto Stock Exchange. But its record in the investment world is far from stellar.

Despite some strength in 1999 and 2000, Canada has been one of the poorest performing major markets for years. For example, over the past 20 years global stock markets as measured by the bellwether Morgan Stanley Capital International World Composite Index (MSCIWCI) have outperformed Canada by, on average, about 3 percent per annum. The secret of overcoming this limitation is to diversify by country or region rather than picking individual country stocks. Furthermore, it has been shown that about 85 percent or so of total global returns are generated by country indices—currency and individual stock movements have only a small effect on performance. Given the substantial barriers associated with global investment, mutual funds are the ideal route to take.

Studies generally support the global asset allocation approach. But where does this fit in the framework? Does global investing become part of long-term asset allocation?

Unlike 15 years ago, there are lots of opportunities to invest globally. For example, a number of global fixed-income mutual funds are domiciled in Canada, including money market and bond funds with a wide array of objectives and target portfolios. However, most investors concentrate on equity funds when diversifying globally.

In the equity category, there are four types of funds:

- *Global funds* invest their assets in equities of various countries, including their own.

- *International funds* invest only in securities of different countries (sometimes limited to a few specific regions), not including domestic funds.

- *Regional funds* invest in stocks from specific regions of the world, such as Europe or the Far East.

- *Specific country funds* invest in securities of a single foreign nation, such as Japan.

Funds are divided into several categories:

- Investment objectives categories (safety, income, growth, aggressive growth)

- Geographical orientation (single country, region, global, international)

- Investment philosophy (active versus passive)

- Investment style (value versus growth; bottom up versus top down)

- Portfolio structure (small versus medium versus large capitalization).

When selecting mutual funds, look for those that have clear readable objectives and that tend to stay with those objectives.

Guidelines for Global Investing

Here are some selection guidelines for global investing:

1. *Global means long-term.* Time is not only on your side, it's essential. Diversification is based on diverse events. Two stocks that tend to respond differently to the same event or that are affected by entirely different factors will show different price behaviour. These stocks are said to have low correlation with each other. Low-correlation stocks reduce the volatility of a portfolio—that is what causes the diversification effect. Foreign securities have low correlations with Canadian securities and this is what reduces portfolio risk.

Foreign securities should represent about 10 percent to 30 percent of your holdings and your strategy should be long-term. Diversification needs time. Your portfolio might suffer in the short term because Latin America or Europe is undergoing a weak period but as the various regions rotate through the investment cycle, the long-run results will smooth out all of this.

2. *Select mutual funds whose managers build portfolios that really match the stated objectives.*

3. *Select mutual funds whose performance generally remains within a specific risk category.*

4. *Select mutual funds from countries with certain characteristics.* Look for mutual funds that invest in countries that are
   • emerging to democracy;
   • experiencing rapid population advance;
   • showing signs of rising incomes, which in turn means increased consumer spending, and interest in Western-style products (this in turn will mean industry growth to supply consumer needs);
   • upgrading their economies.

5. *It's quality rather than quantity that matters.* Invest in mutual funds specializing in countries whose markets have relatively low correlations with that of Canada. European countries such as Germany and France are ideal.

6. *Timing probably won't work.* Don't be constantly switching from country to country in the search for undervalued securities. The danger is that you may miss out on the correlation effects and the advantages of diversification.

7. *Select management styles (active versus passive; value versus growth) that match your tastes.*

8. *Don't base your selection on the absence of load fees or the size of the management expense ratio.* These are important but by no means critical factors.

9. *There is no free lunch in global investing.* Suppose that Argentinean government bonds are yielding 18 percent at a time that Canadian government bonds are yielding 8 percent. Does this mean you can expect an excess return of 10 percentage points by buying Argentinean bonds? You should know by this stage that investing is not that simple. Otherwise why would anyone buy a Canadian government bond when higher rates are available elsewhere? It's a

fact that, at any time, interest rates are high in some countries and low in others. However, through the mechanism of something called interest rate parity, it is not possible to earn higher returns except by chance in the higher-yield country! The great equalizer, however, is the combination of expected exchange rates and interest rates. You see, expected foreign exchange rate movements offset interest rate differentials.

The exchange rate is the number of units of a given currency that can be purchased with one unit of another currency. The spot rate is the price paid for a currency "on the spot." For example a Canadian dollar/U.S. dollar $1.50 exchange rate means it takes C$1.50 to buy US$1.00. Contracts to buy or sell a foreign currency at an agreed-upon future date are called forward contracts and the rates are called forward exchange rates.

If the exchange rate is turned upside down and expressed as the amount of U.S. dollars required to buy a Canadian dollar, the rate is called the external value of the Canadian dollar. If the exchange rate is $1.50, the external value of the Canadian dollar is (1/$1.50) = US$0.667.

Interest rate parity means that the rate of interest, covered for exchange risk, is equal to the domestic rate of interest. In essence a foreign currency will depreciate at a percentage rate approximately equal to the amount by which the country's interest rate exceeds the domestic rate. In a literal sense, it means that there are no bargains in foreign exchange markets.

10. *Direct global investing is probably hazardous to your health*, given the costs, barriers to entry, lack of information, accounting differences, and different regulatory standards. Buy global or international investment funds instead and let the managers make the securities decisions.

Wrapping Up

In conclusion, the paradigms for investors have the following implications:

- Concentrate on setting the right strategic asset allocation for your personal situation (Modern Portfolio Theory and diversification principles).

- Take assurance that passive investing is supported by extensive studies that led to formulation of a major finance hypothesis (the EMT).

- Always focus on a specific implementation strategy (to avoid Gambler's Ruin).

- Extend your asset allocation to global diversification.

5

THE MATH OF INVESTING

The mathematics of finance can seem daunting, especially if you are math-challenged or uninterested. But some knowledge of how all the calculations come together is a necessary basis for your financial decisions. Frankly, you don't need to become a whiz at calculating rates of returns to succeed; all you need is to understand the basic concepts and then harness them for your own uses. We'll look at the key measures in this chapter.

The Magic of Compounding

One of the world's wealthiest bankers, Baron Rothschild, was once asked if he could name the Seven Wonders of the World. "I cannot recall all the world's seven wonders, but let me suggest to you the eighth wonder of the world. It can be utilized by each and every one of us to get what we want," he replied. "It is compound interest."

The concept of compound interest is not difficult. Suppose you place money in an investment that pays interest compounded annually. (Of course, it doesn't have to be interest—it could be dividends, capital gains, rental income, etc. But we'll use interest income to illustrate the point.) During the first year you would earn interest on the principal. However, in subsequent years, you would not only earn interest on the original principal, but also on the interest earned in the first and subsequent years.

Let's say you were committed to saving $100 a month, earning 8 percent interest. In five years, that $100 per month will be worth $7,347.68. Shop at a few more financial institutions and you might get 10 percent interest on the $100 per month (obviously those rates are not available these days but they have been in the past and may be again in the future). At a 10 percent rate, your savings program would net you $7,743.71 after five years.

The longer money is left to compound, the more dramatic the effect on the value of your portfolio. Setting aside $100 per month for 10 years at 8 percent leaves you with a nest egg of $18,294.60. At 10 percent, you would have $20,484.50.

Once you start saving, the feeling becomes addictive, which is why we suggest you set up a regular savings plan and stick to it. But it's important that your saving does not force you to change your lifestyle. Save an amount that you can live with, and over time it will become second nature.

Now let's see what is required to reach millionaire status. Let's begin with a saving program of $200 per month, and an interest rate of 10 percent per year. At that rate, it will take you 37.75 years to reach your million-dollar goal. Earn 12 percent on your $200 per month, and it takes just under 33 years to reach the goal. If you can save $400 per month and earn 12 percent per year, it will take you just over 27 years to reach $1 million; at 10 percent, it will take just under 31 years.

Here's another example. Assume that $1,000 was invested today, earning 10 percent interest, compounded annually. At the end of the first year, your investment would have grown to $1,100. This represents the original investment ($1,000) plus $100 ($1,000 × 1.10) interest earned on the principal. Assume you reinvested the entire amount for another year; the investment would appreciate to $1,210 ($1,100 × 1.10). During the second year, you would make $100 interest on the original investment, plus $10 interest on the interest earned in the first year.

The amount at the end of two years of investment can be broken down as follows:

Original investment	$1,000.00
First year's interest	100.00
Second year's interest on original investment	100.00
Second year's interest on interest	10.00
Total value	$1,210.00

Reinvestment for the third year would produce $1,331.00 ($1,210 × 1.10). The third year's interest of $121 accounts for $100 on the original principal, plus $21 on the interest earned during the first two years. The interest-on-interest component of the investment is what causes the snowballing effect on the growth of money.

To underline the importance of the compounding effect, assume the original $1,000 investment was left to compound for 50 years. At a 10 percent interest rate, the investment would grow to $117,390.85. The interest payable the 50th year would be made up of $100 on the original principal, plus $10,671.89 on the $105,781.96 interest earned during the first 49 years.

Had the interest on the original $1,000 principal been calculated using simple interest, the investment would not have grown nearly as much. With simple interest, the investment only earns interest on the original investment. Interest is not earned on interest received in the previous years. To put this into perspective, our original $1,000 investment would be worth a mere $6,000 at the end of the 50-year period ($100 interest × 50 years, plus $1,000 original principal).

The Impact of Inflation

Let's take a 10-year period, a typical planning period for investors. An investment of $10,000 invested at 8 percent for 10 years will grow to $21,589.25. Now assume that inflation is 3 percent per annum over that same period. What is the purchasing power of your investment at the end of 10 years?

It is calculated as $21,589.25/(1.03)^{10} = $16,064.43. So with an 8 percent growth rate and a 3 percent inflation rate over 10 years, your investment increased by 60.64 percent, or by 4.85 percent per annum in inflation-adjusted returns.

The Rule of 72

We trust you get the picture. It is one thing to plan for the future; it is quite another to understand what it will take to meet your goals.

There are a number of ways to do these calculations. You can use interest rate tables, hand calculators, Excel spreadsheets, and other such tools that are helpful in calculating the future value of a lump sum of money put aside today. But while tables and formulas can be useful in determining the value of an investment at some point in the future, they are not tools that you can always carry with you to the local bank or trust company. Fortunately, there is an approximation method that is a useful way to calculate the future value of a fixed investment today. It is known as the "rule of 72." If you divide 72 by the return on a particular investment, it will tell you how many years it will take for your money to double.

For example, if the current rate of return were 9 percent, your funds would double in eight years (72 ÷ 9 = 8). If the interest rate were 12 percent, your original investment would double every six years (72 ÷ 12 = 6).

Now, assume you invested $10,000 in a bond fund that, historically, has been compounding at an average 10 percent a year. How soon will your money double? The answer is 7.2 years (72 ÷ 10 = 7.2).

How about this: Suppose you have $10,000 you want to double in 10 years to fund your retirement nest egg. What compound rate of return must you earn? Divide 72 by the number of years, and you get 7.2 percent. To double it in five years, you'll have to earn an annual return of 14.4 percent on your investment (72 ÷ 5 = 14.4).

It's simplicity at work, yet the rule of 72 illustrates some powerful investment principles—most notably the magic of compounding. It also drives home the advantages of mutual funds, where dividends and interest can be automatically reinvested into additional shares. Interest makes your investments grow; compound interest makes them grow faster.

And how about the role the rule of 72 plays in assessing the impact of changes in the level of your potential return? Money compounding at 6 percent annually will take 12 years to double. Compounding at 12 percent, it will double in half the time.

The flip side of compounding is the impact inflation can have on your investments. And there, too, the rule of 72 plays a role. An inflation rate of 3 percent means that a dollar today will be worth roughly 50 cents in 24 years. A 5 percent inflation rate means that your cost of living will double every 14.4 years. Tell that to a 40-year-old just beginning to establish a retirement fund!

Measuring Rates of Return: The Past Does Matter

If you understand interest-rate math, you are better equipped to deal with performance measurement.

Mutual fund companies are always reminding us in their ads that "past results are no guarantee of future returns." The same can be said for stocks, bonds, royalty trusts, and even GICs. But that doesn't make history meaningless. It's a matter of knowing how to interpret it.

Given a long time frame, historic asset class returns are a reasonable estimate for a relatively stable security or market index. They are particularly useful in forecasting long-term asset returns.

Mean reversion, or regression to the mean, is a well-documented phenomenon. The theory, first expounded in the 19th century, demonstrates a tendency for many variables to fluctuate widely, but to eventually return to a central value, or "mean." The phenomenon has been associated with numerous subject areas, not all of which involve pure math. These include mean-reverting tendencies in the heights of family members, patterns of economic growth, employment levels, and even Major League Baseball batting averages!

ASSET CLASS RETURNS (PERCENTAGE), VARIOUS PERIODS

PERIOD	CAN. T-BILLS[1]	CAN. BONDS[2]	CAN. STOCKS[3]	INFLATION[4]
1924–1960	N/A	6.05%	10.46%	3.16%
1947–1997	7.23%	9.22	11.24	5.36
1956–2000	5.33	5.28	13.56	4.80

[1]91-day Canadian government T-bills
[2]Long-term Canadian government bonds
[3]TSE 300 Composite Index Canadian stocks
[4]Consumer Price Index

Sources: Scotia McLeod, "Total Rate of Return on Securities," various years; Scotia McLeod, "Handbook of Debt Market Securities, 1961–1997; Boyle, P., H. Panjer, and K. Sharpe, "Rates of Returns on Canadian Securities," Canadian Institute of Actuaries, various years; Kirzner, et al. "Schwab Study," 2001.

Mean reversion is also a key phenomenon in investment finance. Returns on common shares fluctuate substantially from year to year, but have a long-run tendency to regress to 10 percent to 12 percent per annum. Typically T-bills and bonds yield about 4 percent and 6 percent respectively, which means the anticipated performance on a balanced portfolio is about 8 percent per annum. Of course, you do have unusual periods, such as the 1990s when stock returns were substantially above normal, bringing up the averages. The long-term record for the broad Canadian asset classes is shown in the table on the previous page.

Mean reversion suggests these long-term records provide the best estimates of future asset class returns. There is evidence of stability within and among asset classes over these very long time periods. The risk premium of stocks over bonds has declined, although Treasury bills, bonds, and stocks have shown a mean-reverting tendency over the past 50 years. A closer examination of asset class returns will reveal additional information. In the next table, returns and standard deviations are shown for the Canadian Treasury bills, bonds, and stock classes as well as for U.S. and global stocks. The relatively high standard deviations and low return/risk ratios for bonds and stocks over this 50-year period indicates the risk of making short-term forecasts based strictly on these long-term asset class returns.

ASSET CLASS RETURNS, STANDARD DEVIATIONS, AND RETURN/RISK RATIOS, 1956–2000

	CAN. T-BILLS[1]	CAN. BONDS[2]	CAN. STOCKS[3]	U.S. STOCKS[4]	GLOBAL STOCKS[5]
Mean return	5.33%	5.28%	13.56%	14.26%	16.78%
Standard Dev.	1.11	7.18	15.41	15.07	17.11
Return/risk ratio	4.80	0.73	0.88	0.95	0.98

[1] 91-day Canadian government T-bills
[2] Long-term Canadian government bonds
[3] TSE 300 Composite Index
[4] S&P 500 Composite Index
[5] Morgan Stanley Capital International Europe, Australasia, Far East Index (EAFE)

Implications of Mean Reversion

What mean reversion means to you is this: The stock market, like the letter carrier, always delivers—but you have to give it a chance. And you can't try to outguess it. In any given year, it may go down. However, over the past 50 years, common shares have produced exceptional returns. They have been a great hedge against loss of purchasing power, with after-inflation returns averaging about 5.5 percent per annum. In fact, every 10-year period since the Depression has yielded healthy inflation-adjusted returns. As a result, regardless of the investment strategy you choose, you should plan on making equities a significant component of your investment portfolio. The appropriate amount, or allocation, will, of course, vary depending on your taste for risk, your stage in life, and your financial plans. As a general rule, the suggested range of equity inclusion is 30 percent to 70 percent.

What the Numbers Mean

Now we're going to look at returns in the major investment categories over several time periods. This will show you how much the numbers can vary, depending on prevailing conditions. But remember that, over the longer term, we'll always see mean reversion take effect.

Here's an explanation of the meaning of the numbers in the tables.

- The *mean return* is the arithmetic average annual return for the time period. It is calculated for each year as the capital appreciation (or loss) plus any distributions. If, for example, the TSE 300 Composite Index starts the year at 8,500 and ends the year at 9,200, and the dividend yield is 1.5 percent, the annual rate of return R is calculated as follows:

$$R = \frac{9,200-8,500}{8,500} + 0.015 = 0.973$$

That result, 0.0973, is the rate of return for the year, or 9.73 percent.

- The *standard deviation* is a statistical measure of variability (volatility) and, without getting into the mathematics, it measures the degree to which a stock deviates from its average rate of return. A stock with a high standard deviation has a high degree of variability.

- The *return/risk ratio* is the rate of return divided by the standard deviation for a particular period. What it shows is the return per unit of risk incurred for the period. The higher the return/risk ratio, the more favourable the historic performance of the investment.

Asset Class Returns in Five-Year Segments, 1963–1997

In the following series of tables, we'll look at how the asset classes performed under different economic scenarios.

1963–1967 (GROWTH AND PROSPERITY)

	CAN. T-BILLS	CAN. BONDS	CAN. STOCKS	INFLATION
Arithmetic Mean	4.19%	1.85%	11.75%	2.68%
Standard Deviation	0.59	3.28	12.47	0.93
Return/risk ratio	7.06	0.56	0.94	2.89

Comment: This period was marked by high stock returns, reflecting strong economic growth, healthy corporate profits, low interest rates, and moderate inflation.

1968–1972 (MAINLY GROWTH AND PROSPERITY)

	CAN. T-BILLS	CAN. BONDS	CAN. STOCKS	INFLATION
Arithmetic Mean	5.52%	7.72%	10.69%	3.88%
Standard Deviation	1.70	8.29	13.78	0.77
Return/risk ratio	3.25	0.94	0.78	5.04

Comment: Interest rates and inflation rates were starting to rise (a harbinger of things to come), although the economy remained relatively buoyant. Despite a downturn in 1969–70, stocks continued to post solid returns.

1973–1977 (STAGFLATION)

	CAN. T-BILLS	CAN. BONDS	CAN. STOCKS	INFLATION
Arithmetic Mean	7.46%	7.63%	2.91%	8.98%
Standard Deviation	1.50	10.47	17.38	1.67
Return/risk ratio	4.98	0.73	0.17	5.37

Comment: This was one of the worst periods of the century for stocks. Cost-push inflation, reflecting real and perceived shortages for some food products and energy, propelled interest rates higher and choked off corporate profits. The term stagflation, meaning stagnant growth with inflation, was coined.

1978–1982 (GROWTH AND INFLATION)

	CAN. T-BILLS	CAN. BONDS	CAN. STOCKS	INFLATION
Arithmetic Mean	13.71%	9.44%	19.98%	10.32%
Standard Deviation	3.90	20.54	21.99	1.41
Return/risk ratio	3.52	0.46	0.91	7.34

Comment: Inflation rates continue to mount and are accompanied by very high interest rates. However, consumer spending propels the economy to strong advances. Although price/earnings multiples remain low due to high interest rates, strong corporate earnings provide the base for a big stock rally.

1983–1987 (DISINFLATION)

	CAN. T-BILLS	CAN. BONDS	CAN. STOCKS	INFLATION
Arithmetic Mean	9.78%	14.43%	14.60%	4.52%
Standard Deviation	1.14	9.32	15.35	0.69
Return/risk ratio	8.57	1.55	0.95	6.54

Comment: Economic policies designed to curb inflation start to take hold and inflation rates start to subside, bringing interest rates down as well.

1988–1992 (MAINLY RECESSION)

	CAN. T-BILLS	CAN. BONDS	CAN. STOCKS	INFLATION
Arithmetic Mean	10.43%	13.53%	5.65%	4.18%
Standard Deviation	2.53	7.66	14.01	1.60
Return/risk ratio	4.12	1.77	0.40	2.61

Comment: A severe recession in 1990–91, coupled with still-high interest rates, deals stocks a double whammy—reduced earnings per share and falling P/Es mean low stock returns.

1993–1997 (SUPER-PROSPERITY: GROWTH AND DISINFLATION)

	CAN. T-BILLS	CAN. BONDS	CAN. STOCKS	INFLATION
Arithmetic Mean	5.22%	14.74%	18.05%	1.52%
Standard Deviation	1.37	13.16	12.95	0.75
Return/risk ratio	3.81	1.12	1.39	1.90

Comment: Stocks mount a mammoth rally as the corporate cost-reducing restructuring program starts to bear fruit. Falling interest rates and rising earnings per share are bullish for stocks.

Sources: Scotia McLeod, "Total Rate of Return on Securities," various years; Scotia McLeod, "Handbook of Debt Market Securities, 1961–1997."

1998 to the Present

At this stage it's not clear where this five-year cycle will end up. It may indeed be a boom and bust one. Suffice to say that despite the severe sell-off in 2000 and 2001 (to September 30), Canadian stocks have averaged an arithmetic return of 11.1 percent and a geometric return of 10.1 percent. Bills and bonds have averaged 4.9 percent and 4.0 percent respectively.

Long-term asset class returns can be misleading. Although mean reversion is important, over the past decades different cycles are evident, each with its own unique asset class returns. You only have to contrast the return/variance results of the 1973–1977 and 1993–1997 periods to see the differences. In the 1973–1977 stagflation period, Canadian stocks returned an average annual 2.91 percent, as compared to the 7.46 percent return for Treasury bills. Two decades later, in a period marked by growth and disinflation, stocks yielded 18.05 percent, as compared to 5.22 percent for Treasury bills. Furthermore, the return/risk ratio for Canadian stocks fell to 0.17 in the 1973–1977 period, attesting to the low returns and high variability that marked the period. In the 1993–1997 period, the return/risk ratio for stock returns was 1.39, indicative of the high returns earned with less variability during this strong equity market.

Wrapping Up

The mathematics of finance is the basis for intelligent financial decisions. An understanding of the basic math provides you with the tools for measuring the rates of returns on bills, bonds, or stocks or calculating or measuring the performance records of mutual funds. The "magic" of compound interest in particular underscores the reason why you establish a long-term horizon for your investment program.

Perhaps even more important, an understanding of the math will help you to properly assess risk versus return for any investment you may be considering and to realistically measure the relative performance of your investment portfolio over time.

6

KNOW YOURSELF

The first step in any sensible investment program is to understand your investment personality. It can be difficult to pinpoint, but it is essential because personality traits dictate how much risk you can tolerate. That helps you weigh the trade-off between risk and return and make investment decisions that are appropriate and will not leave you tossing and turning at night every time the stock market takes a dive.

Conservative investors are more interested in the safety of their principal than in earning big returns, and they require an income from their portfolios. Aggressive investors are more concerned about their rate of return than the safety of their capital. Income is not usually a priority. Defining an investment personality seems simple enough when we're looking at extremes. But in reality, most people fall somewhere between these two positions. Even conservative investors sometimes have to accept some risk in order to meet their financial objectives. Money market funds or term deposits may not offer enough return to provide the income or growth necessary for the lifestyle they want. Similarly, some more aggressive investors don't have the cash flow or net worth to handle the roller-coaster action of the stock market. Psychologically they can do it; financially they can't! So they compromise by investing in less risky alternatives.

There are probably as many categories of individual investors as there are individual personalities. Unfortunately, if we tried to fine-tune the asset mix to suit all of the possibilities, we would be micromanaging to the extreme. It's better to try making an investment personality assessment that is, as author

George Hartman puts it in *Risk Is a Four-Letter Word*, "approximately right rather than precisely wrong." The questionnaire in this chapter attempts to provide this kind of assessment.

Our Investor Assessment Questionnaire has four basic cornerstones: net worth, financial goals, risk tolerance, and time horizon. All four pieces of this puzzle are interrelated.

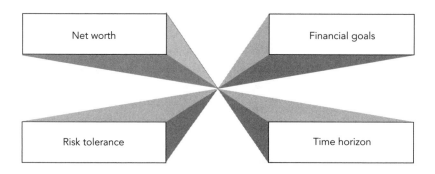

Your net worth (your total assets minus your total liabilities) can influence your risk tolerance. For example, individuals with a higher net worth can be more aggressive, or more tolerant of risk. (They aren't necessarily more aggressive, but they can be.) That's because, with a larger asset base, they can bring more elements of diversification into the portfolio. The greater the diversification, the less volatile their portfolio is likely to be and the more risk it can absorb. So larger portfolios get higher scores on risk tolerance.

Similarly, your financial goals and/or your objectives go hand in hand with net worth. You may have heard the story of the billionaire who had all his money invested in low-risk, low-return U.S. Treasury bills. When asked why, he answered: "Because I feel I can live comfortably on $45 million a year." The billionaire would have the highest possible score on the net worth section of the questionnaire, but would have the lowest possible score on financial objectives.

Financial goals are also linked to time horizons—that is, whether you have short- or long-term objectives. And in turn, your time horizon can influence your tolerance for risk, since risk diminishes over the long term.

With these issues in mind, we have categorized investors into the six personalities listed below. Later in the chapter, after we've helped you identify which type of investor you are, you'll find an investment policy statement for each personality, along with a minimum and maximum weighting of investments in each asset class.

- *Safety:* Investors in this category are uncomfortable with virtually every form of risk. They lean toward securities that provide regular and guaranteed returns, even if those returns are relatively low. Their attitude toward financial planning is apprehensive and, at times, quite pessimistic. Whereas others dream of wealth when they invest, safety investors are motivated by the dread of poverty and the need to preserve capital.

- *Safety/Income:* These investors are also concerned about safety, but require income as well to meet their financial obligations. They recognize the need for a trade-off between the two. Safety/income investors want to make certain their principal is secure, but they have a keen interest in earning income on that principal. In this category, we find many retirees who may be living off a fixed income and require the cash flow from their portfolio to supplement their living standards.

- *Income/Growth:* In this case, investors focus their attention primarily on the income side of the investment equation. However, unlike safety/income investors, these people don't consider their portfolio's income stream to be a critical supplement to their standard of living—at least not yet. Often income/growth investors will reinvest the income stream into more securities within the portfolio, effectively dollar-cost-averaging their investment program. Income/ growth investors understand that financial security depends on achieving some growth within the portfolio. They will spend a lot of time evaluating the return required to meet their long-range financial objectives. These investors often set reasonable goals that, for the most part, can be attained with their investment style.

- *Growth/Income:* This group of investors understands that risk is a natural part of investing. With this in mind, they set out to structure the perfect portfolio, usually a balanced investment scheme. The assets are chosen for their ability to survive the ups and downs of the business cycle. There is one drawback, however: The portfolio is designed to be left alone. Balanced investors are often so absorbed with day-to-day survival that they neglect tomorrow's opportunities.

- *Growth:* This type of investor is not at all concerned about income. Usually, growth investors have a long time horizon (i.e., they are still relatively young) and often a sizeable net worth. Their objective is to maximize the potential growth within the portfolio, albeit with reasonable risks. Growth investors have an appreciation for the trade-off between risk and return, and are willing to assume higher levels of risk for greater expected returns.

- *Aggressive Growth:* We are now at the top of the risk scale. These investors are the quick-draw artists of the investment world, often poised to nimbly move from one opportunity to another. They switch from asset to asset, thriving on risk, seeking the thrills that accompany a profitable trade, and they are willing to accept (or, some would say, to ignore) the risks associated with their investment philosophy. Aggressive growth investors are often young, have a reasonable income base, and, although they tend to look for results over the short term, are seeking some long-term guidance.

Now that you're familiar with the types of investing personalities, it's time to take a closer look at the cornerstones of the Investment Assessment Questionnaire and then answer the questions to determine your Personal Investment Profile.

Setting Your Financial Objectives

Where do you see yourself in 10 years? Retired and enjoying the finer things in life, nestled in the home of your dreams? Content and pleased with your past accomplishments and your aspirations for the future? Or maybe you'll be climbing the career ladder, developing a successful foundation in the career of your choice.

Many of us are unclear about our financial goals, because most of us have never been taught just how important goals are in the context of investment management. In fact, goals are critical. They will define your performance strategy.

It's also important to establish financial goals that are reasonable. You can't simply say, for example, that you want to be a millionaire some day. It may be possible to reach that goal, but how much do you need to set aside, over what period of time, at what rate of return, and with what risk exposure? And having figured that out, is it realistic?

Having realistic expectations is important, because you need to establish some successes in order to maintain a solid footing on your way to financial independence. Failing to meet unrealistic expectations can be discouraging, and that can have a negative impact on your long-range plans.

Take a few minutes with your family and think about some of the financial objectives you'd like to meet. Everything is on the table at this point, from an island vacation, to a new car, to a new cabin cruiser. Name your dream! Remember that financial objectives can be investment-oriented, including such things as growth of capital, protection of principal, and income and tax considerations. There are also short-term and long-term goals, including things like the future education needs of your children, retirement planning, saving for a house, or simply improving your lifestyle. So write down your goals in order of importance, and place them in terms of timing. For example, a trip to Hawaii may be a short-term goal, especially if you hope to take the trip within, say, the next five years. In fact, any goal that comes within the next five years should be included on your list of short-term goals. Anything with a time horizon beyond five years probably should go on your list of long-term goals. Your children's education is a longer-term goal. And, obviously, retirement planning deserves some special attention.

Retirement Considerations

Once you have put together a list of potential goals, try to rank them in terms of importance and then put some realistic prices on them. For example, your retirement income should be at least 70 percent of your current income and, to be safe, you should adjust that number to reflect inflation expectations.

We often get questions about registered retirement income funds (RRIFs). What happens when you are drawing money from your portfolio? Should the design of that portfolio fit within the context of a short-term or long-term goal? What are the odds that you will run out of money before you reach life expectancy? (Some studies conducted at York University attempted to address this issue. What the studies discovered is that although investors may be drawing an income, they still need some assets in their portfolio to provide growth. Without the growth element, there is a real chance that an individual might outlive his or her assets.)

Retired individuals have very long-term goals. When you retire, the real risk is that you will outlive your assets. If you die immediately after you set up your RRIF, there is no financial impact on you. There is on your estate, of course, but not on you personally. So the real risk is that of outliving your assets. And since a RRIF begins to pay out at age 70, and life expectancy is 76 for men and 82 for women, there is a very long time horizon for your investments to meet your goals.

On the other hand, you need to draw income from your RRIF immediately. That affects your time horizon, which raises a very basic question: How long before you need this money? The answer, if you are in a RRIF, is "in less than two years," which would give you a score of 0 in our Investor Assessment Questionnaire. We think that's the right answer to the question, and we suspect that RRIF investors will generally fall within the three most conservative of our investment portfolios. But in each of those portfolios we leave some room for growth. All six investor personalities need some equity in their final asset mix.

The Retirement Planner that follows will help you calculate what rate of return you'll need to meet your goals. However, we recognize that this is a bit more cumbersome than you might like. With that in mind, and if you have access to the World Wide Web, we have an alternative to paper-based calculations.

Go to the **www.quicken.ca** Web site. From there, click on the RRSP Planner, and then click on the question "How Much Should I Invest?" That will take you to a calculator, which will help you decide how much you need in order to retire. You can also use that calculator to help you with Question 2 of our questionnaire ("What is your required rate of return?"). Just plug in your numbers and ask the calculator to give you a rate of return.

RETIREMENT PLANNER

Years to retirement   Years _____

Annual household income   \$ _____

Estimated annual retirement expenses in today's dollars[1]   \$ _____

Total amount required to provide for retirement expenses   \$ _____

Goal for annual contribution to retirement   \$ _____

Required compound annual return to meet retirement goal[2]   % _____

[1]Assume 70 percent of current income

[2]The rate of return you require in order to meet your retirement goal assuming regular annual contributions

Education Considerations

Next to saving for retirement, planning for their children's education is a common goal for investors. In estimating the future cost of a college or university education, some financial advisors attach an assumed rate of inflation to the current tuition level. With cutbacks from all levels of government, particularly in the area of college and university tuition, it's important to make reasonable assumptions regarding the inflation of future education costs.

With that in mind, many advisors inflate current education costs by some fixed rate—say, 7 percent per year, a figure that is reasonably close to the cost increases experienced over the last 10 years. At that rate, a university education that costs \$10,000 a year today will cost almost \$20,000 10 years from now, or just under \$40,000 in 20 years.

However, adjusting costs by any fixed rate can be dangerous. If your child is two feet tall at age one, and four feet tall at age six, that equals a 14 percent annual growth rate. If we maintained that assumption for the next five years, your child would be over eight feet tall at age eleven, and should be receiving scholarship offers to play collegiate basketball.

Also, tuition represents only a small percentage of the total cost of sending a child to university. If the student is attending an out-of-town school, living expenses will account for a much larger share of the total budget, and these costs will increase in line with the overall Consumer Price Index.

So our advice is to use a cost escalator that is somewhere in between the unusually high increases in tuition fees in recent years and the CPI. Around 4 percent is a more accurate estimation of the future cost of a post-secondary education.

EDUCATION PLANNER

Annual cost of the college of your choice	$ _____
Number of years before your child enters college	Years _____
Number of years child will likely attend college	Years _____
Amount needed to meet goal	$ _____

Other Considerations

As we just saw with the example of your child's education, planning with fixed rates can be dangerous. The same is true of your investment objectives and goals–they also change over time. People had much different expectations in the boom days of the 1990s than they did after the bear market of 2000–2001. A regular review is in order annually and, of course, when personal circumstances change–when there is a death in the family, a marriage, a divorce, the birth of a child. At such times, you will need to rethink your priorities.

Finally, it is always important to keep some funds set aside for emergencies. A useful guideline is to have enough savings to cover three to six months' worth of expenses.

Time Horizons

For most of us, the longest-term financial goal is our retirement. In all likelihood, we will be drawing on our retirement income long after having met our shorter-term goals. In other words, our retirement goals will be financed with income left over after meeting our shorter-term goals.

The following worksheets will help you to clarify some of your ideas about the future in terms of three time horizons: short, medium, and long term.

SHORT-TERM PORTFOLIO
(UP TO 3 YEARS)

1. What are your short-term goals, in today's dollars? $ _____
2. What percentage of your yearly gross income is that?   % _____
3. What existing savings can you put toward this goal? $ _____
4. What are your savings as a percentage of your income?   % _____
5. Subtract your savings (4) from your goal (2) to get the
   percentage of your income you need to invest: % _____
6. How many years can you wait to reach this goal?   Years _____
7. Divide the amount you need to invest (5) by the years
   (6) to get the portion of monthly gross income you'll
   have to save: % _____

MID-TERM PORTFOLIO (4–10 YEARS)

1. What are your mid-term goals, in today's dollars? $ _____
2. What percentage of your yearly gross income is that?   % _____
3. What existing savings can you put toward this goal? $ _____
4. What are your savings as a percentage of your income?   % _____
5. Subtract savings (4) from goal (2) to get the percentage
   of your income you need to invest: % _____
6. How many years can you wait to reach your goal?   Years _____
7. Divide the required investment (5) by the years (6) to
   get the percentage of your monthly gross income you'll
   have to save: % _____

LONG-TERM (RETIREMENT) PORTFOLIO (MORE THAN 10 YEARS)

1. Cash value of retirement investments: $ _____
2. What percentage or multiple of your yearly gross income
   is that?   % _____
3. How much have you saved so far? $ _____
4. What are your current as a percentage of your income?   % _____
5. Subtract (4) from (2):   % _____
6. How many years remain before retirement?   Years _____
7. Divide line 5 by line 6 to get the percentage of your
   gross monthly income that you need to invest: % _____

Risk over Time

Now that you've established your financial goals and the rates of return required to achieve them over time, how can you invest your money to realize these rates of return? The investment choices you make are inextricably linked to your level of risk tolerance. That's why our Personal Investment Profile looks at risk and return as two sides of the same coin.

Discussing risk is really talking about the potential for loss. In that context, equity investments are risky because over short periods there is a reasonable chance that you could lose money. However, if you are willing to take a longer-term view, the risk of loss diminishes dramatically. Knowing your time horizon is important, since it will determine the amount of equity in your investment program.

Let's say you were considering investing in mutual funds. If performance were the only criterion for screening potential funds, then it would simply be a case of matching your required rate of return to a fund that has generated that rate compounded over, say, the last five or ten years. Mission accomplished!

Of course, as you might imagine, things are never really that simple. The problem is that our tolerance for risk defines for each of us how well we can adapt to the ebbs and flows of our investment returns. The impact those changes have on us determines our ability to remain invested for long periods.

Stocks are one of the few investment assets that can deliver growth over the long term. But too many individual investors looking for growth are preoccupied with safety of principal, and so are unwilling to assume the risk that accompanies an investment in equities. (On the other hand, veteran money managers will tell you that many investors are reluctant to sell when faced with a loss. Many investors find it difficult to admit to a mistake, or falsely believe that they do not incur a true loss until a security is sold.)

On the other side of the risk/return coin, you have to be able to maintain your positions for the long term, being careful not to take profits too quickly. Many of the same investors who will let their losses run will just as quickly take a profit. There is, of course, some psychological satisfaction in making money. But over the long term this reduces your chances for gains. All too often it takes you out of a market that is performing well. In this case, a little patience is its own reward.

The Investor Assessment Questionnaire that follows begins with your current financial condition (your net worth), and goes on to address the issues we've covered in this chapter: your financial goals, the time horizon you envision for achieving these goals, and your tolerance for risk. Once you've tallied your scores, you will have determined your investing personality and arrive at your Personal Investment Profile, which will give you a foundation for making investment decisions that are right for you.

Investor Assessment Questionnaire

Try to answer each of the following questions as honestly as you can. Where necessary, work with your spouse or partner–investment planning should be a family affair.

Question 1: Net Worth

We'll begin at the beginning–with your current net worth. But before firing up the calculator, you should decide whether or not to include your principal residence.

The bottom line is that you will always need a place to live. Of course, you may decide to rent at some point in the future. In that case, you may want to sell your principal residence and invest the tax-free profits into upgrading your lifestyle. Or you may prefer to retain your residence and use other forms of disposable income to meet your financial needs.

If you fall into the sell-and-invest camp, and are clear about your long-term plans, then by all means, include the principal residence as part of your net worth. For those who fall into the I'll-keep-my-house-forever camp, we suggest you do not include your home as part of your net worth.

Remember that net worth is the total of all your assets, less liabilities.

Is your approximate net worth:

Less than $25,000?	1
Between $25,000 and $50,000?	3
Between $50,001 and $100,000?	5
Between $100,001 and $250,000?	7
Greater than $250,000?	10

Question 2: Financial Goals

Determine your financial goals (e.g., retirement, saving for a home, children's education), then assess the rate of return required to attain these goals.

Is your annual required rate of return:

Less than 6%?	1
Between 6% and 9%?	5
Greater than 9% but no more than 12%?	10
Greater than 12%	15

Questions 3 through 9 will help you determine your ability to deal with risk, or the ebb and flow of the business cycle.

Question 3: Liquidity

How important is it that you have access to your investment capital in case of emergencies or other investment opportunities?

It is extremely important.	1
It is important.	2
It is slightly important.	4
It isn't important at all.	5

Question 4: Safety

After one year of investing, how much would the value of your long-term investment capital have to decline before you would sell it and take a loss?

I would sell if my investment declined by 5%.	1
I would sell if my investment declined by 15%.	2
I would sell if my investment declined by 25%.	3
I would sell if my investment declined by 50%.	4
I would not sell my investment.	5

Question 5: Current Income

How important is it that you receive an income stream from your investments over the period of your investment horizon?

It is extremely important.	1
It is important.	2
It is slightly important.	3
It isn't important at all.	4

Question 6: Reaction to Events (Future Gains)

Here you may wish to be guided by your reaction to the terrorist attacks of September 2001 and the subsequent plunge in the stock market.

How would you describe your reaction to financial news that could have a detrimental effect on your investments?

I would be very anxious and likely sell my investments.	1
I would be fearful and consider selling my investments.	2
I would be uncomfortable but would hold my investments.	3
I would remain calm and definitely hold my investments.	4

Question 7: Portfolio Variability

How important is it that you never experience a loss in your portfolio during a given time period?

It is extremely important.	1
It is important.	2
It is only slightly important.	3
It isn't important at all.	4

Question 8: Performance Review

Which performance numbers most concern you?

Monthly performance numbers	1
Quarterly performance numbers	3
Annual performance numbers	5

Question 9: Speculation

Within the past five years, how often have you invested money into speculative investments?

I have never invested speculatively.	1
I have invested speculatively once.	2
I have invested speculatively twice.	3
I have invested speculatively three or more times.	4

Your time horizon has a great deal to do with risk and with how much equity you can tolerate in your investment program. This last question will help you pinpoint just what your time horizon is.

Question 10: Investment Time Horizon

How long do you plan to hold your investments?

Less than 2 years?	0
Between 2 and 5 years?	3
More than 5 and less than 10 years?	6
10 to 20 years?	10
More than 20 years?	15

Your Personal Investor Score

CATEGORY	INFORMATION FOUND WHERE?	TOTAL SCORE
A. Net worth	Question 1	_____
B. Financial objectives	Question 2	_____
C. Risk assessment profile	Questions 3–9	_____
D. Time horizon	Question 10	_____
Total Score (A + B + C + D)		_____

Determining Your Category

The final tally reveals your investing personality, from which you can determine your Personal Investment Profile (PIP). Your Personal Investment Profile is structured as an aggressiveness index and provides the foundation on which to establish your personal asset mix. The higher the score, the more aggressive the asset mix. The investor categories that follow are distinguished according the six personality types that we listed at the beginning of this chapter. But remember: Financial circumstances and goals change, so take the time to re-evaluate your situation at periodic intervals.

INVESTOR CATEGORIES

SCORE	INVESTOR CATEGORY
0–15	Safety
15–25	Safety/Income
25–35	Income
35–45	Income/Growth
45–55	Growth
55+	Aggressive Growth

Applying PIP to Portfolio Building

The first step when constructing a long-term portfolio is deciding how much emphasis should be given to each asset class. With that in mind, we start the process by defining your "policy statement" for distribution of assets based on your Personal Investment Profile, as shown in the following asset mix chart. The chart shows the average weighting we would expect you to hold in each asset class. Your policy statement is defined as the midpoint for each asset class.

You will also note two other percentages, a maximum and a minimum, on either side of each policy amount. These are the maximum and minimum commitments you should make to each asset class at any point in time. Review your situation each year and update your policy statement based on circumstances at that time. By doing this, you should be able to enhance your returns when the economy is strong and reduce your risk when the economy is slow. In other words, it's another way of trying to smooth your ride through the ups and downs of the business cycle.

PERSONAL POLICY STATEMENTS

SAFETY PORTFOLIO SCORE: UNDER 15

Equities			Fixed Income			Cash		
Min.	Policy	Max.	Min.	Policy	Max.	Min.	Policy	Max.
0%	10%	20%	60%	75%	90%	10%	15%	30%

SAFETY/INCOME PORTFOLIO SCORE: 15–24

Equities			Fixed Income			Cash		
Min.	Policy	Max.	Min.	Policy	Max.	Min.	Policy	Max.
10%	20%	30%	50%	65%	80%	10%	15%	25%

INCOME/GROWTH PORTFOLIO SCORE: 25–34

Equities			Fixed Income			Cash		
Min.	Policy	Max.	Min.	Policy	Max.	Min.	Policy	Max.
20%	35%	50%	30%	50%	70%	10%	15%	25%

GROWTH/INCOME PORTFOLIO SCORE: 35–44

Equities			Fixed Income			Cash		
Min.	Policy	Max.	Min.	Policy	Max.	Min.	Policy	Max.
30%	50%	70%	25%	40%	55%	5%	10%	15%

GROWTH PORTFOLIO SCORE: 45-54

Equities			Fixed Income			Cash		
Min.	Policy	Max.	Min.	Policy	Max.	Min.	Policy	Max.
40%	60%	80%	20%	30%	40%	5%	10%	15%

AGGRESSIVE GROWTH PORTFOLIO SCORE: OVER 55

Equities			Fixed Income			Cash		
Min.	Policy	Max.	Min.	Policy	Max.	Min.	Policy	Max.
50%	75%	100%	0%	20%	30%	0%	5%	10%

Suppose you fall into the Income/Growth category. Your current targets are for a portfolio that is 15 percent cash, 50 percent fixed income, and 35 percent equities. Your ranges are 10 to 25 percent cash, 30 to 70 percent fixed income, and 20 to 50 percent equities.

Remember, your Personal Policy Statement is just the first step in the selection of an ideal portfolio. Later we will add other dimensions of diversification to your portfolio and help you find the right funds or fund alternatives to fill in your portfolio.

Wrapping Up

You cannot hope to be a successful investor if you don't have a clear idea of what you want to achieve, how much risk you're prepared to accept, how much you have to save, and what rate of return you are aiming for. There are many different types of investors with different investment profiles. In order to build a suitable investment portfolio, you need to know what you are trying to accomplish in terms of short- and long-term financial goals and objectives, whether they be that Hawaii dream vacation or retirement planning. To accomplish this you need to quantify your current and potential assets, and quantify your goals. Put all of this together by using our Investment Assessment Questionnaire and you are well on your way to establishing the right portfolio for you.

Without these critical parameters in place, you will founder. It all comes down to the old admonition: "Know thyself." All the financial expertise in the world will be useless without that fundamental building block firmly in place.

7

BUILDING AND MAINTAINING A WINNING PORTFOLIO

In chapter 3, we explained the importance of asset allocation and outlined the various types of asset classes. In chapter 6, you learned how to use information about your risk tolerances, your personal wealth, and your objectives to establish a suitable mix for your own portfolio. Whether that mix is conservative or aggressive or some combination of the two, your critical decision is whether to go with a "do-it-yourself" or a "customized" approach. We favour the former, as you will soon see. Furthermore, after establishing your portfolio mix, how to you deal with the fluctuating values of your portfolio and its drift away from your target? That too will be explored in this chapter.

Homemade versus Store-Bought Diversification

There are different ways of building a suitably diversified portfolio. Should you actively select the components of the portfolio, hand-picking each of the securities? Or should you "purchase" the portfolio directly through asset allocation funds or balanced mutual funds—funds that maintain a proportion between debt and equity securities? Should you mix and match funds or other securities to build your own portfolio based on the asset mix decision that's right for you? Or should you skip right through the process and just buy a balanced mutual fund? How do you use derivative products, which were discussed in chapter 3, to adjust and rebalance a core portfolio and in adjusting the mix? The answer to these and other questions and the rationale for asset allocation are the subject of this chapter.

With the knowledge this book provides, you have all the tools to build your own personalized portfolio. The next questions: Do you have the time? And is it worth the effort?

Let's accept for the moment that there is nothing wrong with good balanced mutual funds. And for beginning investors—with less than $25,000 to invest—a balanced fund is probably the best place to start. Balanced funds provide a built-in asset mix based on the fund manager's view of the world.

Well, maybe the asset mix doesn't completely fit the manager's view of the world. The fact is that balanced fund managers are given specific mandates for structuring and changing asset mixes. For example, the Sceptre Balanced Growth Fund strives "to earn the highest possible return that is consistent with a conservative fundamental investment philosophy." In other words this means the fund maintains a balanced asset mix, somewhere around 50 percent stocks and 50 percent bonds.

That's all right, if you're looking for that type of asset mix. But if you're a growth investor, a 50/50 split isn't likely to meet your long-term needs. And if you are an ultra-conservative investor, 50 percent in equities may be much too high. Your homemade asset mix can deal with that. Put the asset mix decision into the hands of a fund manager, and you eliminate any possibility of making adjustments to suit your circumstances.

You also need to address some issues on the performance side. Look at the table on the next page, which shows the average compounded return over the 10 years to September 30, 2001, for Canadian balanced funds, Canadian equity funds, Canadian bond funds, Canadian money market funds, and U.S. equity funds.

We know that the average Canadian balanced fund returned 8.5 percent, compounded annually. So using our interest rate mathematics from chapter 5, a $10,000 investment in the average Canadian balanced fund made

10 years ago would have grown to $22,609.83: 10,000(1.085)^{10} = $22,609.83. That's what we call store-bought diversification.

AVERAGE COMPOUNDED RETURNS, 1991–2001

Canadian Balanced Funds	8.5%
Canadian Equity Funds	9.3%
U.S. Equity Funds	11.3%
Canadian Bond Funds	7.8%
Canadian Money Market Funds	4.5%

Homemade diversification is when you decide on the asset mix that's right for you, and then find the best people to manage the assets you choose. In the next table, we have structured a simple balanced portfolio using Canadian mutual fund investments plus 30 percent foreign content, as represented by the average U.S. equity mutual fund. Remember that we're trying to compare homemade Canadian diversification with a Canadian balanced mutual fund.

So let's assume you put 30 percent of your capital into the average Canadian equity fund, 30 percent into the average U.S. equity fund, 35 percent into the average Canadian bond fund, and 5 percent into the average Canadian money market fund. (Those percentages, by the way, are a reasonably representative asset mix for a balanced investor.)

Did the homemade portfolio do better than an off-the-shelf portfolio? This is an important question, because if it doesn't beat the off-the-shelf model, why spend the time and effort to build a portfolio from scratch?

HOMEMADE PORTFOLIO

ALLOCATION	PERCENTAGE	AMOUNT	ANNUAL RETURN	VALUE AFTER 10 YEARS
Canadian Money Market Funds	5%	$ 500	4.5%	$ 776.48
Canadian Bond Funds	35	3,500	7.8	7,417.46
Canadian Equity Funds	30	3,000	9.3	7,300.00
U.S. Equity Funds	30	3,000	11.3	8,751.30
Totals	100%	$10,000	9.2%	$24,245.24

Our homemade balanced portfolio produced a compound annual return of 9.2 percent and is worth $24,245.24. That's $1,635.41 more in your pocket, and a 7.2 percent improvement over the store-bought model. And remember, returns compound over time, so the longer the time frame, the greater the potential difference. Plus, our hypothetical homemade balanced portfolio assumes we can only find the average-performing funds in each category.

Why did our homemade model turn in superior results? First, it has to do with asset allocation—a specific asset allocation model is superior to a rough 50/50 asset allocation inherent in a typical balanced fund. Second, it has to do with the 10 to 15 percent of the returns that are attributable to security selection. By finding managers who specialize in specific markets, you define the asset mix decision and let the portfolio managers do what they do best.

By determining your personal asset mix, you tailor your investments to your personal policy statement. And, coincidentally, the numbers tell us that by selecting funds to represent your own personal asset mix, you enhance your overall return. And that assumes as well that you purchase only the median funds in each class, and make no changes to the asset mix for the 10-year holding period.

With the homemade portfolio, you decide the asset mix and let the fund managers decide on security selection. So we argue that the homemade asset allocation program is the right way to go.

The Benefits of an Asset Allocation Strategy

Here is the conceptual justification for going with a homemade asset allocation program.

- *Asset allocation or investment policy accounts for most of long-run returns.* Of the three components of the investment management process, namely, asset allocation (or asset mix), investment selection, and market timing, studies clearly indicate that asset allocation is by far the most important. A well-known study (published in 1986, see chapter 3) indicated that the actual asset allocation selected accounted for 93.6 percent of the variation in returns on very large investment portfolios. Other studies have supported this finding, concluding that the asset allocation decision rather than the security selection and market timing decisions had the greatest impact on total portfolio return and the variability about the total portfolio return.

- *Asset allocation is designed to create optimum investment portfolios.* Securities and portfolios contain both systematic risks (economy-wide or external) and unsystematic risks (related to the individual security). The objective of an asset allocation strategy is to design a portfolio that is not only return efficient but that has only moderate systematic risk and virtually no unsystematic risk.

- *Asset allocation allows for meaningful performance measurement.* An asset allocation policy such as a 20/30/50 mix among cash, income, and growth securities is transparent and allows for performance measurement. Without a clear policy, you cannot set goals and measure against them. Remember, a basic principle of finance is that "what gets measured gets managed."

Rebalancing Your Portfolio

Once you have established the right strategic asset allocation, you need to establish a program for rebalancing the portfolio as it drifts away from your target, as it surely will. Rebalancing is called dynamic asset allocation and refers to the systematic rebalancing to the long-term benchmark asset mix among the various asset classes. Maintenance of the mix can be a challenge. Why does such drift occur? Quite simple—drift occurs because of fluctuating market values.

Suppose you have decided on a portfolio mix of 5 percent safety, 35 percent income, and 60 percent growth, and you start the year with a portfolio as follows:

ALLOCATION	PERCENTAGE	AMOUNT
Canadian Money Market Funds	5%	$ 500
Canadian Bond Funds	35	3,500
Canadian Equity Funds	30	3,000
U.S. Equity Funds	30	3,000
Totals	100%	$10,000

Now assume that over the next 12 months, your Canadian money market funds record a 6.0 percent gain, your Canadian bond funds advance by 5.7 percent, your Canadian stocks increase by 13.3 percent, and your U.S. stocks record a 45.7 percent gain, resulting in an overall portfolio increase of 20 percent. Here's what the portfolio is worth one year later:

ALLOCATIOON	VALUE	ACTUAL PERCENTAGE	TARGET PERCENTAGE
Canadian Money Market Funds	$ 530	4.4%	5.0%
Canadian Bond Funds	3,700	30.8	35.0
Canadian Equity Funds	3,400	28.3	30.0
U.S. Equity Funds	4,370	36.5	30.0
Totals	$12,000	100.0%	100.0%

This typical result reflects the fact that asset classes will more often than not provide returns that don't perfectly match their percentage in the portfolio. Although you have had a good year, your portfolio due to these serendipitous results has now drifted significantly from your target.

In this case, in order to restore the desired mix you would sell $770 worth of U.S. equity funds and buy $200 worth of Canadian equity funds, $500 worth of Canadian bond funds, and $70 worth of Canadian money market money funds to restore the portfolio balance as follows:

ALLOCATION	VALUE	ACTUAL PERCENTAGE	TARGET PERCENTAGE
Canadian Money Market Funds	$ 600	5.0%	5.0%
Canadian Bond Funds	4,200	35.0	35.0
Canadian Equity Funds	3,600	30.0	30.0
U.S. Equity Funds	3,600	30.0	30.0
Totals	$12,000	100.0%	100.0%

How often should you rebalance? Most investors review their portfolio periodically and rebalance at that time. This so-called temporal rebalancing is most commonly done on a monthly, quarterly, semi-annual, or annual basis.

Although temporal rebalancing is the common method, the theoretically correct approach is to rebalance back to original weights in response to price and value fluctuations. For example, rebalancing might be used when there is, say, a 10 percent deviation from the target. There are also costs—possibly substantial ones—associated with switching your funds. These include commissions and loads, and possibly transfer fees, not to mention the "nuisance costs" of signing documents and negotiating instruments.

You might also consider rebalancing if your risk tolerances change, which is likely to happen as wealth increases. If high nominal returns are earned for an extended period, you may become more (or less) risk tolerant. As well, if your objectives change, your desired portfolio asset mix may change accordingly.

The Value of Rebalancing

Overall, the following are the benefits of rebalancing:

- *Rebalancing enforces integrity of mix.* This means that all of the time and effort you put into finding the right mix for you is not wasted, as you are restoring the mix when it drifts from your target.

- *Rebalancing adds value.* Rebalancing dampens returns in a strong market period since you are reducing the equity component. It enhances returns in weak period through counter-cyclical selling. Rebalancing is automatically counter-cyclical—you are selling the stronger asset classes and buying the weaker ones.

- *Rebalancing enforces discipline.* Rebalancing makes you stick with your asset allocation during unfavourable periods.

So, we recommend that you establish a suitable asset mix and then implement a rebalancing program to maintain it.

Wrapping Up

Let's conclude our discussion with the four key principles of portfolio building.

Rule #1: Diversification Is Good

Most investors like to avoid risk, want consistency of performance, hate making mistakes, and like to sleep well at night. Portfolio diversification is the logical outcome of these fundamental principles of human behaviour. Diversifying means spreading the risks so you are protected against unexpected shocks, such as sudden spikes in interest rates, or market crashes, or currency collapses, or unexpected inflation. Putting this into action means setting an appropriate asset mix of safety, income, and growth securities for your portfolio. Since we all have different tastes and financial needs, our asset mixes range from very security conscious (high proportion of cash and fixed-income securities) to aggressive, growth-oriented portfolios (high levels of stock or equity investments).

Applying this first rule is called strategic asset allocation. It's the key to financial success. For it to work, you have to keep it intact.

Rule #2: Stay Diversified

Rule #2 is to always follow Rule #1 by periodically adjusting your actual mix back to your target. Good investment planning doesn't stop at the strategic asset allocation decision. You also have to monitor your program. It's one thing to pick your portfolio structure—it's another to keep it! This second stage of investing is what is called rebalancing, or keeping your desired mix in place.

Rule #3: Asset Allocation Includes Global Diversification

Which of the following do you suppose was the more volatile over the past 30 years?

1. A $100,000 portfolio consisting of a large number of Canadian stocks from many different industries?

2. A portfolio consisting an $80,000 portfolio of Canadian stocks from many different industries, plus a $20,000 portfolio of foreign stocks from many different countries?

The answer is that the second portfolio was much less volatile—and it recorded higher returns as well! Global diversification follows the principle of asset allocation—namely, allocating your portfolio assets to different classes. Global investment has become an integral part of the investment asset allocation process.

Rule # 4: Hold Low-Correlation Assets

Diversification is based on diverse events. Two stocks that tend to respond differently to the same event or that are affected by entirely different factors will show different price behavior. These stocks are said to have low correlation with each other. Low-correlation stocks reduce the volatility of a portfolio—that is what causes the diversification effect.

In conclusion, we believe that a well-diversified portfolio approach best suits the needs of the long-term investor, and the reasoning for this is simple—a properly balanced portfolio allows you to sleep at night and that, by definition, allows you to remain invested for the long term.

The trick is finding the right balance—probably the most elusive concept in the investment business. We all know that to balance is to diversify, but there is a right way and a wrong way to do that. Holding 10 or 20 mutual funds without really knowing what each fund brings to the portfolio is cumbersome and, in the end, probably does more harm than good.

Even if you choose to work with a financial advisor you ought to have some understanding of the process. That way, you'll be able to actively participate in the decision making instead of having to accept everything that's recommended on faith and living with whatever consequences may result.

8

THE DOLLAR DILEMMA: UNDERSTANDING CURRENCY RISK

As commentators on global investing, we are often asked to provide advice on currency purchases. Typically, someone will be planning a trip to New York (or London, or Paris, or Tokyo) and they'll ask: "Should I buy my dollars (or pounds or euros or yen) now, or should I wait?"

Our usual response is, "It's a toss-up!" It's not that we are cavalier or unhelpful. It's just that we believe that predicting foreign exchange rates is like throwing dice. And the events that fuel currency fluctuations (changing interest rates being one of the most significant) are largely unpredictable.

Still, that doesn't mean you should ignore foreign currency risk. Far from it. The key is to look at your investment and your spending needs, and to develop a foreign currency position that meets those needs.

We aren't talking about currency speculation. We are talking about a sensible way to increase your portfolio diversification and to protect against an adverse move in the external value of the Canadian dollar.

Let's look at the potential impact of a foreign currency change—not as investors (that's coming presently) but from a purely practical point of view. For example, let's say you and your family are planning a trip to London next year, and that the cost in British pounds will be about £10,000. If the Canadian dollar falls from its level at the time of writing of C$2.26 per pound (i.e., it takes $2.26 Canadian to buy one British pound) to, say, $2.50 per British pound, the Canadian dollar equivalent cost of your trip will increase from $22,600 to $25,000!

Consider, too, the potential effect of a currency shift on the purchase of imported goods or a foreign vacation property. Clearly, it makes sense, again from a purely practical point of view, to have some of your assets denominated in foreign currencies.

Foreign Currency Risk

Now let's have a look at the investment side of things and you'll see the potential impact of foreign currency fluctuations on your portfolio. Just consider the following.

Over a recent 10-year period (to October 2001), the annual compounded rate of return on Canadian stocks in Canadian dollars was 8.2 percent per annum. A $10,000 investment made at the start of the period would have been worth $21,992 a decade later. However, if you had invested in the Canadian market but measured the returns in U.S. dollars, the results were dramatically different. The annual compounded rate of return was a mere 4.6 percent, which means you earned 3.6 percentage points per annum less than the Canadian dollar version. At this rate, a $10,000 investment would reach a value of only $15,678—a shortfall of $6,314 or 28.7 percent. In other words, the purchasing power of your investment in U.S. dollars was 28 percent less than it would have been if the Canadian dollar hadn't fallen. Does it matter? Absolutely. If you planned to travel, or buy U.S. goods, or to buy a place in the States, the decline in the external value of the Canadian dollar would have been quite serious.

This works both ways. Suppose you buy a U.S.-dollar denominated security (say a U.S. term deposit) with C$10,000, equivalent at the time of purchase to US$6,500, given an exchange rate of US$0.65 or an external value of the dollar of $(1/0.65) = C\$1.538$. Now suppose the investment earns 4.5 percent but the value of the Canadian dollar rises to US$0.68 or $[(1/0.68)$

= C\$1.47]. When you cash in, your Canadian dollar equivalent will be US\$6,500 × 1.045 × 1.470 = C\$9,984.97. A 4.5 percent return in U.S. dollars vanished as the Canadian dollar rose!

As you can see, if you buy a U.S. dollar investment, you are buying a fund that invests in foreign securities denominated in a foreign currency. Changes in the foreign currency relative to the Canadian dollar can have a major impact on your portfolio, either adding to or taking from the performance of your particular security.

Performance Distortions

In order to fully grasp the role of currency within your portfolio, consider how currency risk affects different types of index funds. For the record, index funds are designed to provide mirror-image performance against a specific index. Most U.S. index funds, for example, are designed to track the performance of the S&P 500 Composite Index. Managers do a good job of tracking the index, but when you convert those returns back into Canadian dollars, the return you see isn't always the return you get.

As an example, consider the TD U.S. Index Fund. This is one of the longest-running U.S. equity index funds in Canada. Over a recent five-year period, the fund returned 9.4 percent per annum, while the index it tracks, the S&P 500 Composite Total Return Index, returned 10.2 percent.

Generally speaking, the fund has done a good job tracking the index. The difference in performance can be attributed to the 63 basis point (0.63 percent) Management Expense Ratio (MER). Similarly, the CIBC U.S. Equity Index, which employs the same strategy, came in at 9.3 percent over that same time period.

Other U.S. index funds have not done nearly as well. Take the Scotia CanAm Stock Index Fund, which has been around since 1993. This fund uses a combination of S&P 500 Stock Index futures contracts and Government of Canada T-bills to obtain a return in Canadian dollars similar to the S&P 500 Index. (Futures contracts are described at the end of this chapter.)

To accomplish this, the Scotia CanAm Stock Index fund buys Government of Canada T-bills and then pledges up to 10 percent of these assets to purchase, on margin, S&P 500 Index futures contracts. The fund will carry sufficient S&P 500 futures contracts to enable it to closely match the performance of the S&P 500 Index.

Since it will not use futures contracts for speculative trading, the fund will always set aside sufficient cash or cash equivalents to satisfy the obligations of the futures contracts. Therefore, the fund gives you dollar-for-dollar exposure to the U.S. equity market. But since the bulk of the fund's assets are in Canadian dollar-denominated investments (i.e., Government of Canada Treasury bills), this offering is not considered foreign content within an RRSP. You get foreign exposure without filling up your foreign content allowance.

So we have two funds with similar objectives and different approaches. In both cases, the objective is to track the performance of the S&P 500 Composite Index. The TD fund buys the underlying stocks, while the Scotia CanAm fund uses Treasury bills plus derivatives.

The CanAm Fund's return over the same five-year period was 7.7 percent, representing a tracking error of 2.5 percentage points per annum relative to its S&P 500 Composite Index benchmark. The difference between its performance and the TD and CIBC funds is dramatic when you consider the funds are trying to accomplish the same thing.

So what happened to cause the distortion? It's not that the Scotia CanAm Stock Index Fund was badly managed. On the contrary, it was managed according to the prospectus. The difference in return is almost entirely due to currency translation. For the bulk of the five-year period, the Canadian dollar declined in value relative to the U.S. dollar. (In 1999, as you may recall, the Canadian dollar actually rose relative to the U.S. dollar.)

When the Canadian dollar is weak, it's an advantage for the TD fund, which converts all of its assets to U.S. dollars and is 100-percent invested in U.S. stocks. A weak loonie is a disadvantage for a fund that has most of its assets invested in Canadian dollar-denominated Treasury bills and that does not actively manage currency risk, like the Scotia fund.

One way to avoid such distortions is to buy an RRSP U.S. equity index fund that hedges its currency exposure—caused by having the bulk of its assets in Canadian Treasury bills—back into U.S. dollars. An example would be the CIBC U.S. Equity Index Fund, which uses currency futures and forward contracts to hedge currency exposure.

That doesn't mean you should avoid the Scotia CanAm Stock Index Fund, or any other RRSP equity index fund that does not hedge currency exposure. In the future, it may be that you don't want to be hedged back into U.S. dollars. As we said, in 1999 the Canadian dollar rallied against the U.S. dollar, which had a positive impact on the Scotia CanAm Stock Index Fund relative to the S&P 500 Index (C$) and the TD U.S. Index Fund.

So you have to decide which version you want. For most investors we prefer the natural hedge associated with a pure U.S. exposure.

Natural Hedges

The best approach to dealing with the risks of adverse foreign currency movements is to make sure you hold foreign-currency denominated assets in your portfolio. This is called a natural hedge. Available products include U.S.-dollar denominated bond funds, U.S.-dollar denominated money market funds, and foreign currency term deposits.

Remember that if you are investing through a tax shelter program, your investments are subject to the 30 percent foreign content rule. This means that you are allowed to have a maximum of 30 percent of the "book value" of your investments in foreign property in each of your RRSPs, RRIFs, etc. The term "book value" refers to the original cost of the units and not to the market value of the units at any given time. This means that capital appreciation will not affect book value but any reinvested distributions, sales, and transfers will have an impact. You should recognize, as well, that the 30 percent limit applies to each RRSP you have. If you hold RRSPs at different institutions and/or have multiple RRSPs (such as a regular, a self-directed, and a locked-in plan), you must use the 30 percent rule for each plan. RRSPs that hold foreign property investments in excess of that limit at the end of any month incur a penalty tax of 1 percent per month. Most financial institutions have tracking systems that monitor your foreign property purchases and provide alerts if you have triggered excessive positions. Most provide regular statements setting out the foreign content percentage. Don't rely on them solely—mistakes are made in this area. Since you are deemed by Canada Customs and Revenue Agency (CCRA) to be responsible for keeping track of your positions, we recommend that you keep a close watch.

One method of overcoming the foreign content rule is with clone products. For example the iUnits S&P 500 Index RSP Fund, known as the "i500Rs," is traded on the TSE under the symbol XSP. The fund is designed to track the S&P 500 Composite Index. However, instead of investing in the physical securities, the fund invests in cash and derivatives contracts, specifically in index futures, to match the performance of the underlying S&P 500 Index. This structure means that the i500Rs will be fully qualified investments for RRSPs and other tax shelters, and will not be subject to the 30 percent foreign investment restrictions.

Although traded in Canadian dollars, the i500Rs are managed to replicate the performance of the S&P 500 in *U.S. dollars*. Accordingly, from the standpoint of a Canadian investor, this means you will have the U.S. dollar exchange rate exposure. Overall, the i500Rs will track the Index very closely, but there will be some slippage. The MER is 30 points and the costs of structuring and maintaining the index future replication strategy as well as the forward contracts to create U.S. dollar denomination will add a bit to the trading costs and cause some tracking error.

Another natural hedge is U.S. dollar money market funds, such as the PH&N US$ Money Market Fund. It comes from Vancouver-based Phillips, Hager & North and has been the top-performing fund in its category virtually every year. The fund invests in Canadian issues denominated in U.S. dollars, so it is fully eligible for RRSPs and RRIFs. However, the fund has a high entrance fee, with a minimum initial investment requirement of $25,000 for both registered and non-registered investments (subsequent $1,000).

A smaller-ticket item is the Royal U.S. Dollar Money Market Fund. This fund's performance doesn't quite match that of the PH&N fund, largely because of its substantially higher 1.16 percent MER. Its record is pretty good nevertheless. It's also a more accessible fund, with a minimum investment (whether inside or outside an RRSP) of only $1,000 (subsequent $25).

Another useful natural hedge is foreign bonds and eurobonds. Canadian governments and corporations frequently issue bonds denominated in other currencies, such as euros, Japanese yen, and U.S. dollars. Why? Because many foreign investors don't like the currency risk associated with holding securities denominated in Canadian dollars, so they have been accommodated with bonds in their home currencies. All these bonds are 100 percent eligible for

RRSPs and RRIFs. That's because the foreign content rules don't focus on the currency in which a security is denominated, but rather on the country of origin. Since all these bonds were issued by Canadian entities, they're RRSP-eligible.

For European currency exposure, AAA-issuer eurobonds are ideal. They pay periodic interest (usually semi-annually) and mature at their par value. An important feature is that interest income is not subject to withholding tax at source. You simply include it as interest income (in equivalent Canadian dollars) on your tax return.

Keep in mind that because these securities are denominated in foreign currencies, there may be tax implications when you redeem them. If the Canadian dollar has depreciated during the time you held the units, you will have a foreign-exchange gain that will be subject to the 50 percent capital gain inclusion rule. (Or, if the Canadian dollar appreciates, you will have a loss.) Foreign exchange gains and losses are subject to a $200 exemption in any year.

Risk Management

For investors with large currency exposure, there are a number of products that can be used in portfolio risk management, or as it is commonly called, hedging. These products are classified as derivatives, which include call and put options, futures, forwards, and swaps. Of these, the most useful for retail investors are call options, put options, and futures contracts.

Call options on Canadian dollar futures contracts (see below for a description of futures contracts) are traded on the International Monetary Market of the Chicago Mercantile Exchange (CME). These represent the right to buy 100,000 Canadian dollar futures at a specified price (called the strike price) up to a specified expiration date. The price you pay for this option is called the premium.

Here's how it works. Suppose you have a large U.S. dollar component in your portfolio and you want to guard against a rise in the Canadian dollar. In October 2001, with the Canadian dollar trading around US$0.635, the March 2002 63.5-cent dollar call options were quoted at US$0.84 or US$840 per 100,000 Canadian dollar contract. If you wished to hedge a U.S. dollar portfolio, you could buy one of these contracts at a premium of $840 plus commissions (typically $25 to $100). The contract gives you the right (but not the obligation) to buy a Canadian-dollar futures contract at a price of US$0.635. If the Canadian dollar is trading below the strike price in March, you let the contract lapse, content with the knowledge that the loss on your contract is offset by a rise in the market value of your portfolio. If the Canadian dollar falls by more than your loss on the option contract, you participate in the windfall. On the other hand, if the Canadian dollar rises to say, US$0.66, you can sell your contract, which will be worth $2,500 (0.66 – 0.635 × 100,000) and the profit will fully or partially offset the loss suffered on the portfolio.

Put options can be used in similar fashion to hedge against a decline in the Canadian dollar.

Canadian dollar futures contracts are traded on the International Monetary Market of the Chicago Mercantile Exchange. These contracts call for delivery of 100,000 Canadian dollars on specified dates in March, June, September, and December. If you are holding a U.S. dollar portfolio, you can buy a Canadian dollar futures contract to hedge your risk. If the value of the Canadian dollar rises, the loss suffered on the portfolio is offset by the gain on the futures position. On the other hand, if the value of the Canadian dollar falls, the gain realized on the portfolio is offset by the loss on the futures position. In either case you have reduced or even eliminated the foreign exchange risk.

To trade Canadian dollar futures you need to have a futures brokerage account. Most brokerage firms require minimum deposits of $5,000 to $10,000 (sometimes more) to open an account. Each contract requires about $3,000 or more in margin, which is a performance bond that ensures you will fulfill your side of the contract. All positions are marked to market daily, which means that you will be responsible on a current basis for covering your losses with additional margin.

Unlike options, futures do not trade at premiums and hence are a much cheaper form of insurance protection. The costs are commissions (about $50 to $400 per contract) plus interest forgone on your performance bond (which can be supplied in the form of Treasury bills.) The downside of this form of risk management is that you give up any possibility of a windfall. If the Canadian dollar falls sharply, your portfolio gains are offset by your futures losses. That is the nature of pure risk management.

Options and Futures on Other Currencies

Options and futures are traded on the CME for the British pound, Japanese yen, Swiss franc, and the euro. Futures (but not options) are also traded for the Australian dollar and the Mexico peso.

Wrapping Up

Protecting against a decline in the Canadian dollar is an essential element of financial and portfolio planning. If the Canadian dollar drops and all of your assets are in Canadian dollars you may discover that you can no longer afford that trip to New York or indeed even that second home in Florida. Foreign currency exposure can have a noticeable effect on your portfolio returns.

The ideal approach is to use a natural hedge by buying foreign-currency denominated assets. If you need a more elaborate risk management program, there are options and futures available.

9

SUCCESSFUL MUTUAL
FUND INVESTING

You probably already know what a mutual fund is: a pool of money that a professional money manager invests on your behalf. Each fund operates under a specific set of criteria that determine where it can invest, what fees it can charge, and what kinds of risks it can take. All these are spelled out in detail in a simplified prospectus—a document you must be provided with before any order can be finalized.

One of the most common misapprehensions is that mutual funds and the stock market are interchangeable terms. In fact, there are hundreds of mutual funds that don't own a single stock, and never will. Money market funds, for example, invest mainly in short-term notes issued by governments, banks, and large corporations. Mortgage funds invest in residential first mortgages. Bond funds own debt securities. These funds will never hold a single share of stock.

The distinction is especially important in the wake of the prolonged bear market that began in the spring of 2000. Many investors have been frightened away from mutual funds as a result, concerned about the risk involved.

Let us make one point very clear: Mutual funds can be as safe or as risky as you want. The selection is up to you. In this chapter, we'll provide the basic guidance you need to make the most appropriate choices.

Types of Funds

This is the "you-can't-tell-the-players-without-a-program" section. Before you embark on the process of selecting winning mutual funds, you need to have a clear idea of the different types that are available and what they do. So here's a quick run-down.

Cash type funds invest in highly liquid, low-risk securities such as Treasury bills, bankers' acceptances, and short-term corporate notes. In normal times, they pay the lowest return but also carry the least risk.

Fixed-income funds hold portfolios of debt securities. These can range from top-grade government bonds to corporate high-yields bonds, or "junk bonds" as they are sometimes called. Some of these funds are more risky than others, so you need to understand the specific mandate of the one you're considering.

Equity funds invest in stock markets, either domestic or international. There are many categories of equity funds, ranging from the well diversified (e.g., global funds that invest around the world) to the tightly focused, such as country-specific and industry-specific funds.

Balanced and *asset allocation funds* offer a mix of all three core asset groups. The ratio of stocks to bonds to cash in these funds may vary considerably and in some cases the manager will have the power to move 100 percent into a single asset type, such as equities. Find out what parameters apply to any fund you may be considering before you make an investment.

The Prospectus—The Key to Understanding

Before you buy units in any mutual fund, you'll be given a copy of the "simplified prospectus." These have recently been completely revamped and the new prospectuses contain useful information about every fund that a company offers. Before you make any investment decision, read the section on each fund in which you're interested. Here are some of the most important points to look for:

- *Investment objective:* This is a brief description of exactly what the fund is designed to do. This should tell you at a glance whether it meets your personal goals. This should be immediately followed by a section on *investment strategies* which offers a detailed look at how the managers intend to achieve the fund's goals. This section should tell you about the type of securities the fund will buy, whether it will use derivatives and, if so, how, whether the manager will hold large amounts of cash under certain conditions, and more.

- *Risks:* This section is one of the most important in the prospectus. Read it thoroughly and make sure you understand it. There's no excuse for saying later that you didn't understand how risky the fund was.

- *Suitability:* Here you'll find a description of the type of investor for whom the fund is best suited. If you see a sentence like "You can accept high risk," you are being warned about potentially large swings in unit values. If you don't like taking on a lot of risk, that's a red flag.

- *Past performance:* This section provides information about how the fund has done over time. It's useful to know, but don't assume you can project such results into the future.

- *Financial highlights:* You'll find some useful statistical data here. Note especially the MER (management expense ratio) figures because they represent the annual cost of the fund to you. There are two parts to this equation. One is the fee that's paid to the management company. The other is the day-to-day operating expenses of the fund. It's not unusual for different funds within the same group to charge different management fees. In the case of any fund in which you're interested, see if the numbers are trending up or down. A rising MER will have the effect of reducing net returns.

- *Fees and expenses:* There are a lot of numbers in this section, but check through them carefully. They outline exactly what costs you will have to pay, including sales commissions and annual fees and expenses. If you're buying the fund using a deferred sales charge option, see how much you'll have to pay if you decide to sell. Also, check if the percentage is calculated on your original purchase price or on the market value of the units at the time of sale. If the fund increases in value, the latter method becomes much more expensive. Also, many fund companies charge for early redemption, even on no-load or front-end load funds, so check for this. Sometimes you can find some angles for reducing your commissions here, such as low-load options or negotiable back-end loads.

- *Income tax considerations:* If you're investing outside a registered plan, you'll want to take a close look at the tax implications. In doing so, remember that payments from mutual funds are taxed differently, depending on their source. The prospectus should outline which types of payments can be expected from the fund you're considering. There are several possibilities: capital gains dividends, Canadian stock dividends, foreign stock dividends, rental income, straight interest, and return of capital. You should understand which types of income you can expect to receive and determine whether this makes the best sense for you from a tax point of view. For example, if you want to shelter the maximum possible amount from taxes, you may look for funds that will generate capital gains, Canadian dividends, and return of capital, rather than interest income. Once you've invested, the fund manager will issue an annual reporting slip for tax purposes, showing exactly how much of each type of income you received that year.

A mutual fund prospectus may seem daunting at first glance, but you don't have to read it cover-to-cover. Just go to the specific information on the funds you're considering and then look at the key points we have outlined here. By spending 15 or 20 minutes, you may avoid an investment mistake that could end up costing you hundreds or even thousands of dollars.

Picking Winners

Now that you know the basics, let's get to the meat of this chapter: the process to be used to weed out losers and select funds for your portfolio that will produce solid returns over time. These guidelines will help to set you in the right track.

Mutual funds have a performance record that anyone can look up. But last year's results are no guarantee that the fund is going to win tomorrow. Past performance is simply an indication of form—nothing more.

But the track record at least gives you some idea of how the fund has performed historically. A fund that is consistently in the first or second quartile of its category over several years (in other words, the top half) will likely continue to outperform.

You can find the performance history of every mutual fund in the country in a number of places. Most major newspapers publish monthly surveys of fund performance. Several organizations offer software that tracks fund results and allows you to compare those in which you're interested to the rest of the field. There are several annual mutual fund guides that assess comparative fund performance on a quantitative and qualitative basis, including our own annual *Buyer's Guide to Mutual Funds*. So there's no shortage of performance information. It's simply a matter of taking time to find it.

Just because a fund has a great 10-year record doesn't mean it's still doing well. You have to look at the trend line–how is the fund performs in comparison to others in the same category.

Consider the following examples. In each case, we're looking at the ranking of a fund compared to all others in the same category over several years. See if you can spot the trend patterns.

FUND RANKINGS OVER TIME

	10 YEARS (73 FUNDS)	5 YEARS (136 FUNDS)	3 YEARS (151 FUNDS)	1 YEAR (202 FUNDS)
Fund A Rank	3	108	139	200
Fund B Rank	1	2	1	1
Fund C Rank	48	91	11	19
Fund D Rank	69	113	122	147

The trends are immediately obvious. Fund A is in a long, steady decline. There's nothing in that trend line to encourage you to believe that next year it's going to finish near the top of the charts. Fund B shows itself to be a winner no matter what time frame you look at. Fund C is a case where something positive is happening. Over the past three years, it's been transformed from a weak performer to one that's in the top 10 percent in its class. And finally, Fund D is clearly a chronic also-ran–a fund that underperforms the competition no matter what time frame you look at.

Most Canadians are cautious by nature when it comes to their money. They don't like a lot of risk, and this feeling was reinforced by the bear market that opened the 21st century.

That's why it's essential to look at volatility when you're trying to pick the best funds for your personal needs. Fortunately, the information is easy to find. Most of the business papers include volatility (also called variability) rankings in their monthly mutual fund reports, so you can tell at a glance how much risk is inherent in the fund.

Even more useful is the average risk information that's available on mutual fund Web sites such as Globefund (**www.globefund.com**). Go to their Reports section, call up any fund, and click on the name. That will take you to a statistical page that shows you, among other things, the three-year risk rating of the fund company compared to the average for its category and its benchmark index. If you want to choose low-risk funds for your portfolio, this is one of the most valuable reference tools we've found.

Some types of funds will outperform others at certain stages in the business cycle. For example, you can make good money in a recession, especially in the early stages, by putting money into bond funds. That's because the Bank of Canada usually moves aggressively to lower interest rates when the economy turns sour, in hopes of encouraging investment and consumer spending. Bond prices rise in a falling interest rate environment, so bond funds will do well. We saw that phenomenon most recently in 2001.

Stock funds are normally the best performers when the economy is beginning to turn the corner into a recovery phase. The typical pattern is that stock prices get beaten down to bargain-basement levels during a recession. When economic conditions start to look better, cheap shares attract investor attention and the markets take off.

By putting all these factors together, you can zero in on specific funds that meet your personal requirements.

Building a Successful Portfolio

Choosing good funds is only part of the battle, however. You have to bring them together in a combination that ensures that the sum (the total portfolio) is greater than the individual parts. That's what lies at the core of successful mutual fund investing.

The ideal fund portfolio should achieve the following:

• Provide potential for steady growth at an average annual rate of at least 8 percent to 10 percent annually over the long term.

- Limit downside risk in falling equity markets.

- Provide some currency protection.

- Be well diversified by asset class, style, and geography.

- For non-registered portfolios, be tax-efficient.

You should review these criteria every time you consider a new fund for inclusion in your plan. If the fund doesn't meet at least two of the objectives, it should be bypassed.

Let's review each criterion in detail.

Growth

The biggest mistake many fund investors make is to succumb to greed. It's the reason that many people got clobbered in the high-tech crash. They saw the huge returns that tech-weighted funds scored in 1998–99 and overloaded their portfolios in that direction. At the same time, they underweighted poorly performing value funds and fixed-income funds.

A reasonable average annual return over the long haul (say 10 years plus) is 8 percent annually. With careful management, 10 percent is achievable. If you aim higher than that, you will have to accept a degree of risk that would make many people uncomfortable.

Downside Risk

If you feel that your fund portfolio suffered higher losses than you would have liked in the market tumble of 2000–2001, then you may have built in too much risk. The answer is to rebalance your asset mix to put more emphasis on low-risk securities, such as money market funds, mortgage funds, bond funds, balanced funds, and value-oriented equity funds.

However, don't go to the extreme of making your portfolio so safe that you reduce your return potential to less than 8 percent annually. Yes, you can bullet-proof your portfolio with ultra-secure funds, but in doing so you will compromise your returns. The key is to find the right balance.

Currency Protection

There is no way of knowing where the loonie will go in the future. But we can say two things with certainty:

1. Our currency has been devalued by about one-third against the U.S. dollar in the past decade.

2. Every prediction that the loonie is about to rise to US$0.70 and higher has proven wrong to date.

Of course, all this could change. But if past trends continue, the Canadian dollar will gradually lose more ground against the greenback in the coming years. That's why every fund portfolio should contain some currency protection. This is not a case of speculation; it's a matter of hedging against continued devaluation of the loonie.

Currency protection can be achieved by holding mutual funds that invest in U.S. dollar securities. These include U.S. equity funds, foreign bond funds, and U.S. dollar money market funds. Although many of the equity funds can be purchased in either Canadian or U.S. currency units, in fact it doesn't matter which you choose. As long as the securities in the portfolio are denominated in U.S. dollars, you will get the benefit of any gain that currency makes against the loonie.

Of course, our dollar may turn around and start to rise, so you wouldn't want to hold your entire portfolio in U.S. dollar funds (which you could, even in an RRSP). Decide on a U.S. dollar percentage that is appropriate for your plans (at least 25 percent is recommended) and be sure that you choose funds that will provide that.

Diversification

Several types of diversification need to be considered in building your fund portfolio. Asset mix diversification is the most basic. This is simply the way in which you combine cash (money market funds), fixed income, and equity funds in your portfolio. There is no "ideal" asset mix but a 10/40/50 allocation is a reasonable target for a balanced portfolio. Review chapter 6 to determine the appropriate level of asset allocation for your investment profile.

Geographic diversification is essential. Canada is a small market with a weak currency. To tie up most or all of your fund assets in this country is therefore a mistake, unless you prefer to let patriotism rule over pragmatism. At least 40 percent of your fund portfolio should consist of U.S. and international funds.

Style diversification is increasingly recognized as a key to superior fund performance. People with a good percentage of value funds in their equity mix withstood the market turmoil much better than those whose portfolios were heavily growth oriented. However, growth funds will come back at some point in the future. The ideal portfolio has a mix of both, with some occasional fine-tuning to adjust the balance towards the better-performing style. We will explore this issue in greater detail in the next chapter.

Tax Efficiency

For non-registered portfolios, you need to take tax efficiency into account in the fund selection process. The last thing you need is to be stuck with a big tax bill each year. For income-oriented portfolios, you should consider dividend funds and income trusts funds. They will generate income that is taxed at an advantageous rate compared to interest income from bond funds.

Study the distribution history of any equity fund carefully before purchase. Distributions are taxed annually and a fund with a record of high distributions may add a significant amount to your tax bill. Also, consider "umbrella funds," which allow you to switch money among various "classes" without triggering capital gains tax liability. Several companies now offer them.

When you are buying funds for your "perfect" portfolio, think carefully about the purchase options. You want a selection of funds that provides the flexibility to make changes without triggering expensive penalty charges. Therefore, avoid back-end load funds if possible. No-load funds are the ideal choice, but there are other alternatives. Some companies offer "low-load" funds. They're mainly for institutional investors, but if you're a good client you may be able to buy that way. Also, some financial advisors will sell front-end-load units at zero commission, just to get your business or because you have a large account.

If you must buy funds on a deferred sales charge (DSC) basis, choose fund families that offer plenty of switching options and make sure you will not be charged a fee when you want to move your money within the same organization.

If you can master these basic rules you can indeed build your Perfect Portfolio. We've created an example of how one such portfolio might look. Your own numbers may be somewhat different, depending on your objectives, but if you use this is a model you won't go far wrong.

A Sample Portfolio

Here is a sample fund portfolio that takes into account the criteria we have just discussed. This is a balanced portfolio that uses a basic asset mix of 10 percent cash, 40 percent fixed income, and 50 percent growth. A more aggressive portfolio would increase the growth content while reducing the fixed income segment accordingly. The Model column represents the basic allocation. This remains constant. The Current column represents any fine-tuning you may do to reflect prevailing market conditions. At the time of writing, we favoured value funds over growth funds in our equity balance. Be sure to review your Current column at least quarterly.

SAMPLE PORTFOLIO

TYPE OF SECURITY	MODEL	CURRENT
Canadian Money Market Funds	5.0%	5.0%
U.S. Money Market Funds	5.0%	5.0%
Canadian $ Bond Funds	20.0%	20.0%
U.S. $ or Foreign Bond Funds	20.0%	20.0%
Canadian Equity Funds (value)	12.5%	15.0%
Canadian Equity Funds (growth)	12.5%	10.0%
U.S. Equity Funds (value)	7.5%	10.0%
U.S. Equity Funds (growth)	7.5%	5.0%
International Equity Funds (value)	5.0%	7.5%
International Equity Funds (growth)	5.0%	2.5%
Totals	100.0%	100.0%

Wrapping Up

The secret to a successful mutual fund portfolio is twofold. First, you must know how to select funds that have an above-average chance of superior performance. You won't always get it right, but if you go about the process with discipline and monitor your funds carefully, the odds of success will be greatly enhanced.

But that's only part of the process. The funds you select must be used as building blocks to create a portfolio that is fully integrated and that will achieve a number of specific goals, the most important of which are above-average growth potential and minimal risk.

By combining these two critical elements, you should be able to create a fund portfolio that will comfortably generate an average annual return of at least 8 percent while providing peace of mind in all economic conditions.

10

THE MYTHS AND TRUTHS
OF HEDGE FUNDS

A hedge asset is one that has low or no correlations with other specific asset classes. For example, a market-neutral hedge fund isolates unique risk and eliminates market risk by buying stocks and shorting the market in a specific proportion. Take the following case: Suppose that an investor's particular talent is in evaluating oil companies. The investor has a superior analytic model and approach that allows him to identify undervalued oil companies. Assuming that the model really works, what is the danger? Quite simply, what if the expert selects and buys the target stocks and then the market crashes, taking all investments with it. To eliminate the systematic pull of the market and to isolate the expert's oil picking abilities, the proper strategy is to buy the stocks and sell short a market index or an oil and gas index in a suitable proportion. This will reduce or eliminate the market effect, avoid Gambler's Ruin (right strategy, wrong execution), and isolate the expert's oil company selection abilities.

That's what a true hedge fund does—it isolates talent from luck. The reward system normally reflects this as well, since hedge fund managers are normally compensated primarily on the basis of performance rather than assets. Most hedge funds are private trusts with high minimum investments of rarely less than $150,000, and often as much as $1 million. They are normally organized as trusts and the advisor normally has incentive bonuses. They are typically domiciled offshore, although managed by domestic advisors. Hedge funds are sometimes confused with speculative or performance funds, which are funds that seek exposure to specific risks such as currency or sectors. However, speculative funds do not seek to eliminate the external risks associated with systematic market and economic changes and cycles. Hedge and performance funds have low, sometimes negative, correlation with traditional investments such as stocks and bonds.

Most investors regard hedge funds as an esoteric type of security that is available only to the super-rich. Hedge funds carry an aura of high-powered traders speculating in everything from international currency movements to soybean futures, employing highly risky leveraging and short-selling strategies in the process.

There's also a degree of mistrust surrounding these funds, much of it a legacy of the 1998 failure of Long-Term Capital Management, a huge hedge fund backed by some highly influential people, including a former vice-chairman of the U.S. Federal Reserve Board. The Russian economic collapse in the late summer of that year wiped out almost half of the fund's capital and created a crisis that for a time threatened to set off a domino effect throughout the U.S. financial system. Only a complex bail-out orchestrated by Fed chairman Alan Greenspan prevented the situation from getting completely out of hand.

As a result, many people regard these funds with a combination of suspicion and fear. They don't understand how hedge funds work, and they don't see how an ordinary investor can benefit from them.

In fact, hedge funds (which are really a form of a broader category known as absolute return investing) may indeed have a role to play in your portfolio. So let's dispel some of the myths and explain the truth about these little-understood securities.

Opposite Ends of the Spectrum

The weak performance of most conventional investments in 2000–2001 focused attention on the polar extremes of investment strategy, namely index (or passive) investing versus absolute return investing. The contrast is very dramatic and reflects alternate philosophies of investment.

Index or passive investing is based on the view that the market for securities is efficient (see our discussion of Efficient Markets Theory in chapter 4). The best strategy flowing from that view is to attempt to match the performance of an underlying index as closely as possible. For example, if you were interested in investing in Canadian securities and you wanted to take a passive approach, you would consider buying the i60 units that are traded on the Toronto Stock Exchange and that are designed to match as closely as possible the performance of the S&P/TSE 60 index. An index product is totally transparent—it will yield a profit when the underlying index rises and a loss when the underlying index falls. It's as simple as that.

An absolute return investment is the direct opposite of an index or passive investment. These investments are designed to eliminate or substantially reduce the market index effect. The investment philosophy paradigm is that managers can identify undervalued or overvalued securities. Such strategies are called market neutral or absolute return strategies and are employed by "absolute return funds" or ARFs.

ARFs are funds whose returns are not tied to a specific benchmark but instead are expected to have positive returns most of the time. Losses are expected to be rare and to be associated with unusual events. The "hedge fund" is a specific example of an ARF. Although hedge funds have received a lot of attention recently—some good, some bad—they have actually been around for quite some time. The concept itself is over 50 years old.

Genesis: Two Paths and the Road Not Taken

The hedge fund is an elusive concept and comes in many forms and guises. Some funds that call themselves hedge funds aren't that at all, but merely speculative funds. To understand what a hedge fund is you have to go back to the roots and to an understanding of risk and how to minimize it.

The bedrock of portfolio building is found in two basic paradigms of finance: Modern Portfolio Theory and its derivative, the Capital Asset Pricing Model. These models were discussed in chapter 4. To summarize, these models link risk and expected return of a security (and, more important, a portfolio) to the return on a market index. The "beta" measures the degree to which a security and portfolio fluctuate with a market index. In a properly diversified portfolio, the unique risk associated with one specific security is minimized, leaving only the systematic or economy-wide risk associated with a market index. This recognition of, and focus on, systematic risk represented the road most often followed by investors over the years.

The alternate path of portfolio building was set out in 1949 by one Alfred Jones, who was working on formulating his own investment strategies. A multi-careered person (he was an associate editor at *Fortune* magazine in 1940), Jones described an alternate view of investing, namely how to isolate the market exposure of individual securities. Jones outlined how an investor could eliminate market risk by buying securities and shorting the market in specified proportions. This approach captures the essence of hedge funds: the key is to isolate the analytic talent of the hedge fund manager from the fluctuations of the market.

This is Jones's basic equation:

$$\text{Market exposure} = \frac{(\text{long exposure} - \text{short exposure})}{\text{capital}}$$

Jones's approach served as the genesis of the modern hedge fund, and in fact he launched one in partnership form in 1949. The fund apparently had a successful run. Ultimately, Jones' success led to public awareness of the hedge fund concept.

A Taxonomy of Hedge Funds

A host of investment strategies are employed under the name of absolute return funds or hedge funds. Most such funds are highly specialized, sometimes with unclear objectives, and rely on the specific expertise of the manager.

You can visualize the ARF universe on a spectrum running from pure market-neutral funds to partially market-neutral funds, to fully directional or speculative funds.

Pure market-neutral hedge ARFs are the easiest to understand. They typically hold both long and short positions in securities, usually in the same sectors of the market. This is done by pairing up positions, such as being long (which simply means owning shares) in a stock that is believed to be undervalued in, say, the gold mining sector, while shorting an overvalued stock in that same sector. Market-neutral ARFs are designed so that their performance is expected to be absolutely uncorrelated with bond and stock markets, which means they will move counter to the indexes.

The next stage of ARFs are those that take hedged positions (are long/short) but are only partially market neutral. These would include ARFs that have long/short positions but have a bias in a particular direction (usually bullish). For example, a fund with $20 million in capital could borrow $8 million and buy $28 million worth of stocks while selling short $16 million worth of stocks. The fund's gross investment of $28 million would have a net market exposure of $28 million − $16 million = $12 million, making the portfolio 60 percent net long relative to its $20 million of capital. Of the $28 million gross investment, $12 million would be unhedged and $16 million ($16 million long and $16 million short) would be hedged and thus theoretically market neutral. So the fund would be biased towards the bullish (up) side of the market by $12 million.

Other funds in this category include event-driven isolation hedge funds, which focus their investments on special situations, perhaps distressed firms, leveraged buy-outs (LBOs), or takeovers; convertible hedge funds, which hold long convertible/short common share positions; and takeover arbitrage funds, which generally buy target firms and sell short the takeover firm.

At the extreme are funds that take directional positions in the market. These tend to be opportunistic, directional, or event driven. Some are momentum- or trend-based strategies. These are often called hedge funds but really fall into the speculation fund category. By their nature, they may nevertheless have relatively low correlation with conventional bonds and stocks.

Structure of Absolute Return Funds

Most investors know little about ARFs primarily because most are designed for institutions and people with high net worth. Most are sold by private placement or limited partnership and typically cannot or do not advertise. These "exempt market" funds are not offered by prospectus and are not subject to the regulations that govern ordinary mutual funds. Accordingly, the typical cautions and warnings associated with mutual funds are not required. ARFs usually require a substantial minimum investment, as much as $150,000 (varies by province) under the securities exemption that assumes the buyer is "sophisticated," although sometimes the minimum investment is as much as $10 million.

The traditional ratio of 85 percent/15 percent between the choice of asset class and the skill of the manager is reversed for such funds, with the emphasis landing squarely on the manager's ability. Indeed, the rewards in place for hedge fund managers are designed to be highly lucrative so as to attract the best. Management fees and incentive bonuses are very high. On the other hand, hedge fund managers who don't produce get fired quickly.

How ARFs Should Perform

Absolute return funds, despite the notoriety associated with the hedge fund version, are actually much less aggressive than many believe, as long as they are structured properly. Given the long/short positions in stocks, this means that in a strong equity market they should underperform, since the shorts (even if the fund manager had done a good job of finding overvalued ones) will increase in value due to the systematic pull of the market. This underperformance will dampen the overall returns because if the value of a stock that has been shorted actually rises, the investor loses money (a short position is a bet the stock will drop).

In a down market, a hedge fund should outperform since the short positions should at least offset (and perhaps more than offset) the losses on the long positions. Furthermore, the variability (volatility) of the fund, given the long/short positions, should be less than a market index. Often, the objectives of such funds are described as earning the 91-day T-bill or five-year government bond rate plus two or three percentage points, regardless of market conditions.

Overall, a well-designed hedge fund should

- underperform in a rising market

- outperform in a declining market—and show positive returns as well

- have relatively low standard deviations.

The Hedge Fund Record

Tracking performance of hedge funds is difficult. There are many different types of ARFs and only a few index providers. The data is skimpy and suffers from survivorship bias. (Survivorship bias refers to the observation that poorly performing funds tend to disappear and are excluded from performance calculations. Accordingly, longer-term results are biased to the upside because the weaklings have been closed or merged out of existence.)

Despite the short sample period and data deficiencies, a pattern does emerge. For example, over the decade from 1991 to fall 2001, the Zurich Market Neutral Median Index, a leading hedge fund index compiled by Zurich Capital Market, averaged 10.9 percent per annum, as compared to 9.49 percent for the TSE 300 Composite and 16.76 percent for the S&P 500. The index had a very low correlation with the S&P 500 (0.186) but a higher one with the TSE, possibly because of Nortel's dominance of the TSE for some of that period. It's also interesting to note that the Zurich index has been highly consistent and stable—its standard deviation has been about one-third that of the TSE and S&P.

Another broad index is the CSFB/Tremont Hedge Fund Index. The Tremont Index annual compounded rate of return over the period January 1994 to the present has been 11.5 percent, as compared to 9.03 percent and 16.5 percent for the TSE and S&P Indexes, respectively.

What to Look For in a Hedge Fund

If you are selecting an exempt market hedge fund, we recommend looking for answers to the following questions:

1. *Does the fund have a transparent statement of objectives?* What is the fund manager trying to accomplish? What are the specific strategies to be employed? Are deviations from the strategy allowed? What are the profit targets and benchmarks? You want to avoid having the wrong fund for your purpose and will probably need to interview the manager.

2. *What is the fund's track record?* If the fund manager is not prepared to supply a documented, audited record of past performance, drop it from your list.

3. *What is the fund's correlation with other conventional asset classes?* The fund manager should be able to provide a correlation matrix setting out the relationship between the fund's rate of return and that of stocks and bonds.

4. *What is the fund's managerial incentive program?* Is there a high-water mark beyond which the manager shares in the profits? Is it cumulative and reasonable?

5. *Does the fund hold strictly liquid measurable assets?* Strict, objective marking-to-market is a key feature of a proper hedge fund. Hedge funds that hold illiquid positions can be problem since they will include the risk associated with fund manager window dressing, subjective manual closing, and other such allocation problems.

Hedge Funds for Retail Investors

Although generally aimed at the institutional market, a few hedge funds are now targeted at the retail investor. These include the following:

FUND	MANAGER	STRATEGY	MINIMUM INVESTMENT
US Market-Neutral Portfolio	@rgentum	Market neutral	$500
Canadian Long/Short	@rgentum	Partially market neutral	$500
Global Market Neutral	Transamerica Life	Fund of funds	$1,000
Newcastle Market-Neutral	Newcastle Capital Mgmt.	Fund of funds	N/A

The @rgentum Canadian L/S Equity Portfolio is a tiny mutual fund from the innovative @rgentum group (their operating slogan is "Where Tradition Meets Technology"). It is structured as a classic long/short hedge fund. Its objectives are consistent with ARFs, namely generating positive returns regardless of market direction. Its return objective is to outperform T-bill yields and to approach the returns on Canadian stock market index returns. The risk objectives are to have a lower standard deviation than the market and little correlation with traditional investments. The portfolio objective is to maintain a long to short exposure of 62 percent to 38 percent. The focus in on mid- and large-sized companies with an average market float of $250 million.

The fund is managed by ChabotPage Investment Counsel, and thus far the fund's long/short strategy is off to a great start. Over a recent one-year period, the fund realized a 29.1 percent return, as compared to the massive 25.1 percent loss on the TSE 300 Composite Total Return Index and an average loss of 6.5 percent for Canadian equity mutual funds. The MER is high at 2.95 percent, but if the fund continues to perform the way it has, you won't mind paying the fee.

The fund is highly affordable—minimum initial and subsequent investments for both registered and non-registered investing is $500. The fund is fully RRSP-eligible. The fund is not available for Yukon, North West Territories, or Nunavut residents.

Note that the @rgentum funds have linked up with the University Avenue fund organization. At the time of writing, some structural reorganization was planned, so check with a financial advisor before making any investment decision, as the fund may not be available for purchase at this time.

Another fund in the family is the @rgentum U.S. Market-Neutral Portfolio. The record is much less stellar than the @rgentum Canadian L/S Equity Portfolio but it's worth a look. Its objectives are similar to those of the @rgentum Canadian L/S Equity Portfolio. Its specific goal is to earn returns in excess of T-bills with less volatility than the market and little or no correlation to the U.S. stock market. The MER is 2.95 percent. Initial and subsequent purchases are $500 for both registered and non-registered portfolios.

An exchange-traded fund is also available for retail investors. The Newcastle Market-Neutral Trust (NMN) is a closed-end investment fund (rather than a mutual fund) that is traded on the Toronto Stock Exchange and invests in a portfolio of hedge funds. It's structured as a fund of funds and invests in a portfolio of ARFs.

The fund is managed by Newcastle Capital Management, whose CEO is David Patterson. NMN's primary objective is to pay $0.40 per unit per quarter (8 percent per annum based on the original issue price). The fund's market-neutral stance means that its objectives include ensuring the performance of the fund is independent of fixed-income and equity markets. The fund also has the objective of maintaining a volatility level that is less than that of a mid-term bond portfolio and less than half that of major North American stock markets.

The fund suffered through the general hedge fund disaster of 1998, when Long-Term Capital Management collapsed in the wake of the "Volga Virus."

However, the last few years have been solid. The fund recorded total returns of 17.4 percent and 30.1 percent in 1999 and 2000 and was ahead by 22.2 percent to the fall of 2001, at a time when equity markets were plunging.

The Newcastle portfolio contains a number of different hedge funds, recently 40 of them. The fund's largest positions are in convertible arbitrage, merger arbitrage, market neutral equity, and fixed income arbitrage. The fund's recent leverage level was just over 30 percent.

Wrapping Up

Absolute return funds have their place in a portfolio. The manager is permitted to concentrate on the securities or sectors of his or her knowledge base. Residual risk is eliminated as cheaply as possible. In this way, much of the dead weight of other fund strategies is mitigated. Including an ARF in an overall investment strategy provides portfolio protection and permits the investor to risk manage basic disasters. Finally, ARFs can isolate opportunities. Because the fund manager is investing based on his or her expertise, the competition from traditional managers is limited.

Overall, hedge funds have the potential for solid returns over the long run since the return from these funds is not usually dependent on the performance of bond and equity markets. The record thus far supports this.

A properly designed hedge fund should have the effect of reducing your overall portfolio risk, since it will have low or zero correlation with the rest of your positions.

Most important, ARFs can be expected to generate positive returns regardless of how the broad markets are doing. Assuming the fund you own fulfills that basic mandate, it can be a very useful counterbalance in rough times.

11

WHEN STYLE IS SUBSTANCE

It used to be said of the late Pierre Trudeau, "The style is the man himself." In other words, Trudeau's flamboyant manner and his gift for the right turn of phrase at a critical moment were more than surface affectations. His style was an accurate public reflection of the type of politician, and human being, that he was.

We begin this chapter with that point because style is often seen as frivolous and transitory. Certainly it can be, when the word is applied to a fad or passing phase. But there are times when style is indeed substance, and that is certainly the case when it comes to investing.

In the last chapter we referred to the importance of style diversification in the portfolio-building process. We feel this issue is significant enough to examine it in greater depth, particularly since the concept is new to many investors and the application of it is often haphazard, if it is applied at all.

Style Basics

The more you learn about the fundamentals of investing, the more you'll hear about various styles. You may read that a particular money manager is a value investor while another is a sector rotator. You'll come across terms like *top-down* and *bottom-up*.

It all sounds technical and rather confusing, and the practical use of style in diversifying a portfolio may not be obvious. But if you really want your investments to perform at maximum efficiency, you have to know the basic styles and what they mean in real terms.

Let's start with stocks and equity mutual funds and look first at the two most basic approaches, top down and bottom up.

Top Down

The top-down approach places the emphasis on markets and sectors, rather than on individual stocks. For example, a top-down manager for a Canadian stock fund will use an analysis of the current economic situation as a starting point. From there, he or she will seek to identify those sectors of the economy that are best positioned to outperform under the most likely scenario. The fund's portfolio will be most heavily weighted to those sectors, and underweighted in areas the manager believes will do poorly. Once all that is done, the actual stocks are selected, usually from industry leaders in the most promising sectors.

For example, during the later stages of an economic recovery, resource stocks and consumer issues often do very well. Since interest rates are usually rising in that situation, utilities, which are highly interest-sensitive, may do badly. So a top-down manager who normally would give oil and gas stocks a 10 percent weighting in the fund's portfolio might increase that to 15 percent. Utilities stocks, which might normally get a 12 percent weighting, could be cut back to 8 percent.

Conversely, if the economy is slumping a top-down manager will focus on more defensive sectors. These would include banks, utilities, consumer staples, pharmaceuticals, and the like.

Managers of top-down international funds take the same approach but do it on a country-by-country basis. A European fund manager, for example, might decide that Scandinavia, Britain, and Spain have above-average prospects for the coming year. Germany and France might be seen as below average. The manager would adjust the portfolio composition to reflect that view.

A global top-down manager has greater scope. He or she might decide to underweight Europe significantly if the prospects there appear weak and overweight the portfolio towards, for example, North America and the Far East.

Bottom Up

True bottom-up investors aren't indifferent to what's happening in the economy, but they don't view it as the number-one priority in stock selection. A bottom-up investor or money manager takes the position that what *really* matters is the quality of a company. If it's a well-managed firm with solid growth potential, then that fact will eventually be reflected in the share value.

Bottom-up managers are essentially fundamentalists. They spend a lot of time analyzing company balance sheets, talking to corporate executives (especially presidents and chief financial officers), and visiting factories or mining sites or laboratories to see for themselves what's actually happening. In some ways, their style is more difficult than that of a top-down manager because there's a higher degree of subjectivity involved. Is that company president really telling me the full story? Is this sales team capable of cranking up revenues by 30 percent next year? Is the new capital expenditure going to pay off as quickly as the chief financial officer calculates?

The economy is tough enough to predict, although the broad trends tend to be fairly evident at any given time. The bottom-up manager goes beyond that, to make big bets on people and products—variables that are even more uncertain than the economic winds.

Top down and bottom up are basically different ways to select stocks. The next level of investment style gets more sophisticated, because it involves deciding what type of stocks will be chosen by the method being used. This is the level at which the character and the priorities of any investment portfolio are established.

Value Investing

We have already introduced you to two of the world's greatest value investors, Sir John Templeton and Warren Buffett, in chapter 2. Actually, they are both disciples of the man regarded as the father of modern value investing, Benjamin Graham. Buffett acknowledges his debt in a preface he wrote to the fourth edition of Graham's classic stock selection guide, *The Intelligent Investor*, regarded as the bible of value managers.

"I read the first edition of this book early in 1950, when I was nineteen," Buffett wrote. "I thought then that it was by far the best book about investing ever written. I still think it is . . . .

"To me, Ben Graham was far more than an author or a teacher. More than any other man except my father, he influenced my life."

In *The Intelligent Investor*, Graham sets out the basic principles of value investing, which are directed at seeking out stocks that represent a combination of low risk and excellent value. Many, many successful securities portfolios have been built on these principles. As you might expect, Warren Buffett's fabled Berkshire Hathaway company in the U.S. (an investment firm) employs the Graham teachings in its stock selection approach—buy cheap and hold forever, if possible.

The main drawback to value investing from some people's perspective is the emphasis it places on buying out-of-favour stocks that are trading at below the company's break-up value and then waiting until the market recognizes the hidden gem and bids the price up to realistic levels. Sometimes that process can take a long time, even years, so a portfolio or a mutual fund that's built on a value investing approach may not be the best choice for an investor seeking fast growth. Value managers constantly stress the importance of discipline and patience. The latter attribute is often difficult for investors in a world where instant gratification became a way of life in the closing years of the 20th century.

Even those investors and money managers who espouse the principles of value investing diverge over how to apply them in practice. At one extreme are the "deep value" investors. These are people who apply extremely rigorous tests to the process of stock selection. They are not simply looking for companies that are cheap compared to the broad market; they want companies that they can buy for 50 cents on the dollar. That doesn't mean a focus on bankrupts, but rather on companies whose stocks are trading well below book value. This can happen if a firm has so-called hidden assets on its balance sheet, such as prime urban real estate being carried at book value. Or it may be because the company operates in a sector or a country that is temporarily out of favour. Or it may be because the company is undervalued and a likely takeover target. One of Canada's best-known deep value managers, Peter Cundill, produced handsome profits for investors in his Mackenzie Cundill Value Fund in 2000–2001 when he loaded up with shares in high-quality Japanese companies at bargain-basement prices.

At the other end of the scale are "relative value" managers and investors, who assess the reasonableness of a stock's price by comparing it to similar companies in the same type of business.

Some of the top value-oriented funds in Canada include the Templeton funds and the Mutual Beacon Fund from Franklin Templeton; the Mackenzie Cundill funds; the Trimark funds operated by AIM; the ABC Funds, run by deep-value manager Irwin Michael; the AGF International Value Fund run by another Graham disciple, Charles Brandes of San Diego; and the AIC Funds, which have been faithfully constructed to replicate the Warren Buffett style. Some AIC funds actually have Berkshire Hathaway shares as their largest single holding.

Growth Investing

The growth investor or fund manager doesn't really care whether a stock is selling at a bargain price. His or her main interest is in how fast the share price is likely to run up. So a growth portfolio will consist mainly of stocks of fast-growing companies with high earnings potential—hot stocks, if you like. You'll often find a lot of small- and mid-cap companies in a growth portfolio, because they offer the best opportunity for fast price movement.

As a result, growth portfolios are best suited for more aggressive investors seeking maximum capital appreciation. But be careful, because a growth-oriented style tends to be more risky than one that is based on a value approach. That's because many of the stocks in a growth portfolio may trade at high multiples relative to the overall market—valuations well in excess of where they should be based on traditional ratios such as share price to profits (known as a price/earnings ratio). Investors often bid up the price of quality growth shares in anticipation of future earnings increases. If they fail to materialize, the stock can drop in a big hurry—as we saw with the high-tech sector in 2000–2001. So growth-oriented portfolios may produce big gains when markets are bullish, but are likely to generate above-average losses in bear markets.

Some of the top growth-oriented mutual fund companies in Canada are McLean Budden, Altamira, AIM, and the Hirsch funds.

A more conservative variation on the classic growth approach is the GARP style of investing. The initials stand for Growth At a Reasonable Price, and what this approach comes down to is a blend of growth and value. The investor or fund manager identifies companies with above-average growth potential and then sets price targets for acquiring the shares. If the stock is too expensive, the investor waits patiently until it comes within buying range, which it almost always does. GARP has become a popular style in the mutual fund business in recent years, with companies like Fidelity, Phillips, Hager & North, and GGOF's Guardian Group among the leading practitioners.

Sector Rotation

Sector rotation takes the top-down investing approach to the next level. A sector rotator focuses primarily on cyclical companies—those that tend to perform especially strongly at certain points in the business cycle. The idea is to overweight the portfolio with stocks that are likely to do better than the market in general, thereby generating above-average returns for investors. Some of the favourite areas for this style of investing are automobile manufacturers, steel companies, forestry companies, mining firms, energy stocks, and airlines.

Following the top-down approach, when economic conditions are bad, the sector rotator overloads the portfolio with defensive stocks—shares in companies that aren't as vulnerable to recessionary conditions.

A top sector-rotation manager can produce outstanding returns for mutual fund investors. But there's a fair amount of educated guesswork involved in the process and timing is a critical factor. If a manager takes a big position in a certain sector too early, the result can be a prolonged period of indifferent returns.

That's exactly what happened to the managers of Mackenzie Financial's Industrial Group of Funds through much of the 1990s. Funds like Industrial Growth and Industrial Horizon aren't technically sector rotation funds. However, the managers acted as if they were. They built the resource sector of their portfolios in anticipation of big moves in those stocks. The problem was that the great resource rally never happened, except in the energy sector. The result: Industrial Growth Fund, once the largest mutual fund in Canada, was among the worst performers in its category over the decade to the end of March 2001, with an average annual compound rate of return of just 2.2 percent.

The Toronto-based firm of Elliott & Page is regarded as one of the top sector-rotation money managers in Canada. The Elliott & Page Equity Fund (now closed to new investors) has a long track record with results that are about average for the Canadian Large-Cap category over a decade.

Momentum Investing

Perhaps the best way to describe the momentum investing style is as a cross between the growth and sector-rotation approaches: focusing on the hottest stocks in the hottest sectors. Momentum investing worked extremely well during the high-tech run-up in the 1990s—some of the mutual funds that use this approach posted huge gains. But because most were still heavily in technology issues when the market collapsed, they were hard hit by the downturn. That's the risk of momentum funds: timing is everything and can be very difficult.

The AIM group offers several momentum-based funds, as does Talvest. The Synergy Canadian Momentum Class has also been a good performer in strong markets. Synergy is a fund company worth noting because it is the only one that was specifically built around the principle of style diversification and offers dedicated growth, value, and momentum funds to investors.

Indexing

All of the styles we have described so far are said to be "active." Index investing is "passive," in the sense that the practitioner does not do any stock picking. Instead, the portfolio is structured to reflect the performance of a particular stock market index. Several index mutual funds are sold in Canada; most use either the TSE 300 or the S&P 500 as their benchmark. There are also a number of exchange-traded funds (ETFs) that use indexing. Some of these funds allow investors to buy a sub-index of the market. In Canada they are sold under the name iUnits and trade on the Toronto Stock Exchange. Examples include iEnergy, iGold, and iMidCap.

Indexing is often touted as a core approach to portfolio building. However, it's important to note that, historically, index products tend to outperform in strong markets and to underperform in weak ones. That's because they cannot employ the defensive tools available to investors and fund managers who use an active approach, including asset allocation changes and a higher emphasis on defensive stocks. If you are going to use indexing, we recommend that it be confined to a certain percentage of your total portfolio.

Fixed-Income Styles

Style diversification is not employed as frequently by individual investors in the fixed-income section of a portfolio, but you should be aware of the approaches that are used. They include the following.

Interest Rate Anticipation

The primary goal of the investor or manager is to identify interest rate trends and adjust the holdings of the portfolio to take advantage of them. So, for example, if analysis indicated that rates were likely to rise in the coming months, the manager of a bond fund would seeking to "shorten term." That would involve increasing the weighting of short-term bonds within the portfolio, which are less vulnerable to interest rate risk, while decreasing long-term bond exposure. Conversely, when rates are expected to drop, a bond fund manager will "lengthen term" as a means of increasing the fund's capital gains potential.

Investors can employ this approach within their personal portfolios, if they have confidence in their ability to forecast rate movements. This can be done by buying and selling individual bonds or by switching the weighting of different types of bond funds as the situation warrants. A number of bond funds specialize in short-term issues. They're easy to pinpoint; just check the mutual fund listings under Canadian Short-Term Bond Funds. There is no specific category for funds that specialize in long-term bonds, but two of the leaders of this type are Altamira Bond Fund and Spectrum Long-Term Bond Fund.

Credit Analysis

In some cases, the creditworthiness of a company is more important to its bond price than interest rate movements. This is especially true in the case of high-yield bonds (or junk bonds, as they are often called). In fact, the market price of these bonds often bears very little relationship to interest rate trends. In the fall of 2001, for example, the price of many high-yield bonds plummeted over concerns that the economy was plunging into a deep recession that would undermine the financial stability of the issuing companies and compromise their ability to make interest payments. The ultimate disaster scenario for a bond investor is a default, when the issuer is not able even to repay the principal. That's the risk faced by junk bond investors, as well as the mutual funds that invest in them.

Credit analysis plays a critical role in determining the vulnerability of a high-yield bond to default in the event of rough times. Few individual investors are capable of this kind of sophisticated analysis, which is why investing in junk bonds is best done through mutual funds that have a proven track record in the field. One of the best has been the Trimark Advantage Bond Fund.

Bond Indexing

Some bond fund managers follow an indexing approach similar to that employed by index equity funds, but they employ some active decisions as well. The benchmark most often used in this situation is the Scotia Capital Markets Universe Bond Index. The bond portfolio is structured to track the index in general terms, but the manager has some leeway to deviate from it, depending on conditions. The highly successful Phillips, Hager & North Bond Fund uses this approach.

Other bond funds may use a different index; for example, the TD Short Term Income Fund closely tracks the Scotia Capital Markets Short-Term Bond Index.

You can also buy ETFs that will perform in much the same way as a bond index. There are two now available: iG5 units (TSE: XGV), which use a five-year Government of Canada bond as the benchmark, and iG10 shares (TSE: XGX), which track the 10-year Canada bond.

Applying Style Diversification to Your Portfolio

In chapter 9, we provided a sample asset allocation that included both growth and value components in the equity section. We suggest that you not try to fine-tune style diversification beyond that unless you are very skilful at the process.

In determining your relative holdings, keep in mind that securities that fall into the GARP, sector rotation, and momentum categories all qualify under the broad heading of growth.

In general, it is a good idea not to overweight too heavily towards either the growth or value side at any given time. Styles, like markets, tend to be cyclical, and each approach will have a period in which it outperforms. No one, however, has been able to predict with any degree of accuracy when one style will come into favour with investors so we advise maintaining a foot in both camps at all times. For example, growth securities generally did very well during the late 1990s, spurred by the dazzling performance of technology stocks. Value stocks and funds underperformed. When the high-tech bubble popped in 2000, however, most growth-oriented securities went into a nose-dive. Value stocks, by contrast, enjoyed a resurgence.

So while there may be times when you want to overweight towards one style or another, you should never allow your portfolio to get too far out of balance. Changes in the economic climate can occur with lightning speed.

Using style diversification in the fixed-income section of a portfolio is more complex, and this is best done through mutual funds and/or ETFs.

Wrapping Up

Style considerations have become very important in the process of building a successful investing portfolio, and you need to understand how each approach differs and what pluses and minuses it brings to a portfolio.

The most commonly used styles for equity portfolios are value, growth, momentum, sector rotation, and indexing. Of these, value is the most conservative and normally carries less risk. A momentum style is considered to be highly aggressive but can produce impressive returns during bull markets.

The styles most commonly used for fixed-income securities are interest rate anticipation, credit analysis, and bond indexing.

At the very least, investors should look carefully at the relationship between the growth and value equity positions they are holding at any given time and ensure that one is not disproportionately high in relation to the other. Normally, a reasonably equal balance between growth and value is recommended.

12

SPECIALTY FUNDS: THE
RISK/OPPORTUNITY
BALANCE

Take a close look at your mutual fund portfolio. The odds are that it contains at least one and possibly more of what are known as "specialty funds." If so, ask yourself why you own it. Chances are that the answer you'll come up with is something like: "It seemed like a good idea at the time."

Most specialty funds owe their existence to a passing investment fad. They were created because people were interested in or excited about a specific type of investing—fund companies are always on the lookout for new ways to attract your dollars. Perhaps they even performed well for a time. But now they linger on like leftovers after a feast. And, like leftovers, they start to smell bad after a while unless they're cleaned up.

There are several forms of specialty funds. Here's a run-down.

Sector Funds

Sector funds focus on specific area of the economy. In Canada, there were only two types of sector funds for many years: natural resource funds and precious metals funds.

Natural resource funds concentrate mainly on shares in energy and mining companies, although they may also have positions in forestry companies, precious metals operations, and companies that service the resource sector.

Precious metals funds are really a sub-set of the resource funds. They may invest in companies in the gold, silver, diamond, platinum, and uranium businesses, and may also hold gold bullion and other precious metals directly.

The 1990s changed the sector fund landscape completely, however. A wide range of sector funds became available to investors in this country. They included a broad range of science and technology funds. Within that grouping are a number of funds that concentrate on a single area: telecommunications, biotechnology, e-business, etc. Health care funds, which had been a sub-set of the science and technology category, were spun off into their own group in fall 2001. We also saw the creation of funds that focus on other areas, such as financial services (now also an official category), consumer products, real estate, and leisure and recreation. Some of the new funds were oriented towards Canadian companies, but most were global in scope.

As of the fall of 2001, Globefund listed 180 entries in the Global Science & Technology category, 81 in the new Health Care category, 38 in the Financial Services category, and another 110 in the Specialty category, which is largely made up of sector funds. As well, there were 54 natural resource funds, 22 precious metals funds, and 16 real estate funds, bringing the total to 501. That's a lot of choice for Canadians.

Most of these funds have not been around long enough to establish a meaningful track record. But the evidence we have is not encouraging, as we'll explain shortly.

Trend Funds

These funds have portfolios that are structured to catch some supposed new wave and allow investors to ride its crest. Included in this group are baby boomer funds, demographics funds, New Economy funds, and the like. There aren't a lot of these yet, but some, like the CI Global Boomernomics Fund, have captured a huge amount of interest, pulling in more than $3 billion, including all spinoff versions.

This type of fund is so new that we really don't have a handle on what to expect over the long haul. Global Boomernomics did show a respectable three-year average annual return of 7.7 percent to the end of September 2001, but its more recent figures are well below average. The jury is still out here, but our view is that these funds will eventually be seen as yet another fad with no staying power.

Asia/Europe Country-Specific Funds

The funds in this group focus on a single nation. The concept originated with Japanese equity funds during the 1980s when Japan's economy was booming and the Nikkei Index was going through the roof. Today, hardly anyone is interested. Most of the remaining funds in this category are very small—only three have assets in excess of $100 million. As far as long-term performance goes, results have been terrible. Only one fund showed an average annual profit over the 15 years to September 30, 2001: AGF Japan. Its average annual gain? A mere 1.7 percent. You would have done far better with a money market fund. The same story applies over 10 years. In the most recent five-year period, only Fidelity Japanese Growth Fund showed a profit—and it was only 0.1 percent a year.

The second wave of Asia/Europe country-specific funds focused on China, at the time when it was projected that the Chinese economy was on track to surpass that of the U.S. sometime early in this century. Since then, we've also seen funds that specialize in India and Germany.

None has stood the test of time. Of the country-specific funds with a five-year record to the end of September 2001, only AGF Germany showed a profit, with an average annual gain of 3.7 percent. Again, money market funds did better. The top-performing China fund was AGF China Focus, which just managed to break even over the period.

Regional Funds

Regional funds include European, Asian, Latin American, and emerging markets funds. There are about 300 funds of this type available.

There is some argument for the existence of broadly based regional funds, such as those that cover all of Europe or Asia. However, the reality is that only the European category has performed well over time, with an average annual compound rate of return of 8.6 percent over the decade to September 30, 2001. Not a single Asia-Pacific fund even managed to break even over the five years to the end of September 2001, and only two showed a ten-year profit. The best was Talvest Asian Fund, with an average annual gain of 3.9 percent. Again, money market funds did better.

Latin American funds and emerging markets funds are both products of the early 1990s, when the value of shares in developing countries skyrocketed as investment capital poured in. Some of these funds produced eye-popping gains in the early going, causing even more money to flow in. But once again, staying power has proved to be a serious problem.

Only one emerging markets fund, CI Emerging Markets, showed a winning record over five and ten years during the time frame we've been studying. No Latin America fund has a ten-year record and only one, TD Latin American Growth, was in the black over five years, by just 1 percent annually.

Why We're Concerned

History has shown us that while macro economies can experience ups and downs, the broad impact of such movements tends to be diluted. However, specific economic sectors or geographic areas may experience explosive short-term boom periods, which are followed by bust cycles that may continue for years.

This has been one of the problems of resource funds for years. Because the stocks in which they invest are cyclical in nature (oil and gas, mining, forestry), resource funds as a group follow a similar pattern. So investors will experience times when their funds are doing extremely well and other periods when they record double-digit losses year after year. The long-term effect for the buy-and-hold investor is mediocre performance. Over the decade to September 30, 2001, the average Canadian natural resource fund returned 6.4 percent annually, according to figures published by *The Globe and Mail*. The average precious metals fund fared even worse, with an annual gain of

5.8 percent. By comparison, the average broadly diversified Canadian equity fund, which from time to time may have held resource and precious metals stocks, gained 9.2 percent annually. Investors who kept their money in natural resource or precious metals funds thus incurred far greater volatility for much less return—not a winning combination in any circumstances.

When the technology boom took flight, many people opined that tech stocks and funds would not be subject to these boom and bust cycles. Technology, the reasoning went, is the key to the future, and these products will be in high demand for years. The collapse of 2000–2001 gave the lie to that myth. Science and technology funds that enjoyed double- and even triple-digit annual gains in the late 1990s fell like rocks. Over the five-year period to the end of September 2001, the average science and technology fund recorded an annual gain of a mere 2.3 percent. The average U.S. equity fund returned 7.9 percent a year. (We use the U.S. as the benchmark here because most technology funds are top-heavy in U.S. stocks.) None of the technology funds has been around long enough to have a 10-year track record but our guess is that by the time they achieve that milestone, we'll see a similar story.

As we have seen, most specialized funds based on geography, with the exception of the European Equity category, show a similar pattern.

The preponderance of evidence suggests that specialized funds are not useful buy-and-hold choices. Most are highly volatile, and we have yet to see evidence that any of these specialty areas (again with the exception of Europe) can outperform an average broadly based equity fund or a benchmark index fund over the long haul.

Yet many investors hold such funds in their accounts, not because the funds are part of a cohesive strategy but because they were acquired in the expectation that they would juice returns. Investors keep holding on to them, despite dismal performance in most cases.

The problem is inertia. Many people review their accounts only once or twice a year. If they see securities that are well down from their original book value, the first reaction is to hold on until the stock or mutual fund gets back to a break-even position and then sell. That could be a long time coming, and in the meantime the security may generate below-average returns.

Ask yourself this question: Can I predict with any reasonable degree of accuracy what segments of the economy are likely to outperform in the next one, three, or five years? If the answer is no, then you should not be in sector funds, unless you have a financial advisor whom you think can manage this difficult task (and few can).

Then ask yourself: Do I have the ability to identify which world markets are likely to be among the top performers in the coming period? If the answer is again no, then you should not be in specialized geographic funds, with the exception of those that focus on Canada, the U.S., and Europe—and even then you should diversify.

The decisions of which sectors to buy and which areas of the world to emphasize are better left to professional money managers. They don't always get it right, but they have the tools and the training to have a better chance of success than the average investor.

Our bottom line is that specialized equity funds should not be part of most investment programs. These funds tend to be purchased for the wrong reasons (expectation of high short-term gain) and then held for the wrong reasons (anticipation of eventually breaking even). Neither is a strategy for success.

You will be better off building a portfolio of well-managed, broadly based funds and letting the managers make the calls on where to place the money.

Exceptions to the Rule

So does this mean you should never invest in sector funds, trend funds, or specialized geographic funds? No. But you need to have a specific strategy in mind if you plan to go this route.

If you want to use these funds in an effort to boost returns, we suggest you treat them like stocks. That means buying them when they're cheap and selling them when they're expensive. This approach flies in the face of the traditional advice for mutual fund investing, which is to buy for the long term. But we have yet to see any evidence that such guidance makes any sense in this case. On the contrary, all the statistical indications to date are that adopting a buy-and-hold strategy for funds of this type will result in below-average long-term performance and, quite possibly, to actual losses.

So these funds are better treated like stocks, which is why we have dubbed them "opportunity funds." They are best suited for active traders, who will use a buy low, sell high approach, monitor the funds and the underlying sectors or regions carefully, and take profits when appropriate. If you are comfortable running your fund portfolio (or a portion of it) in that way, then sector funds may be of some interest to you. Perhaps you will decide to take a position in a science and technology fund at a time when the sector has been beaten up and no one wants to hear about it. Just remember to get out once the big run-up has occurred. Don't ride the fund back down again once the wave breaks.

Similarly, emerging markets funds, Latin America funds, Far East funds, etc., will go through boom periods, which will offer opportunities to smart traders. But most fund investors will only decide to get in once the boom has pretty well run its course. Few have the nerve to buy at the bottom, when pessimism abounds.

It takes a savvy, aggressive investor to make money in these funds. If you're in that category (or your financial advisor is), then fine. But most people should take a different direction.

Wrapping Up

Most specialty equity funds were spawned out of investment fads and have not proven to be good long-term performers. Yet Canadians have billions of dollars tied up in these assets. If you are holding some of these funds in your portfolio, you should take a hard look at each one and ask why it is there, what role it is playing in your master plan, and what kind of return it is producing. In most cases, we advise avoiding specialty funds and choosing funds that offer broad market diversification. Let the professional managers make the calls on which sectors and regions to move into and out of, and when.

13

MUTUAL FUND
PERFORMANCE AND
MARKETING HYPE

Performance measurement is hardly an exact science, and there are no guarantees that the past will reflect the future. However, that shouldn't deter you from the task of measurement. There is a famous story about the great economist Frank Knight. Professor Knight was walking around the University of Chicago campus and saw a plaque dedicated to Lord Kelvin. The plaque read: "That which cannot be measured cannot be known." Knight, on seeing the plaque, said: "Oh, well, if you can't measure it, go ahead and measure it anyway."

Let's say you bought a Canadian equity fund last year because it had a great track record, with an annual compounded rate of return of 14 percent over the past five years. You thought: "If the fund keeps it up, I can move those retirement plans forward." So despite the fine print in the newspaper ad warning that "past returns are no guarantee of future results," you jumped in, and set out to hone your golf swing.

One year later, the fund has lost 9.7 percent of its value and you are disappointed, frustrated, and angry. You might be able to accept this if the Canadian market had lost ground during the same period. But looking at the statistics, you see that the TSE Composite Index was up by 11.4 percent over the same time frame.

How is this possible? How can a manager with a great five-year track record fall to pieces when you buy into the fund? How can a manager specializing in a market that's up more than 11 percent lose money? It happens, of course, and all too often. If the fund manager picks the wrong stocks or the wrong style, you can be left in the dust.

Next time you will know better. Maybe you will just go out and buy a balanced mutual fund! The manager will make a simple decision to over-weight stocks or bonds depending on the economic cycle. With that kind of management, you should never be too far removed from the market.

But then you discover there's more to balanced funds than meets the eye. A quick scan of the statistics shows you that there are over 350 Canadian balanced funds from which to choose, with one-year performance numbers ranging from –21.5 percent to +33.7 percent. How is this possible? You would think that one balanced fund is pretty much like another, especially if you are buying Canadian balanced funds. After all, how hard can it be to make a choice between Canadian stocks and Canadian bonds? Apparently it's harder than you might imagine.

To understand why there is such disparity, you need to dig beneath the surface. You'll discover some of the things the mutual fund industry doesn't tell you that will reveal a lot about why funds act the way they do. Like why, for example, more expensive actively managed funds have not done any better than low-cost index funds in some cases. And while you can make an argument that index funds track the market both up and down, you can't escape the fact that, in any given year, 80 percent of money managers under-perform their passive benchmark index.

That's a tough fact to digest until you realize how mutual fund companies rate their portfolio managers. They're not measured against a benchmark index; rather, they are evaluated in terms of how they stack up against their competition. At the end of the day, money managers are not competing against an index—they are competing against their peer group. When you look at the marketing material of a mutual fund, do you see any mention of what the fund did against its benchmark? Not likely. What you see is the quartile ranking and the performance numbers that got it to that level.

Whether the fund company focuses on the quartile rankings or performance numbers in its marketing depends, to a large extent, on which story has the most impact on the consumer.

So if active management can't guarantee results, how do fund companies entice you to buy their particular funds? They employ savvy marketing techniques, such as performance skews and window dressing. They create myths around issues relating to tax efficiency, index funds, and cash flow.

Summarized below, you'll find out about some of the things that the mutual fund industry doesn't tell you, and how you can use this vital information to pick better investments in the future.

Performance Skew

Did you happen to notice how many equity mutual funds were promoting their historical performance numbers at the end of January and February 2001? Part of that, of course, relates to the buying patterns of consumers. January and February bring the RRSP rush, so marketing budgets naturally go into high gear. But coming on the heels of a bad year (2000 was a particularly weak one for most growth funds), many funds concentrated on their much more impressive three- and five-year results rather than the one-year numbers.

In contrast, the year-over-year numbers to February 2000 were particularly impressive for some fund categories. And what about the five-year performance statistics for U.S. equity funds from the beginning of 1995 to the end of 1999? It was one of the best five-year runs for the U.S. equity markets in history. The numbers told an even more compelling story if the U.S. equity fund was holding technology stocks. If you noticed, a lot of U.S. equity funds were promoting their five-year track record at the end of 1999 and in early 2000.

You may have also noticed the stellar one-year returns at the end of January 2000 for the average Canadian labour-sponsored fund. It was the best year on record, and the marketing departments wanted to promote that success along with the hefty tax breaks accorded to investors in labour-sponsored funds.

Another period of stellar returns came between November 1998 and November 1999. The one-year numbers for international funds came to the forefront. Why? Because November 1998 marked the end of the Asia crisis.

The international markets–particularly the Asia Pacific basin–were just starting to recover from a massive tailspin. In some cases, returns over that year just got the funds back to where they were before the crisis. But the numbers from the beginning of November 1998 to the end of October 1999 were compelling.

Notice many performance statistics for bond funds during the year 2000 RRSP campaign? Probably not! The bond market was the weak link in the financial markets from 1997 to the end of 1999. It was especially difficult for bond funds during 1999, when only 15 out of 162 Canadian bond funds had a positive return. Mutual fund companies promoting the bond funds were only doing so as safe haven investments, and in the process were highlighting their quartile rankings. Did you know, for example, that 44 Canadian bond funds were ranked as first-quartile performers in 1999, but 29 of them actually had negative returns?

And then we get into 2000 and 2001. The period from March 2000 to October 2001 represented one of the worst bear markets for stocks since the Great Depression. Suddenly mutual fund companies stopped focusing on one-year returns. No wonder. They were awful. The average Canadian equity fund lost 18.6 percent over that time. Better to focus on the three-year number (average annual gain of 8.8 percent) or the ten-year return (average 9.2 percent annually).

The moral of the story? You have to be careful when buying any fund on the basis of past performance, at least as described in the fund's promotional material. Even though there are standard performance measures in the industry, there is some discretion as to what is published and how it is published. Fund performance reflects the base and terminal period selected, the horizon examined, even the measures used.

The warning labels attached to the performance statistics may be your best defence against getting caught up in performance skew.

Window Dressing

Marketing a fund is an elaborate endeavour, geared not only to getting consumers to buy into the company, but also to keeping them interested and invested. One of the ways fund companies keep investors in the loop is by providing quarterly updates that, among other things, show unitholders what assets are being held in the fund's portfolio. If you are investing, for example, in a Canadian equity fund, the fund company will list the securities in the account at the end of the quarter.

Now suppose you are a fund manager who thought Nortel Networks was overpriced in 1999. You never held the shares in your portfolio. (If a manager did not own Nortel Networks in 1999, performance numbers would have suffered.) In 1999, Nortel and BCE Inc. represented approximately 38 percent of the S&P/TSE 60 Index. Would you want your unitholders to know you missed the boat on Nortel Networks? The only way they could ever find that out is to look at the holding summary in the quarterly report, if they decided to read it. Many investors do not.

That's where window dressing comes into play. A fund manager may want to make sure that they own some of the best-performing stocks, even if they did not own them long enough to produce any impact on the bottom line. The trick is to buy some shares before the end of the quarter so that they show up on the manager's books when he or she sends the quarterly report to shareholders. This practice has become more widespread in recent years as investors gain more access to information. Almost all mutual fund companies now have Web sites, where you can access information about a particular fund, including the most recent quarterly statistics on the portfolio.

Financial advisors also buy mutual fund software to track the performance of all available mutual funds in Canada. These software packages—the biggest being Morningstar Canada—allow financial advisors to rank funds using any number of criteria, including the fund's holdings. For example, a financial advisor could rank prospective Canadian equity funds based on their holdings in Nortel Networks. The advisor simply asks the software to rank the funds from highest to lowest in terms of the fund's exposure to Nortel.

If you are looking at a prospective fund because of its holdings, then beware of window dressing. If the fund's performance numbers don't match up with the holdings inside the fund, it's likely the manager has simply bought the high-profile stocks so that they show up in the fund's portfolio.

Remember as well, it works both ways. After the Nortel collapse in 2000, many fund managers made sure that Nortel disappeared from their portfolio prior to their next quarterly report!

The Tax Efficiency Myth

One of the more interesting marketing concepts is tax efficiency. Some funds show historical returns and then tout how the fund is 100 percent tax efficient. The implication is that you will receive all of the historical returns after tax. Well, not quite. Most mutual funds are set up as trusts. When the manager purchases and sells securities, gains and losses on those transactions are reported to the unitholder at year-end.

The problem with tax efficiency ratings is in how consumers interpret them. If a fund has a three-year, 100 percent tax efficiency rating, it simply means that the fund has not reported any capital gains during the previous three years. This record can be caused by a couple of things. It may be that the investments inside the fund have not performed well over the previous three years, and the manager is still holding out for a longer-term target price. If so, that would be seen in the three-year performance statistics. It could also mean, assuming the manager has a good three-year track record, that the fund has huge unrealized capital gains exposure that will have to be recognized for tax purposes at some point in the future and you will inherit this tax liability if you buy in now!

All too often, investors buy into the tax efficiency concept only to be hit with a whopping capital gains tax in the year they sell the fund. In some cases, the capital gains tax can be greater than the return of the fund during the time you were holding it. Nothing can make investors more frustrated than paying tax on capital gains they never realized. That's one of the reasons investors should avoid purchasing tax-efficient mutual funds in the last quarter of any year, especially if those funds have a very good three-year performance record. The gains on that three-year record will have to be paid at some point in the future. You also have to ask if the manager of a well-performing fund is likely to sell some of the securities that produced the stellar return if it ends up triggering a huge tax hit for unitholders.

Think about that for a moment. You are managing a successful, 100 percent tax-efficient fund with a stellar three-year return. Chances are good that you have been attracting a lot of new investors recently, because they like the story. Are you going to capture some of those gains by selling some of your positions if it has an impact on the new unitholders? If so, you'll cause them to pay tax on gains they never actually receive. So perhaps you, the manager, will decide not to sell, because you want to maintain the loyalty of your new unitholders. In some cases, you may end up holding those securities when your gut is telling you it's time to sell. If so, then tax issues are becoming the driving force behind the fund, not the investment merits of the securities being held inside the fund.

In short, think of tax-efficient funds as tax-deferred funds—at some point, you will have to pay the piper.

Index Funds—Dangerous in a Bear Market?

If you buy an index fund, you will receive the returns of the benchmark index. By that, we simply mean that a Canadian equity index fund will likely track the performance of either the S&P/TSE 60 Index or the TSE 300 Composite Index. A U.S. equity fund will track the performance of the S&P 500 Composite Index or perhaps the Dow Jones Industrial Average. International index funds tend to track the Morgan Stanley Europe Australia and Far East Index (EAFE). The point is that your performance will match the underlying index—no better, no worse.

You also pay less to own an index fund. The annual management expense ratio is usually less than 1 percent, which is about 40 percent of what you pay to buy an actively managed fund in the same category.

We'll explore indexing in greater depth in chapter 16 but, briefly, the argument against index funds is the same as the argument in favour of them: You will match the performance of the underlying index, both up and down. In other words, there is no professional manager to help reduce exposure to the market when the index is falling. If the benchmark index falls by 10 percent, your fund will also fall by 10 percent, give or take a few basis points to account for the MER. On the assumption that investors are risk-averse, falling as much as the benchmark index is not a very appealing result. Hence, many investors have the notion that index funds are less attractive in a bear market.

The problem with this view is that it has more to do with perception than reality. Investors rarely hold index funds independently. In most cases, index funds are held within a portfolio. Within the context of a portfolio, investors can control their exposure to the financial markets by simply overweighting or underweighting the cash component inside the portfolio.

Think about it this way. Suppose that in 2001 your portfolio held only two securities: the S&P/TSE 60 iUnits (which trade on the Toronto Stock Exchange under the ticker symbol XIU) and Treasury bills. The MER on the S&P/TSE 60 iUnits is 17 basis points (0.17 percent) per annum. There is no cost to hold Treasury bills.

Now suppose you agreed with the manager of XYZ Canadian Fund who put 30 percent of his portfolio in cash, which he saw as a cushion to protect the portfolio should the Canadian market fall dramatically. For providing that professional management, the XYZ fund charges a 2.5 percent management fee. You put 70 percent of your portfolio into the S&P/TSE 60 iUnits and invest the rest of the portfolio in Treasury bills. Are you not in the same position as the XYZ fund but with an average portfolio MER of 0.119 percent per annum?

Now you could argue that the fund manager of XYZ would produce a better return on his stock selections than the S&P/TSE 60 iUnits. Well, he might. Buy he would have to outperform our "homemade" portfolio by 2.38 percent per annum just to break even.

Within the context of a portfolio, index funds are no more dangerous in a down market then they are beneficial in an up market. With an index fund you are assured that the money committed to the index fund is 100 percent invested in the underlying index. With a portfolio approach, this means you have control over your asset mix at all times.

Cash Flow Considerations

Mutual funds in a bear market raise another concern. How do fund companies manage cash flows? If performance wanes, funds can be subjected to redemptions. That's when more money is leaving the fund than is coming into it in the form of new sales.

Investors have always been told that managers maintain some cash reserves in their portfolio to manage redemptions, because having cash allows the fund to meet the redemptions without having to sell securities.

The worst thing that can happen is that a fund manager will have to sell securities to meet net redemptions. Selling profitable positions can trigger capital gains for the unitholders who stay in the fund. Selling losing positions can be a benefit from a tax angle, but the manager may be forced out of a position before he or she is ready. Neither situation is good for the manager, the fund, or the unitholder.

This is one area where actively managed funds have an advantage over index funds. An index fund, by definition, is always 100 percent invested in the underlying market. If there are more redemptions than there are new contributions, the manager has to exit a position, because there is no excess cash reserve. In this case, the index fund manager will trigger gains or losses to the unitholders who remain with the fund. It's one of the downsides of indexing.

On the other hand, index funds have a distinct advantage when the fund is taking in more contributions than withdrawals. As money flows into the fund, it is invested immediately. There are some management issues in terms of the size of the contribution and how quickly it can be invested, but for the most part, index funds do a good job of handling new contributions.

It is not nearly as easy for actively managed funds. When new money comes in, it isn't always the best time to make new investments. When you think about it, new money flows in after the fund has been on a hot streak. The fund has posted some impressive performance numbers based on investments held inside the portfolio. Obviously, they have gone up in value but you have to ask: Are those securities still good investments at today's prices?

This timing question can be a problem for a manager. The fund may, for example, hold Nortel Networks at a cost of $10 per share. At $25 per share the manager doesn't want to sell, but buying more shares may not be the answer either. If he or she doesn't spend the new contributions, the money is held as cash in the portfolio. If contributions are coming in at a fast pace, the cash component of the portfolio begins to have greater influence on the performance of the fund. That can be a negative because, over time, cash is the worst-performing asset.

A Useful Tool

The issues of measuring a mutual fund against the peer group and performance skew present a serious challenge to investors. A useful tool was developed by the Fundata Group in 2001. Eric Kirzner, one of the co-authors of this book, was the technical expert.

The Fundata FUNDGrade Mutual Fund Rating System ranks mutual funds as follows:

SCORE	DEFINITION
A	Superior past performance
B	Strong past performance
C	Average past performance
D	Sub-par past performance
E	Poor past performance

Funds are ranked both against their peers in their asset class category and against suitable benchmarks for the category. (For example, Canadian equity funds are measured against the TSE 300 Composite Index.) The benchmark for each fund group is that of the Investment Funds Standard Committee (IFSC).

Here are some of the key features of the rating system:

- *A "high-water" hurdle:* To score an A grade, a fund must not only substantially outperform the category average, it must also beat the benchmark for the category. By ranking against both the average of the asset class in which the fund competes and the benchmark, the fund categories that have overall relatively poor performance are appropriately downgraded. Accordingly, a fund needs to outperform both the group average and the benchmark to earn an above-average rating. If none of the funds in a category beats the benchmark, the highest grade a fund can receive is a C.

- *Time-weighted adjustments for return, risk, and consistency:* The rate of return, risk, and other factors are time weighted, using sum-of-the-years digit calculations. The use of time weighting means that more recent fund performance is rated more heavily than more distant performance. Recent results are likely to be more indicative of the current fund manager's policy, strategy, and success (or lack thereof) than more distant results.

- *Survivorship bias adjustment:* Most of the current mutual fund performance surveys suffer from survivorship bias. For example, if the survey starts with the current list of mutual funds and looks back at how they have done over the past 10 years, this means that funds that disappeared over that time period would not be included. Often it's the poorer-performing funds that disappear. Any backward-looking study is likely to suffer from this effect. The problem with survivorship bias is that it is likely to overestimate overall returns. Objective group averages are shown both with and without survivorship adjustments. The adjustment for survivorship bias means that the investor gets a clear picture of actual returns over the period examined.

Back testing was conducted on the historical record for all fund categories using 25 years of past data spanning the period 1975 through 2000. Overall, the Fundata FUNDGrade model discriminates by identifying top performers based on past results.

The Fundata score is included in all Southam Mutual Fund performance rankings tables. You will also find it in *Gordon Pape's Buyer's Guide to Mutual Funds*, written by the authors of this book.

Wrapping Up

So the mutual fund industry doesn't tell you a lot of things—that doesn't make the industry bad. As with any business, you market the best you have to offer, and avoid the issues that might make the buyer think twice about investing in a specific fund.

On the other hand, it's useful to understand these issues. It makes you a better consumer. And when you settle on a specific fund, you will have done your homework. In the end, you may become a longer-term investor, more likely to stick with a fund through the ups and downs of the business cycle. We think that's important. We also think that an informed consumer is a better client for the mutual fund business.

Using past performance to assess the future is a tricky business but, as in Professor Knight's comment, it is often the best we have. Measurement is the key—remember, what gets measured gets managed!

14

THE PROS AND CONS OF
LEVERAGING

Borrow against your house and invest in the booming stock market. That became the mantra of many financial advisors and some well-known financial commentators during the heady days of the Great Bull Market of the 1990s. Books were written on the subject, including one that singled out co-author Gordon Pape for sharp criticism because of his cautionary approach. In his book *The Strategy: A Homeowner's Guide to Wealth Creation*, well-known author Garth Turner said: "I have great respect for financial writer Gordon Pape, but his strategies are among those that now alarm me greatly. He counsels people to be intensely risk-averse at a time when too many Canadians will end up being both old and poor because they did exactly what he advises." Specifically, Turner singled out a newspaper article titled "Leveraging—a dangerous road to riches," which warned of the pitfalls of using home equity lines of credit to invest in the stock market.

That article appeared in 1997 and was certainly out of sync with Mr. Turner's investment philosophy at that time. But our views remain the same today, and we believe that recent stock market history has validated those concerns. We leave it to the reader to judge.

Certainly, many financial planners were happy to jump on the leveraging bandwagon. Some genuinely believed it to be the right course for their clients at a time when the conventional wisdom was that stock markets could continue to rise for the next decade and beyond. Others were at least partially influenced by the fat sales commissions and trailer fees such a strategy would generate. A person who took out a $200,000 line of credit against his or her home and invested it in mutual funds created a very attractive profit for the advisor who handled the sale. That may seem like a harsh judgment, but it was a motivating factor, perhaps the primary one in some cases.

Now, just a few short years later, many people have been left financially devastated as a result of leveraging decisions made in the late 1990s. It's time to rethink the whole idea.

The Math Looks Great

Leveraging is a technical term meaning borrowing to invest. For years, it was mainly used for brokerage margin accounts. These are arrangements in which an investor buys stocks "on margin," putting up only a percentage (say 50 percent) of the total cost. The broker effectively provides a loan for the balance. If the stock falls sharply in value, the investor may get a "margin call." That means he or she must put up more cash, or sell. Margin calls can add fuel to a market plunge as margin investors are forced to liquidate their positions.

Trading on margin has always been regarded as high-risk territory, best left to speculative investors who understand the risks involved. But the appearance on the financial scene of home equity lines of credit in the 1980s changed the dynamics fundamentally. These lines of credit meant that ordinary people who had benefited from the big run-up in housing values during the inflationary 1970s and 1980s suddenly had access to large amounts of cash. In most cases, these weren't sophisticated investors—in fact, they knew little of the investment process. But they had home equity, and they could suddenly tap into it. Some financial advisors saw it as an opportunity.

The math of leveraging has always been seductive, and no more so than at a time when markets are soaring. Effectively, you use other people's money to enhance your own profits and get a tax break for doing so. So it was easy to make a compelling case for borrowing against your home equity to invest. A financial advisor could sit down with a client and offer what seemed like an irrefutable case for using the family home for investing.

Here's how such a conversation might have gone back in, say, August 1999:

Advisor: I'd like to show you a way that you could make an after-tax profit of more than $60,000 over the next five years. Are you interested?

Client: Sure, as long as it's not too risky.

Advisor: It's not. Now, I believe you had your house appraised recently. What is it worth?

Client: They said $300,000.

Advisor: Is it mortgage-free?

Client: Yes.

Advisor: Okay. You can get a home equity line of credit for two-thirds of that amount, which will work out to $200,000. I can handle the arrangements for you.

Client: At what interest rate?

Advisor: Prime plus a quarter percent. Right now, that works out to 6.5 percent. You won't find a cheaper rate. But you won't actually pay that much.

Client: Why not?

Advisor: That's one of the beauties of this strategy. The interest is tax deductible. Let's see. *(He checks his file.)* Your marginal tax rate is 50 percent. Let's figure it out. *(He punches numbers into a calculator.)* That means that on a $200,000 line of credit, you'll be charged $13,000 a year for interest at the current rate. But because the money is used to invest, that charge is tax deductible. The actual after-tax cost to you is only $6,500.

Client *(dubiously)*: That still seems like a lot.

Advisor: Maybe, but that's only one side of the equation. We take that money and put it into equity mutual funds. I have some terrific ones in mind. You know how well the stock market has been doing lately?

Client: I've been reading about it. Those technology stocks—I can't believe some of the stories!

Advisor: Believe them. It's just the beginning. I was at a presentation last week given by one of the fund managers. He said the growth rate in those companies could be better than 20 percent a year over the next decade. Now, I think we should be more conservative than that, so let's say we invest that money in some equity funds and that they give us an annual return of 15 percent on average. I've prepared a projection for you, based on a $200,000 investment—I figured that would be about what you would have available. Let's look at it. *(He passes over a sheet of paper with the following numbers.)*

Amount invested	$200,000
Annual return at 15%	30,000
After-tax cost of loan interest	6,500
Tax on profit at capital gains rate	11,250
Net after-tax profit	12,250
Net profit over five years	$ 61,250

(Note: the numbers today would be even more impressive because the capital gains inclusion rate has been reduced to 50 percent— it was 75 percent in 1999. Also, lower interest rates mean lower loan costs.)

Advisor: What do you think?

Client *(whistling)*: Wow.

Advisor: Yeah. Pretty awesome.

Client: You really think those profits are possible?

Advisor: Hey, nothing is guaranteed. But I think there's a good chance you could do even better.

Client: Then let's do it.

There's no way of knowing how many people actually decided to go this route in the hopes of big profits from their home equity. All we can say with any degree of certainty is that a large number of them now wish they had never heard of the idea.

Let's see what might have happened to someone who decided to use leveraging and invested in a portfolio of equity funds at the end of December 1999. Of course, much will depend on the specific funds that were chosen, so let's look at two different approaches.

The Aggressive Approach

With an aggressive approach, the financial advisor and the client were swept along by the tide of the rising market and the tremendous enthusiasm over high-term. This was the prevailing mood of the time. The portfolio was constructed accordingly, as follows:

20%	AIM Global Technology Fund
20%	CI Global Telecommunications Sector Shares
20%	AGF Aggressive Growth Fund
20%	Elliott & Page Growth Opportunities Fund
20%	Janus American Equity Fund

In calendar 2000, here's what happened in each case:

AIM Global Technology: −27.9%

CI Global Telecommunications: −31.1%

AGF Aggressive Growth: −14.2%

E&P Growth Opportunities: +21.7%

Janus American Equity: −19.1%

Based on our portfolio weighting, the value of the portfolio on January 1, 2001, would have been $169,760, for a net loss for the year of $30,240, or 15.1 percent. The after-tax interest charges would have added to the total loss.

But that was nothing compared to what was to come. The markets continued to head south in 2001. By mid-October of that year, here's what had happened to the individual funds on a year-to-date basis:

AIM Global Technology: −52.5%

CI Global Telecommunications: −55.8%

AGF Aggressive Growth: −43.7%

E&P Growth Opportunities: +3.4%

Janus American Equity: −31.4%

Disaster! The portfolio's value has fallen to $115,669, a loss of more than 42 percent from its original value of $200,000, and this in less than two years. Only the Elliott & Page fund has made a profit; all the rest are dramatically down. And our investor was still paying carrying charges on the loan. How long is he likely to hang on in these circumstances, despite the advisor's pleas for patience?

Unfortunately, this type of portfolio is not untypical of the fund selection that might have been made in the market euphoria of the day. It is a classic illustration of the dark side of leveraging. The strategy can magnify your profits when stock markets are rising. But it has a similar effect on losses when markets are falling, especially if it is being aggressively managed.

The Balanced Approach

Now let's assume the advisor was wiser and recommended a more balanced approach. He still counselled putting the money into equity funds, but chose more diversified funds that were less exposed to the high-tech bubble. Here is the selection that he advised for his client:

20%	Mackenzie Ivy Canadian Fund
20%	AGF American Growth Class
20%	Templeton Growth Fund
20%	Fidelity European Growth Fund
20%	Trimark Canadian Small Companies Fund

Here we have a nice mix of growth and value funds, along with good international diversification. Let's see how the funds fared in calendar 2000.

Mackenzie Ivy Canadian: +20.4%

AGF American Growth: –14.6%

Templeton Growth: –0.8%

Fidelity European Growth: –7.7%

Trimark Canadian Small Companies: +16.5%

Here the result after the first year is much better. The gains in the Ivy and Trimark funds slightly outweigh the losses in the other three, providing a net profit within the portfolio of $5,520 for the year. That's almost (but not quite) enough to cover the after-tax cost of the loan interest.

Now comes the deep bear market of 2001. Let's see how these funds fared for the year to mid-October:

Mackenzie Ivy Canadian: −4.8%

AGF American Growth: −27.5%

Templeton Growth: −9.1%

Fidelity European Growth: −23.5%

Trimark Canadian Small Companies: +18.9%

Although four of the five funds lost money during the period, the results were nowhere near as bad as for the aggressive approach. The portfolio value at this point would have been $190,334, for an overall loss of less than 10 percent since the original investments were made. Of course, the investor would have laid out thousands of dollars in after-tax interest costs as well, which wouldn't have made him happy. But in this case, he might have been prepared to hang in and wait for better times given the fact the funds he owned had, collectively, held up reasonably well in very difficult markets.

The moral is obvious. If you are going to indulge in leveraging, take a balanced, or a conservative, approach in selecting your securities. You'll limit the upside potential to some degree, but you'll also reduce the downside risk considerably.

Why Leveraging Is Not for Everyone

Our problem with leveraging doesn't relate to its potential value as an investment tool. Rather, we're concerned that people are being persuaded to borrow against their homes or other securities without truly understanding the risks involved and the potential distress that losses may cause, especially if the money is aggressively invested.

In short, it's a psychological concern. Consider this. Suppose our fictional investor with the aggressive portfolio had gone home that night and told his wife what he had done. She may have expressed concern, but his arguments (or, more precisely, those presented by the advisor) would have persuaded her.

However, as stock markets began to weaken in the ensuing months, both of them would have become increasingly worried. After all, it was their home on the line. By the early autumn of 2001, the breakfast-table conversation may have degenerated into a running argument over whether they should hang on or take the loss and get out immediately, before any more damage was done. After the market plunge following the September 11 attacks, it would hardly be a surprise if the worry had degenerated into something approaching panic. You can hear it now: "We saved and scrimped all those years to pay off our mortgage and now we're right back where we started!"

The advisor's reaction would probably be to hang on, that a recovery was inevitable. But given the mood of the moment, would the couple have been receptive to such counsel? Many wouldn't. They'd flee.

Of course, over time that would likely prove to have been the wrong move. Even the aggressive portfolio, with its big losses, will probably bounce back eventually. But emotion plays a major role in investment decisions, especially in situations like this when money has been borrowed against the family home.

That's why we believe that leveraging is a suitable strategy only for very knowledgeable investors in most cases. Unless you're prepared to deal with what could be severe short-term losses and stick with the approach for the long haul, you're not a good candidate.

If you decide that you do indeed have the financial know-how and the stomach for leveraging, here are some suggestions that may be helpful:

- *Invest when markets are low, not high.* There's a natural tendency to avoid the stock market when the bear is in control and stocks are being ground down. Conversely, when markets are rising, everyone wants their share. That's why it's so easy to convince people to use leveraging when everything is on the rise and almost impossible to get anyone to listen when markets are in the doldrums. Of course, that's far and away the best time to use this approach. Stocks have been beaten down so badly that there is little downside left. Profit potential is at its maximum—historically, the early legs of a new bull market are the strongest. Interest rates are low, so the cost of borrowing is minimized. There can never be a better combination for the dedicated leverager. It's overcoming the generalized doom and gloom that's the real problem.

- *Take a balanced approach.* We've seen an illustration of the difference between an aggressive and a balanced approach in a terrible stock market. Those numbers should be all you need for guidance as to the route we recommend.

- *Take profits and pay down the debt.* If you do use leveraging and have success, don't keep reinvesting the profits. That's like betting all your winnings on every new roll of the roulette wheel. You expose yourself to a higher degree of risk every time, and sooner or later you'll lose. Instead, use the capital gains and/or dividends to pay down the loan. That way, if the market goes into the tank, your exposure will be reduced.

- *Don't mortgage the family home.* There's too much emotion attached to it. People can live with temporary losses against collateral such as GICs, bonds, or other securities. They have much more difficulty coping when the family home is on the line.

- *Pay the lowest possible interest rate.* Even though the interest is tax deductible, you still have to pay some of it out of your own pocket. If the loan is substantial, that could amount to several thousand dollars every year. So shop for the best deal available.

RRSPs—A Leveraging Exception

There is one type of leveraging that often makes sense for investors—the RRSP loan. These loans are offered by financial institutions every RRSP season to enable people to top up their contributions. The loans carry a low rate of interest (prime or slightly more) and are usually repayable within a year.

The bad news is that the interest charges in this case are not tax deductible. But the advantage of the tax refund that is generated as a result of this loan more than offsets that negative.

This is one of the few situations in which it is almost impossible to lose money through leveraging. Let's look at a typical scenario. We'll assume that Joe Jones has RRSP room of $10,000, but has only managed to save $3,000 towards his contribution. His choice is to contribute only the $3,000 or to borrow $7,000 and make his full $10,000 contribution. The money in the plan will be invested conservatively and he's looking for an average annual return of 8 percent. The interest rate on the loan is 6 percent. His marginal tax rate is 40 percent. He repays the loan in monthly instalments over 12 months. Here's how the numbers tumble:

	WITHOUT LOAN	WITH LOAN
RRSP contribution	$3,000	$10,000
Tax refund	1,200	4,000
Return at 8%	240	800
Total first year benefit (refund plus profit)	1,440	4,800
Interest charges	0	230
Net gain	$1,440	$ 4,570

As you can see, the RRSP loan strategy produces a go-ahead of more than $3,000 in the first year alone. Of course, that gain will be magnified going forward since there is more money in the plan earning tax-sheltered income. Over 25 years, that extra $7,000 will grow to almost $50,000 at 8 percent compounding. That's a nice extra chunk of cash for retirement.

There are a few things to keep in mind if you decide an RRSP loan is the right strategy for you:

- *Make sure you can handle the payments.* Never borrow money if it's going to place you in a financial bind. Be sure you can comfortably repay the lender.

- *Use your refund to pay down the loan.* This will give you a head start and, by reducing the principal, cut your monthly payments considerably.

- *Pay off the loan within a year.* The math is extremely strong in the first year. It breaks down after that because the advantage of the tax refund is not repeated.

Of course, making a full contribution without resorting to a loan is the best route. But if a loan is the only way to make a maximum RRSP contribution and you can handle the payments, go for it.

Wrapping Up

In general, we do not recommend leveraging as a strategy for anyone who is not an experienced investor. The psychological impact of a heavy loss is often too much for people to cope with, and in such cases they may decide to bail out, thus locking in their losses. If you do decide to use leveraging, we suggest taking a balanced approach to limit risk.

This means avoiding a "go-for-broke" style that emphasizes higher-risk stocks and/or equity mutual funds. While this type of aggressive approach increases profit potential, it also greatly magnifies the risk of loss in falling stock markets, as we saw in our illustration. A balanced method of selecting securities can still focus on equities but will concentrate on more conservatively managed funds and/or blue-chip stocks.

If you do decide to employ leveraging, we recommend that you take profits periodically and use the money to retire part of the loan. This will reduce risk going forward.

Although we generally discourage leveraging except for very experienced investors, we make an exception for RRSP loans. Because of the tax refund generated by the contribution, these loans are almost risk-free and produce a multiplier effect that can greatly increase the end value of a retirement plan over time.

15

PACKAGED PORTFOLIOS: HOW GOOD ARE THEY?

Throughout this book, we've stressed the importance of building your own investment portfolio, using the guidelines we've laid down. We believe that's the only way to create and manage an investment plan that is perfectly tailored to your specific goals and risk tolerance level, and that will allow you to fine-tune your asset mix with precision according to changing circumstances.

However, we acknowledge that many investors find this a difficult and time-consuming process. Those who use a financial advisor can delegate the portfolio-building task to that person and simply monitor the results occasionally to ensure everything is on track. But many people don't use a professional advisor, for various reasons. They're the do-it-yourselfers, the investing world's equivalent of car owners who repair their own engines. Sometimes, they're very successful at it. But sometimes the engine sputters and dies, just when you need it the most.

The investment industry, always sensitive to what it perceives as a new need for investors, has responded predictably by creating pre-packaged portfolios, supposedly designed to suit each investor's situation. Don't know how to construct your own portfolio? Don't have the time or the patience? Just buy one off the shelf!

Two Types of Packages

There are two basic types of packages available: the "wrap" account and the mutual fund packages, referred to in the trade as "funds of funds." Let's look at each.

Wrap accounts are offered through brokerage firms and other financial advisors. The odd name relates to the fact that the client pays a single fee for the full service, usually a percentage of assets under management. There are no sales commissions, transaction charges, etc.—all the costs are "wrapped" into the one annual fee.

Every brokerage firm and large financial planning company offers some type of wrap account. Typical is the Sovereign program from RBC Dominion Securities. It offers the choice of a number of different investment "pools"— in effect, private mutual funds run by top managers selected for Sovereign by the well-known Frank Russell organization. These pools cover the full range of investment options, including Canadian equity, U.S. equity, overseas equity, global equity, Canadian fixed income, money market, and more. Risk management is also part of the total equation. The RBC Dominion broker works with the client to decide on the appropriate allocation to each pool, thus establishing a personal asset mix.

We frequently receive questions about the effectiveness of Sovereign and other wrap programs. Unfortunately, we cannot provide any meaningful answers. The performance numbers of the pools within the programs are not public information (clients can, of course, obtain the data). Also, each client will have a different asset mix, so portfolio returns will vary.

If you are interested in exploring the wrap account concept, we recommend you take the following steps:

1. Ask the broker or planner to provide you with the performance results of each of the individual pools within the program over one, three, five and ten years, and since inception.

2. Also ask to be provided with the benchmarks for each pool and the returns on those benchmarks for the corresponding period. Every pool should have a benchmark against which performance is measured; for example a Canadian equity pool might be measured against the TSE 300 or the S&P/TSE 60, depending on its investment mandate.

3. Compare the results of the pools against the benchmarks. If the pools outperform on a regular basis, it indicates the program is working well.

4. Ask the advisor what asset mix he or she would recommend for your account. Then ask that a projection be run showing the return your account would have earned over the past few years had your money been in the wrap program. Be sure you obtain a net return, after the deduction of the wrap fees.

5. Compare the return against what your portfolio has actually been earning. If the wrap account would have performed better after expenses, then it's worth considering.

Mutual Fund Portfolios

As the number of mutual funds proliferated in the 1990s, fund portfolios were introduced to help confused investors create a balanced account. Unlike wrap accounts, most of these portfolios are designed in such a way that their performance can be tracked and meaningful comparisons can be made to the results generated by the average balanced fund, for example.

Some of the trackable portfolios are composed entirely of funds offered by a single company. These include the STAR portfolios (Mackenzie Financial), Investors portfolios (Investors Group), Spectrum portfolios (Spectrum), Royal Select funds (Royal Bank), MatchMaker portfolios (Bank of Montreal), and FundSmart portfolios (TD Bank).

Other portfolios are built using funds from a number of companies. These include Keystone (from Mackenzie Financial), Azura (operated by Evolution FM), and Artisan (operated by Assante).

This isn't a complete list by any means, but it gives you an idea of the wide range of products that are available.

At one point, fund companies apparently believed that these packages represented huge potential sales. However, investor reaction to these plans has been tepid. The Scotia Leaders Program, which was launched in 1996 based on the selections of mutual fund author Ranga Chand, is no longer being marketed. The same is true of the CIBC Choice Funds Program, which had been advised by co-author Gordon Pape. Mackenzie's STAR portfolios, which were heavily marketed at the time they were launched, have not pulled in the kind of dollars originally anticipated. Virtually all the portfolios have assets under management of less than $100 million and several are actually below $10 million, which makes us wonder how long it will be before they are merged.

Despite this mediocre success, some people may be tempted to go the package route instead of building their own fund portfolio using the principles we've outlined elsewhere in this book. But before you make that decision, you should know more about what's available in the fund package market, and what you can expect in terms of performance, safety, and cost.

Here's the scoop on some of the main packages now on the market competing for your investment dollar. We only deal with the trackable programs here, because they are the only ones that offer readily available comparisons with each other and with benchmarks.

Mackenzie STAR

One of the pioneers in popularizing the package concept is Gordon Garmaise who, along with his wife Ena, founded Garmaise Investment Technologies, a Toronto-based company that creates tailored portfolios and develops systems for helping people choose which one is best for their needs.

Garmaise, who holds a Master of Science degree in finance and economics from MIT, worked with Mackenzie Financial to launch the first portfolio system that really caught the public's attention. Named STAR, the program offers 29 portfolios (including segregated versions) in four categories, using only Mackenzie funds. They range in risk from conservative to highly aggressive.

The STAR program consists of the following categories:

- *Registered:* Eligible for registered plans; contains foreign content up to the allowable limit. However, don't be misled here. Gordon Garmaise says that these funds actually contain 48 to 58 percent foreign content. This results from the fact that the domestic funds held within the portfolios add more foreign holdings to the total mix, even though they are considered 100 percent Canadian for purposes of the 30 percent limit. So if you buy one of these packages, you will actually be getting a lot more foreign exposure than you might realize.

- *Canadian:* Eligible for registered plans; contains no foreign content funds but provides foreign exposure through derivatives. Total foreign content is about 25 percent.

- *Investment:* Not intended for registered plans; contains a blend of Canadian and foreign funds. Total foreign content is about 65 percent.

- *Foreign:* Contains only foreign content and no Canadian exposure.

The STAR portfolios have been around long enough to allow for some comparisons against regular balanced funds. The results vary, but only a couple have been consistently better than average. Most tend to fall into the high- to middle-third quartile, which is not bad but not sensational either. However, Garmaise cautions not to judge the portfolios on return alone. Risk also has to be taken into account and is a critical component in shaping the overall portfolio composition.

"You have to really control the downside in these portfolios," Garmaise says. "People tend to remember their losses much more than their gains. Limiting those losses when markets decline is one of the most important services we can render."

But he admits, "In the past we underperformed somewhat, partly because some of our portfolios turned out to be not as well diversified as we expected."

To put things back on course, the STAR portfolios went through a major overhaul in July 1998, with several funds being dropped from the mix, others downgraded, and new funds added.

"We learned a lot in the first three years," Garmaise says. "The program is even better now."

There is some evidence that this contention is correct. Several STAR portfolios performed much better since the overhaul than they had previously. But you have to use the correct benchmarks to compare. The STAR Canadian series matches up against the Canadian Balanced category. But the others, including the registered series, should be compared against the Global Balanced category, Garmaise says, because of the high foreign content they contain. So let's take a look at how they fared, to September 30, 2001:

STAR CANADIAN BALANCED PORTFOLIOS

PORTFOLIO	RATE OF RETURN	
	1 Year	3 Years
Average Canadian balanced fund	−8.4%	5.6%
STAR Can. Balanced Growth & Income	−5.0%	3.4%
STAR Can. Conservative Inc. & Growth	2.2%	4.9%
STAR Can. Long-Term Growth	−5.5%	4.1%
STAR Can. Maximum Long-Term Growth	−12.8%	4.7%

Source: The Globe and Mail.

Take a close look at these results. Most of the STAR Canadian portfolios beat the average one-year return of the Canadian Balanced category. But not one came close to matching the three-year result. In fact, in most cases you would have done much better by just putting your money into one of Mackenzie Financial's balanced funds and letting it go at that. Ivy Growth & Income, for example, generated an average annual compound rate of return of 7.6 percent over the same three-year period.

Now let's look at the STAR global portfolios, including those in the registered group:

STAR GLOBAL BALANCED PORTFOLIOS

PORTFOLIO	RATE OF RETURN	
	1 Year	3 Years
Average global balanced fund	−16.1%	1.0%
STAR Reg. Balanced Growth & Income	−4.5%	2.7%
STAR Reg. Conservative Inc. & Growth	−1.9%	2.0%
STAR Reg. Long-Term Growth	−11.5%	0.4%
STAR Foreign Balanced Growth & Income	−9.2%	3.2%
STAR Foreign Max. Long-Term Growth	−11.8%	2.2%
STAR Inv. Balanced Growth & Income	−5.4%	1.8%
STAR Inv. Conservative Income & Growth	−2.5%	4.4%
STAR Inv. Long-Term Growth	−14.5%	0.7%
STAR Inv. Maximum Long-Term Growth	−14.6%	4.5%

Source: The Globe and Mail.

Here the picture looks much better. All of the portfolios did better than the average global balanced fund over one year, and all but two had a better three-year record. Significantly, most of the portfolios also did better than the Mackenzie Ivy Global Balanced Fund, which had a one-year loss of 12.1 percent and a three-year average annual return of just 0.6 percent.

Of course, we're looking at pure return numbers here, without the relative risk factor taken into account, a point on which Garmaise places a great deal of emphasis. And it is true that many (but not all) of the STAR portfolios carry below-average risk for their categories.

The other point to consider with STAR, and with all other single-company portfolios, is the difficulty of achieving a high level of performance when your selection process is limited. Every organization, even one as large as Mackenzie, has weaknesses, and these can show up in this type of situation. A STAR portfolio, no matter how carefully constructed, is only as good as the performance of its underlying Mackenzie funds.

The STAR portfolios charge an extra 10 basis points (0.1 percent) over the usual management fees for the component funds. That makes them cheap by portfolio standards.

Bottom line: The STAR portfolios are performing much better since the 1998 overhaul. However, the only true domestic category, the Canadian portfolios, tends to be somewhat weak. Also, those who choose the Registered category need to understand exactly what they are buying, as the foreign content holdings are surprisingly high.

Keystone Portfolios

Gordon Garmaise's second project with Mackenzie is the Keystone portfolios. The principle is the same as with STAR, but in this case several other companies also provide funds that can be used in the mix. They include AGF, CI, Beutel Goodman, Saxon, Sceptre, and Spectrum.

"The advantage here is that we can add funds in areas where Mackenzie might not have a good alternative," Garmaise explains.

There are two types of Keystone portfolios available: the Registered series, which is designed for RRSPs and other registered plans, and the Investment series, which is intended for non-registered portfolios.

Here again, we see the same phenomenon we saw with STAR. The registered portfolios contain much more foreign content than you might expect, making the appropriate benchmark the Global Balanced category.

Here's a sampling of how they have fared, again to September 30, 2001. We've included comparable STAR portfolios for comparison.

KEYSTONE PORTFOLIOS PERFORMANCE

PORTFOLIO	RATE OF RETURN	
	1 Year	3 Years
Average global balanced fund	−16.1%	1.0%
Keystone Reg. Balanced Growth & Income	−11.8%	3.0%
STAR Reg. Balanced Growth & Income	−4.7%	2.7%
Keystone Reg. Conservative Income & Growth	−8.5%	2.7%
STAR Reg. Conservative Income & Growth	−1.9%	2.0%
Keystone Reg. Long-Term Growth	−15.2%	6.7%
STAR Reg. Long-Term Growth	−11.4%	0.4%
Keystone Inv. Balanced Growth & Income	−10.8%	3.8%
STAR Inv. Balanced Growth & Income	−5.4%	1.8%
Keystone Inv. Conservative Income & Growth	−7.5%	3.2%
STAR Inv. Conservative Income & Growth	−2.5%	4.4%
STAR Inv. Long-Term Growth	−14.5%	0.7%
Keystone Inv. Long-Term Growth	−14.3%	6.0%

Source: The Globe and Mail.

The results here prove the point we have been making. In five of the six head-to-head tests with comparable portfolio compositions, the multi-company portfolio (Keystone) beat the single-company portfolio (STAR) over a three-year period, which is a more meaningful result than one-year numbers. Also, all the Keystone portfolios beat the average for global balanced funds over three years. However, only two of the six Keystone portfolios were better than the average Canadian balanced fund over that time frame. If you are buying a Keystone Registered portfolio for Canadian content exposure, keep that in mind.

Like STAR, Keystone charges a premium of 10 basis points (0.1 percent) over the regular management fees of the funds.

Bottom line: Your chances of achieving above-average returns are better with Keystone than with STAR over a longer time frame. But, as with STAR, be sure you understand exactly what you are buying.

Artisan Portfolios

There are 14 portfolios offered in the Artisan line-up. They are run by Assante Asset Management and are distributed through a network of financial planning companies owned by that firm. These are third-party portfolios that include funds from AIM, Altamira, Fidelity, Dynamic, CI, and AGF. Each portfolio is designed to meet a specific investment need. The balanced entries range from Most Conservative to Most Aggressive. As well, there are some targeted portfolios such as New Economy and Canadian T-Bill.

The mix of funds you get will depend on your choice of portfolio. For example, if you purchase units in the Artisan Growth Portfolio, you will be buying a basket of outside funds that includes, among others, AGF Global Government Bond, BPI American Equity, Fidelity European Growth, Dynamic Canadian Growth, and Altamira Bond. The weighting in each portfolio is determined by Assante, which is a Winnipeg-based company.

The MER of the Artisan portfolios is relatively high, coming in at over 3 percent in most cases (the T-Bill Portfolio is 1.34 percent). This means you are paying a hefty premium for the package versus simply buying the underlying funds. You have to decide if buying the funds this way is worth the added cost.

As with Keystone and STAR, you may be getting more foreign content here than you expect, so ask before you buy.

The portfolios were launched in January 1998, so we now have some three-year numbers for comparison purposes. Here are some comparisons (to September 30, 2001) with the Keystone balanced portfolios, which use the same general approach.

ARTISAN PORTFOLIOS PERFORMANCE

PORTFOLIO	RATE OF RETURN	
	1 Year	3 Years
Artisan Moderate Portfolio	−10.6%	4.4%
Keystone Reg. Balanced Growth & Income	−11.8%	3.0%
Artisan Conservative Portfolio	−7.6%	3.5%
Keystone Reg. Conservative Income & Growth	−8.5%	2.7%
Artisan Growth Portfolio	−15.5%	3.6%
Keystone Reg. Long-Term Growth	−15.2%	6.7%
Artisan Maximum Growth Portfolio	−25.8%	1.3%
Keystone Reg. Maximum Long-Term Growth	−19.9%	1.5%

Source: The Globe and Mail.

Neither group shows a clear-cut advantage in this match-up. The conservative Artisan portfolios win out over three years, but the more aggressively managed Keystone portfolios have the advantage.

Bottom line: So far the Artisan funds are decent performers. But you will pay a premium price to have your funds packaged for you in this way. Any financial advisor could emulate the portfolios, or you could do it yourself.

Investors Group

There are seven fund-of-funds portfolios in the Investors Group line-up. All invest exclusively in other Investors Group funds, and all are designed to offer varying levels of risk. Some have been around for several years so we have a pretty good idea of how they compare to funds in their peer group and to other Investors Group funds of the same type. Here are some examples, using figures to September 30, 2001:

INVESTORS GROUP CANADIAN EQUITY

FUND/PORTFOLIO	RATE OF RETURN			
	1 Year	3 Years	5 Years	10 Years
Average Canadian equity fund	−18.6%	8.8%	6.5%	9.2%
Investors Retirement Growth Portfolio	−3.8%	7.8%	5.0%	7.6%
Investors Retirement Mutual Fund	4.7%	10.1%	5.4%	7.6%
Investors Canadian Equity Fund	−8.8%	7.6%	3.4%	8.0%

Source: The Globe and Mail.

In this case, the Retirement Mutual Fund did better than the Retirement Portfolio for the one-, three-, and five-year periods. Over a decade, the two produced the same average annual compound rate of return. However, all significantly underperformed the average for all Canadian diversified equity funds.

INVESTORS GROUP GLOBAL EQUITY

FUND/PORTFOLIO	RATE OF RETURN			
	1 Year	3 Years	5 Years	10 Years
Average Global equity fund	−25.2%	3.5%	5.1%	9.0%
Investors Growth Portfolio	−12.3%	4.3%	7.1%	10.3%
Investors World Growth Portfolio	−23.0%	0%	−0.2%	N/A
Investors Global Fund	−15.4%	2.4%	6.7%	9.1%

Source: The Globe and Mail.

The Investors Growth Portfolio looks quite good in this comparison. It outperformed the average for the Global Equity category in all time periods, and also did better than the Investors Global Fund, which makes up 40 percent of its portfolio. The World Growth Portfolio does not look good at all, no matter which time frame you consider.

INVESTORS GROUP CANADIAN BALANCED

FUND/PORTFOLIO	RATE OF RETURN			
	1 Year	3 Years	5 Years	10 Years
Average Canadian balanced fund	−8.4%	5.6%	6.2%	8.5%
Investors Income Plus Portfolio	3.1%	6.1%	7.1%	7.4%
Investors Retirement Plus Portfolio	1.2%	5.7%	5.4%	7.2%
Investors Mutual of Canada	−11.4%	8.8%	7.8%	9.3%

Source: The Globe and Mail.

When we look at the Canadian Balanced category, it is quickly apparent that the two Investors Group portfolios are not the best place to be over the long term. Both portfolios produced worse results than the average Canadian balanced fund over 10 years, although they were better in the shorter terms. The stand-alone Investors Mutual of Canada Fund did significantly better than either of the portfolios for all time periods except one year, plus it outperformed the averages over those same time periods. It is the better long-term choice among these Investors Group products; however it has a higher risk level when markets fall.

The MERs of the portfolios are generally in line with those of regular Investors Group funds, so cost is not a major concern here.

Bottom line: Returns from the Investors Group portfolios are respectable but they generally fail to match the averages for their respective categories. In some cases, you would do better by selecting a stand-alone fund from those offered by the company.

Spectrum Portfolios

Like Investors Group, the Spectrum organization offers several portfolios constructed from their own line of funds. They're called The Portfolio Series and they range from very conservative to quite aggressive in their approach. As is typical with package programs, investors complete a questionnaire, the results of which direct them to the portfolio best suited to their needs. These are the choices:

- *Canadian Income Portfolio:* This is the most conservative of the group and consists of 80 percent income funds (including the Spectrum Dividend Fund) and 20 percent equity funds. Gain for the year to September 30, 2001, was 4.9 percent, which was worse than the average bond fund due to the weakness in the stock markets. However, the three-year return is slightly better than average for the Canadian Bond category. The plan offers monthly income. However, the MER of 2.06 percent is high for a portfolio of this type.

- *Canadian Conservative Portfolio:* The mix here is about 60 percent income funds and 40 percent equity funds. One-year gain was –1.3 percent, above average for the Canadian Balanced category. However, the three-year average annual return of 5 percent was worse than the norm. Income distributions are paid quarterly. The 2.24 percent MER is slightly below average for the category.

- *Canadian Balanced Portfolio:* This one also uses a mix of 60 percent income funds and 40 percent equity funds, although the parameters are more flexible and the fund selection is somewhat different. That's reflected in the results; this portfolio lost 9.1 percent in the year to September 30, 2001, below average for the category. But it has fared much better in the longer term, with an average annual gain of 9.1 percent over a decade. This is the one of the oldest of the Spectrum portfolios and its track record over the years is quite good. The stand-alone Spectrum Diversified Fund has done even better than this portfolio over the past five years, but this one wins out handily over a decade. The MER of 2.39 percent is about average for the category.

- *Canadian Growth Portfolio:* This one is for more aggressive investors. The split is 20 percent income funds and 80 percent equity funds. That means this portfolio should do well when stock markets are rising, but will look sickly when they are falling. The latest one-year numbers confirm that, with a loss of 16.7 percent. The MER is on the high side at 2.56 percent.

- *Canadian Maximum Growth Portfolio:* Here's one for the bulls. The portfolio invests only in a selection of Spectrum equity funds, with no fixed-income representation. Not surprisingly, it posted the worst numbers in this group last year, losing 22.4 percent in the 12 months to September 30, 2001. MER is 2.66 percent, which is high for the Canadian Equity category.

- *Global Growth Portfolio:* Spectrum offers one international portfolio in its line-up, an aggressive mix of 80 percent equities and 20 percent income. It doesn't have a long record but its one- and three-year results are better than average for the category. The MER is about average at 2.78 percent.

Bottom line: We've repeatedly made the point that portfolios are only as good as the individual funds that go into them. Spectrum's in-house portfolios are a case in point. When we reviewed them in mid-2000, they were among the best fund packages we found, because the underlying funds were doing well. In fall 2001, they were just so-so, again reflecting what was happening underneath.

MatchMaker/FundSmart

These are investment services offered by the Bank of Montreal (MatchMaker) and TD (FundSmart). The BMO program uses only Bank of Montreal funds, while the TD plan includes both the company's funds and those from some outside companies, including Altamira, AGF, Fidelity, AIC, and Dynamic.

We think the TD program has more potential, but it has not been around long enough to form any conclusive opinion.

BMO's MatchMaker offers 12 Strategic portfolios that are rebalanced periodically. As in the other programs, the idea is to optimize returns while keeping risk within tolerable levels. Each Strategic portfolio contains a minimum of five funds. As with many of these portfolio plans, investors complete a questionnaire that is designed to direct them to the most suitable portfolio.

The MatchMaker portfolios have been around long enough to establish a five-year track record. Here's a sampling from the Canadian Balanced category. The funds with Registered in the name are RRSP-eligible. Two versions of each non-registered portfolio are offered. Those designated "1" are more conservative than those designated "2." (You may have noted one of the problems with all these portfolios—the names are often similar, potentially leading to confusion.)

MATCHMAKER DOMESTIC BALANCED PORTFOLIOS

PORTFOLIO	RATE OF RETURN		
	1 Year	3 Years	5 Years
Average Canadian balanced fund	–8.4%	5.6%	6.2%
MatchMaker Registered Balanced 1	–6.9%	4.4%	5.9%
MatchMaker Registered Growth 1	–13.0%	4.9%	4.5%
MatchMaker Registered Balanced 2	–10.7%	4.1%	5.9%
MatchMaker Registered Growth 2	–19.4%	2.4%	3.4%
BMO Asset Allocation Fund	–5.9%	7.4%	7.3%

Source: The Globe and Mail.

None of the portfolios outperformed the Canadian Balanced category average over any time period. However, as with STAR and Keystone, that may be misleading because the actual foreign content within these portfolios is well in excess of 30 percent in many cases. These funds all look much better when stacked up against the Global Balanced category. However, we believe that many people who buy these portfolios don't realize the high degree of foreign content they contain and would see the Canadian Balanced category as a better benchmark.

If that's what you are actually looking for, then you should probably ignore MatchMaker and invest in the stand-alone BMO Asset Allocation Fund, which is in the same family and which has a better track record than any of the portfolios we've looked at.

Bottom line: There is no evidence that the BMO packages can outperform the peer group average on a long-term basis (but it does depend on which peer group you select). Certainly, they don't fare well against a stand-alone fund from the same company in this study.

Wrapping Up

There are two basic types of package deals: wrap accounts and funds of funds. Wrap accounts are difficult to judge in terms of value for money and require some careful analysis before making a commitment.

On the whole, the mutual fund packages have not been particularly impressive, although none has been absolutely awful and a few have fared reasonably well.

These plans are best suited for investors who prefer the convenience of one-stop fund shopping and buying a package that is tailored to fit their investment goals (at least in theory). We believe, however, that you can build your own portfolio more effectively using the principles contained in this book.

16

MAKING INDEXING WORK
FOR YOU

When you are building investment portfolios, one of the most important considerations is identifying your selection style. The major style decision is whether to use an active, passive, or mixed approach to investing. Active investors seek out and invest in undervalued securities, or buy mutual funds that are managed by security selectors who follow an active approach. Passive investors believe that security prices fully reflect all available information and the search for undervalued securities is fruitless. They follow an index strategy, and this has changed the financial landscape for modern investors. Since it has become so important for many people, this chapter will explore the entire approach in depth.

What Indexing Is All About

Indexing is considered a passive investment strategy because you don't strive to select quality individual stocks, bonds, or other securities. Instead, you either buy index-based products, such as mutual funds, or structure a portfolio that mirrors (or "tracks") a market index, bond index, or specialty market sector index. In either case, you are purchasing a set of securities assembled to replicate the targeted index.

Canada has been an important incubator for indexing strategies. One of the world's first index mutual funds was introduced in this country in 1978: National Trust's TSE 300 Index Fund. The world's first successful exchange-traded index fund was the Toronto 35 Index Participation Fund (TIPS), introduced by the Toronto Stock Exchange (TSE) in 1989.

TIPS was the prototype for this rapidly expanding market, which now includes SPDRs, iShares, iUnits, DIAMONDS, QQQs, and numerous other exchange-traded index funds. These products were previously called "index participation units," or IPUs. The broad term "exchange-traded funds" (ETFs) or more specifically "exchange-traded index funds" (ETIFs) has recently taken hold.

In spite of the TSE's early leadership role, investor interest in indexing was much slower to develop in Canada than in the U.S. and U.K. In the late 1990s, however, the high returns on index funds relative to actively managed funds began to build indexing momentum in this country. As a result, a large number of new index mutual funds have been introduced in Canada over the past few years.

Market Indexing Roots

Proponents of passive investing point out that an investment strategy of randomly selecting common shares to buy and hold has returned about 10 to 11 percent a year over the past 60 years. This result cuts right to the core of passive investing and market indexing.

Market indexing has its roots in the investment finance combination of Portfolio Theory and Efficient Markets Theory, both of which were discussed in chapter 4. As you'll recall, under Portfolio Theory, as designed by Nobel Prize–winner Harry Markowitz, investors should only be concerned with two elements of their portfolios—the anticipated return, as measured by the average or expected rate of return, and the risk, as measured by the standard deviation or variance of the rate of return. By diversifying across asset classes, you reduce risk by eliminating the unique risk associated with individual securities, and also reduce your exposure to interest-rate, exchange-rate, and inflation risks, without reducing expected return.

As we've noted, Canadian investors were slow to warm up to the concept of indexing. We suspect this seeming disinterest reflects a lack of understanding of passive investing by individual investors, fear on the part of investors that they may be missing out on the next big winner, and possibly a disinclination to promote index products by brokers and financial advisors. (The latter circumstance may reflect the fact that index products pay lower commissions and trailer fees than active products.)

An impelling motivation for passive investing is the "Gambler's Ruin Principle," which refers to having the right idea but utilizing the wrong implementation strategy. For example, one of the top-performing markets in 1999 was Malaysia, which recorded a 47 percent return. If you held an iShares Malaysia ETIF, you would have matched that performance, at least relatively closely. However, if you went on your own, you might have chosen the wrong investment vehicles or selected the wrong mix of stocks (perhaps overweighting in weak sectors) and missed out on the Malaysia stock rally. If you want to invest in Malaysia—or anywhere else for that matter—for portfolio diversification reasons, you should consider an index product.

To that end, if you are concentrating on getting the right strategic asset allocation mix rather than on security selection and market timing decisions, you may well find an indexing strategy ideal for your purposes.

The Efficient Markets Theory (EMT) states that security prices reflect all publicly available information, on average neither overestimating nor underestimating the true value of securities. The theory implies that you cannot expect to earn excess profits by employing conventional analytic techniques that use information available to everybody. For example, if you believe in the theory, you would expect published news reports about companies to be a simple confirmation of information rather than something to be acted upon. If you believe in market efficiency, you will find indexing the right approach.

Indexing: The Cost Issue

With an indexed portfolio, you make trades only when there is a change in the underlying index. Therefore, if you are managing your own indexed portfolio, you pay fewer commissions and incur fewer incremental tax liabilities than you would if you were using an active approach.

Taxes on security gains are deferred until the security is actually sold. Thus, an indexed portfolio may go several years without a taxable sale, whereas an actively managed portfolio will probably incur tax liabilities every year. You get the same benefits if you purchase index funds or other index products since the fund manager will be making fewer trades, requiring fewer bid/ask spread costs; will have a lower overall outlay for commissions and taxes; and, because no research or decision making is required, will charge you far smaller management fees than active managers. Active management incurs higher commissions, taxes, management fees, and higher bid/ask spread costs. One estimate is that the trading costs for active portfolios are about six times greater than for passive investing.

Index fund managers do not need the large staff of research analysts and portfolio managers required by active funds. Furthermore, there are monitoring and search costs for active fund managers. The contracts between active fund managers and their stakeholders may be complex and expensive, since active managers may be granted substantial discretion. On the other hand, index managers do not need close supervision or daily monitoring, and are rarely fired. Accordingly, you should expect to see far lower management fees and expense ratios with index funds and products than for active funds.

The goal of an index fund manager is simply to complete a portfolio that will emulate the target index. Thus, his or her trades are considered to be "information-less" and, as a result, the market impact costs are likely to be lower than those associated with active managers, who are assumed to be trading based on some research findings or on special information.

Indexing strategies are transparent and unambiguous. Typical active equity fund managers maintain cash reserves of 5 to 10 percent. These cash reserves transform the allocation to something other than a 100 percent equity portfolio. For example, a fund based on a stock index that has cash reserves of 10 percent is actually a 10 percent safety/90 percent equity portfolio. Cash reserves make it more difficult for you to determine a fund's true asset allocation and may act as a drag on the fund's returns. Furthermore, you are paying active management fees on the cash component of the portfolio. In contrast, a typical index fund has a very small or negligible cash reserve.

Index Products and Defensive Protection

One knock against index securities is that since they are fully invested (except for index mutual funds that have small cash reserves), they don't provide protection against a bear market. In contrast, many fully managed equity mutual funds hold cash as a tactical trading strategy, providing the option of increasing this component as conditions warrant. The argument is that in a bear market, an insightful fund manager will increase the cash component, thus cushioning the blow and allowing the fund to outperform market indexes, or at least lose less than the indexes.

There are two fallacies inherent in this argument. First, the fund manager has to be right about assessing when a bear market has struck and knowing when to increase the cash component. Studies show that fund managers haven't been too successful at this type of market timing. Second, by increasing the cash component, the fund manager is changing the asset allocation. Say an investor is holding a 20/30/50 portfolio, made up of a money market fund, an income fund, and an equity fund. If the fund manager increases the cash component of the equity fund by 10 percent, the investor is now holding a 25/30/45 asset allocation. Presumably, an investor who wants a change in the mix can do so independently.

If you believe in these paradigms, you should concentrate your attention on your portfolio mix (safety/income/growth combinations) rather than individual stock selection.

The Record

Indexing takes a lot of the emotion and drama out of investing. In recent years, index products have outshone active investments over many time frames. For example, over the five years to June 30, 2000, Canadian market indexes outperformed the average and median Canadian equity fund by an average of about 5.2 percentage points a year, well above the average management expense ratio (2.3 percent) of equity funds. The most dramatic case was in the year ending June 30, 2000, when the average mutual fund missed the TSE 300 Composite Total Return Index by a whopping 20.3 percent.

Over that same time period, index mutual funds performed much better than their active counterparts, having missed the TSE 300 Composite Index by an average of 1.3 percentage points per year. Exchange Traded Index Funds (ETIFs) such as iUnits S&P/TSE 60, or "i60s" as they're called, and their predecessor, TIPS 35 and TIPS 100, have almost perfectly matched their underlying indexes.

On the other hand, in 1996 and 1999, the average Canadian equity mutual fund beat the TSE 300 by 0.6 percent and 0.2 percent, respectively. And in the 12 months to September 30, 2001, the average Canadian equity mutual fund's loss of 18.7 percent was dwarfed by the massive 33.1 percent loss on the TSE 300 Composite Index.

Over the past 10 years, the record for active investing is much better. The average Canadian equity mutual fund has underperformed the TSE 300 Composite Index at a rate of about 0.3 percent per year—meaning that the average fund actually beat the index, but the cost of doing so ate up the profits and then some.

Keep in mind that, if anything, the mutual fund sample results are biased upwards, since the funds that merge or otherwise disappear do not appear in the sample (a phenomenon known as survivorship bias). Typically, such funds are weaker-than-average performers.

Implementing a Strategy

How do you carry out an indexing strategy? There are a number of useful vehicles. Let's look at each in turn.

Exchange-Traded Index Funds (ETIFs)

One of the most efficient investment products for passive investors is the exchange-traded index fund (ETIF). These are exchange-traded units of a fund that holds a basket of stocks, which in turn mirrors the composition of a specific underlying market index. ETIFs trade just like stocks and are priced on the exchange on a bid/ask basis.

The ETIF universe has expanded dramatically in recent years, fuelled primarily by new product introductions from the two key index product designers and managers, Barclays Global Investors and State Street Global Advisors.

ETIFs provide the investor with the ability to buy or sell the underlying index at any time during the trading day at prevailing market prices, thus generating liquidity. In contrast, the standard index mutual fund is valued at the end of the trading day, which is the only time the investor can buy or sell units.

The first successful ETIF was the Toronto Index Participation Shares, or TIPS, introduced by the Toronto Stock Exchange on March 9, 1990. As we've noted, the TIPS structure was so sound that it has served as prototype for subsequent U.S.-based ETIFs, including SPDRs, based on the Standard & Poor's 500 Composite, and DIAMONDS, based on the Dow Jones Industrial Average. The original TIPS was linked to the Toronto 35 Index. A second ETIF, TIPS 100, was subsequently introduced and was linked to the TSE 100 Index.

Both TIPS series were merged into the S&P/TSE 60 Participation Units or "i60s" in March 2000. This ETIF, introduced by Barclays Global Investors in 1999, is pegged to the S&P/TSE 60 Index. The S&P/TSE 60 Share Index was introduced December 31, 1998, and is a capitalization-weighted index comprised of 60 of Canada's largest companies. The S&P/TSE 60 is an actively managed index. An S&P selection committee manages the inclusion of companies in the index using fundamental valuation criteria. The key criteria are size (assets and market capitalization), liquidity, and sector leadership. The index is designed for institutional investors since it contains stocks in which institutions want to actually invest.

The i60s are almost identical to their TIPS predecessor. They trade at approximately one-tenth the value of the S&P/TSE 60 Index. If, for example, the S&P/TSE 60 Index is quoted at 894.50, the i60s will trade at about $89.45

The i60 Fund holds common shares of the companies making up the S&P/TSE 60 Index in the same proportion as reflected in the Index. The management expense ratio (MER) is 17 basis points. By contrast, index mutual fund MERs are generally in the 50- to 110-point range, although some less expensive options have appeared recently.

There are now close to 100 ETIFs traded in Canada and the U.S. The i60 is the most popular of the ETIFs based on a Canadian index.

U.S. ETIFs

SPDRs

The Standard and Poor's Depositary Receipts, or SPDRs, are pegged to the S&P 500 Composite Index. They trade under the ticker symbol SPY.

The S&P 500 Index is a capitalization-weighted, broadly diversified index that comprises over 80 industry groups. The index is composed of stocks that are traded on the New York Stock Exchange, the American Stock Exchange, and the Nasdaq Stock Market.

SPDR units are traded in minimum increments of 1/64 of a dollar, or $0.016625. Like TIPS, and now i60s, SPDRs are quoted and traded in one-tenth the value of the S&P 500 Index. For example, if the S&P 500 Index is at 1,098.73, the core value of a SPDR will be US $109.87.

The SPDR Trust expires in 2018. The dividends and other distributions of the 500 companies of the S&P 500 Index are collected and invested by the trust and then distributed on a quarterly basis to the unitholders. Dividends received from SPDRs are not eligible for the dividend tax credit, because only dividends from taxable Canadian corporations qualify. Furthermore, they are subject to tax withholding at source if they are held outside a registered plan. The rate is 15 percent, so if you earn a dividend of $1,000 on your SPDR units, the U.S. government will withhold $150. You can recapture the tax as a foreign tax credit on your tax return.

Mid-Cap SPDRs

There are some variations of SPDRs based on S&P 500 components and other Standard & Poor's indexes. Introduced on May 4, 1995, Mid-Cap SPDRs are based on the S&P 400 MidCap Index, comprised, as you would assume from the name, of 400 mid-cap U.S. companies. The expense ratio is about 0.25 percent. Ticker symbol is MDY.

Select Sector SPDRs

Introduced on December 22, 1998, select sector index products are subsets of the S&P 500 Composite Index. There are nine different ETIFs, based on each of the following: basic industries (ticker symbol: XLB), consumer services (XLV), consumer staples (XLP), cyclicals/transportation (XLY), energy (XLE), finance (XLF), industrial interests (XLI), technology (XLK), and utilities (XLU). The expense ratio for each of the sector SPDRs is about 0.65 percent.

DIAMONDS

DIAMONDS was the first financial product based on the Dow, introduced January 20, 1998. The Dow Jones Industrial Average is a large-cap index of 30 blue-chip companies traded on the New York Stock Exchange. The expense ratio is about 0.18 percent. Ticker symbol is DIA.

The NASDAQ-100 Shares

Introduced in 1998, this product is based on the Nasdaq 100 Index of 100 mid- and large-cap companies traded on National Association of Securities Dealers stock exchange. The index has a heavy high-tech and Internet emphasis. Ticker symbol is QQQ.

Global ETIFs

Non-U.S. ETIFs are available in the form of iShares Morgan Stanley Capital International (MSCI) Index Funds. Originally issued as MSCI World Equity Benchmark Shares (WEBS) in May 1996, iShares represent a basket of securities that replicates the total return performance of a specific MSCI market index. All of these MSCI indexes are total return indices with net dividends (after withholding taxes) deemed to be reinvested. (The MSCI World Composite Index, launched in 1969, is the most widely used world performance index.)

There are 21 different series of iShares that include Australia, Austria, Belgium, Canada, the ECU, France, Germany, Hong Kong, Italy, Japan, Malaysia, Mexico, the Netherlands, Singapore, South Africa, South Korea, Spain, Sweden, Switzerland, Taiwan, and the United Kingdom.

Although iShares can be highly useful in adding a global equity component to your asset allocation mix, it's essential to recognize that tracking errors (degree to which performance deviates from the index) on iShares are much higher than on the Canadian and U.S. ETIFs. The increased tracking error is caused by the following factors:

- *Cash drag.* Cash drag is the impact that a cash holding has on the performance of a portfolio. If a fund manager holds 5 percent of a portfolio in cash and earns 4 percent on that money while the remainder of the portfolio earns 15 percent, the cash holdings will drag down the return. iShares hold a small portion of their portfolio in cash.

- *Advisory fees.* At present, the advisory fee is running at a rate of about 0.85 to about 0.98 percent per iShares portfolio.

- *Portfolio sampling.* Although iShares are designed to replicate the specific underlying MSCI index, the approach used by the investment advisor—Barclays Global Fund Advisors—is to hold a basket of securities that closely matches the index. The portfolio is allocated to a subset of the market, and results may therefore vary positively or negatively from the index.

- *Regulatory restraints.* Under the U.S. Single Issuer Rule, which is applicable to iShares, no issuer in a portfolio can represent more than 25 percent of the portfolio. For example, the Mexico iShares is affected by this rule. Telefonos de Mexico, which has two issues in the MSCI Mexico Index of over 30 percent in aggregate, has to be underweighted in the iShares portfolio to meet the rule. Accordingly, the Mexico iShares portfolio is underweighted in the telecommunications sector.

- *Revenue differential.* All iShares record dividends on the ex-dividend dates, whereas the MSCI index estimates monthly dividends as $\frac{1}{12}$ of the previous 12 months' dividend. Thus, the tracking error can vary substantially from month to month.

Index Mutual Funds

Index mutual funds are an alternative to ETIFs. Index mutual funds, like other equity mutual funds, invest in portfolios of common shares. However, the objective of an index fund is to track—as closely as possible—an underlying market index.

Like other mutual funds, the net asset value per unit (NAVPU) of an index fund is calculated at the end of the day—unlike ETIFs, whose units continuously trade at market price on an exchange. Also unlike ETIFs, which accumulate dividends outside the fund and pay them out to shareholders quarterly, index mutual funds reinvest dividends as they are received. Index mutual funds, when they do make distributions to unitholders, offer distribution reinvestment plans; ETIFs at present do not have such plans.

Canadian-based index mutual funds that track U.S. and global equity indexes are also available, as are RRSP-eligible versions that use T-bills and derivatives to replicate the underlying index. These are known as synthetic funds.

As of October 2001, there were 12 index mutual funds focusing on the Canadian market. Seven are conventional, open-ended funds; one, the Royal Premium Index Fund, is a low-MER, high-minimum-investment ($250,000) fund; and the others are segregated or protected funds.

Segregated funds generally have higher MERs than the standard funds, reflecting an effective "put option" held by the investor. The segregated funds provide varying degrees of protection to unit holders by guaranteeing a minimum fund performance over specific time periods.

There are six relatively new Canadian-based mutual funds that invest in U.S. portfolios. The fund with the longest record is the TD U.S. Index Fund, pegged to the S&P 500 Index. The tracking error has been about 1.1 percent a year over the past five years. This is the original index fund launched by Green Line. Their renamed TD line-up now has eight such funds covering all the major regions of the world. TD also has an RRSP-eligible version (using T-bills and derivatives) and a Canadian dollar version of the U.S. index fund.

There are also a few Canadian indexed global mutual funds. For example, the CIBC International Index Fund is pegged to the well-known Morgan Stanley Capital International Europe, Australasia, and Far East Index (EAFE). EAFE is as representative an index of non-North American investing as you can find. The major components of the 1,075-company EAFE are the United Kingdom, Japan, Germany, France, and Switzerland. The CIBC fund is a physical security-based portfolio. The fund manager's target is to track the EAFE index within 75 basis points.

There is also a fully RRSP-eligible version of this fund, the CIBC International Index RRSP Fund. It also tries to track the EAFE index within 75 points. However, this fund uses a combination of Canadian T-bills and equity index futures to replicate the index. This use of cash and derivatives means that the fund is fully eligible for an RRSP or RRIF. This version of the fund has potentially adverse tax consequences if held outside an RRSP.

Index-Linked Notes and GICs

Although we have focused primarily on the equity side of index investing, you can also employ index products for the fixed-income component of your portfolio. In addition, you can invest in both income and growth sectors through the use of a single specialized security. The vehicles involved in these approaches are index-linked notes, index-keyed term deposits, and index-linked guaranteed investment certificates (GICs). They have different names, but they all use the same underlying principle: each pays a guaranteed floor interest rate, plus an increment (if any) that is tied to the performance of a single market index or a portfolio of market indexes.

For example, the CIBC introduced three-year and five-year GICs that come in four versions, each representing a mix of GIC, bond, and equity. The GIC payoff is tied to the GIC yield, the income component to the CIBC Wood Gundy Bond Index, and the equity yield to the aggregate performance of a Toronto, a U.S., a Japanese, and a pan-European market index.

The underlying indexes used for index-linked GICs range from the TSE 300 Composite Index to the Eurotop 100 Index. Some of the payoffs at maturity are based on the closing level of the underlying index. Others base the payoff at maturity on the average of the closing monthly levels of the underlying index over the term of the investment. With some products you get the entire increase in the index, while with others you receive a percentage of any increase. Some payouts are capped, thus restricting the maximum potential profit. The large number of investment options provides the investor with multiple strategy choices. However, making a choice requires a clear understanding of the products and their associated MERs.

An index-linked GIC is actually a term deposit plus a "call option" on the underlying market index. Most of these products can be difficult to analyze and even more difficult to value. For example, one bank-issued GIC is linked to the markets of the G7 countries. This three-year product pays a floor rate of interest, plus an increment that is pegged to an aggregate index of G7 markets, subject to a 65 percent participation rate in any market increase over the product's three-year lifespan. In other words, you get a combination of safety, income, and potential capital appreciation—but projecting the precise outcome is virtually impossible.

Indexed Bond Products

Indexed bond products are tied to the performance of an underlying bond index or to a bond itself. A small but growing number of Canadian mutual funds are tied to specific bond indexes. For example, the CIBC Bond Index Fund tracks the ScotiaMcLeod Bond Universe, while the CIBC Short-Term Bond Index Fund targets the ScotiaMcLeod Short-Term Bond Index.

In November 2000, Barclays Global Investors introduced the iG5 Fund and the iG10 Fund. Units in these funds trade on the TSE and are designed to replicate the return on five-year and ten-year Government of Canada bonds, respectively. The iG5s and iG10s are the first exchange-traded funds based on bonds. They are managed according to a predetermined set of rules, and hold only a single bond at a time. However, one bond is all you need when you are investing in the default-free portion of the bond market. If you are holding Government of Canada bonds, the only diversification you need is temporal; a single bond is sufficient for any given maturity because there is no credit risk.

The key feature of these bond funds is their cost-effectiveness, due largely to the economies of scale gained by trading large quantities of single bonds. Transaction costs in trading iGs are minimal compared to the high bid/ask spreads and other fees individual investors face when buying and selling bonds in small amounts (such as $5,000 or $10,000).

As time passes, the current bond's term to maturity shortens. Accordingly, each of the iGs is rebalanced periodically to bring the maturity back to the five- and ten-year targets. This means you may, from time to time, be holding a product with a term to maturity closer to four or nine years.

The current MER for the iGs is 25 basis points (0.25 percent). The interest income on the iGs is distributed semi-annually, a schedule comparable to distributions on the underlying government bonds.

FPX Index Portfolios

Another opportunity for passive investing is with ready-made passive portfolios. Richard Croft and Eric Kirzner have designed a set of indexes that are published daily in the *National Post*. These "FPX indexes" are passive and investable measures of representative diversified investment portfolios and should be used as benchmarks to measure the performance of your own personal portfolio, or as fully investable portfolios if you instead choose to buy one of them. The FPX Indexes are described in detail in the next chapter.

Wrapping Up

When you are building investment portfolios, one of the most important considerations is identifying your selection style. The major style decision is whether to use an active, passive, or mixed approach to investing. Active investors seek out and invest in specific securities that they believe are undervalued, or they buy mutual funds that are managed by security selectors following an active approach. Passive investors believe that security prices fully reflect all available information and the search for undervalued securities is fruitless. They follow an index strategy.

The studies and performance samples provided in this chapter should be enough to convince you that a passive investment approach is worthy of some consideration.

Our favourite and most direct product for the index approach is the ETIF. So think about i60s, SPDRs, DIAMONDS, QQQs, and other such colourfully named yet effective products when structuring your portfolio. If you decide to use any of these securities, as always we recommend a diversified approach.

Index-based securities can be used as core holdings to which, if you wish, you can add some carefully selected, actively managed mutual funds to create a portfolio that's well suited to your needs.

17

UNDERSTANDING AND
USING FPX

All investors—from individuals such as yourself to the managers of huge institutional funds—face a basic decision, namely that of setting an investment strategy. What method will be used to make actual security selections? As we discussed in the previous chapter, there are basically two broad choices: passive investment or active selection.

The relative merits of each approach to security selection have been the focus of much research and debate. As we've explained, index, or passive, investing is based on the view that markets for securities are efficient and the resulting strategy is that of attempting to match the performance of an underlying index as closely as possible. For example, if you were interested in investing in Canadian securities and you wanted to take a passive approach, you would consider buying the i60 units that are traded on the Toronto Stock Exchange and designed to match as closely as possible the performance of the S&P/TSE 60 index.

Whether to adopt a passive or an active style, or a combination of both, will be among the most important decisions of your investing career. If you decide to take a passive approach to investing, your strategy will be to match the returns on one or more of several broad-market indexes. Your objective will be to do so with as small a tracking error as possible.

Enter the FPX Indexes

Until recently, few tools of measurement were available to passive investors. However, in 1998, in order to assist passive investors' selection and to provide active investors with a measuring stick to gauge the performance of their portfolios, Richard Croft and Eric Kirzner (a co-author this book) helped plug the gap. They designed a set of passive indexes for the *Financial Post* (now part of the *National Post*) as performance measures for diversified investment portfolios. These indexes have proved to be very popular and are published daily in the *National Post*. We believe you will find them useful as performance measurement and comparison devices.

The FPX Indexes are based on conventional strategic or long-term asset allocation models, with debt/equity mixes spanning the range of 30/70 to 70/30. To be a proper index of market performance and to serve as a useful benchmark, we believe each index should have the following characteristics:

- *Investable:* You can actually buy it.
- *Reportable:* You can describe its performance with a number.
- *Transparent:* You know and understand how it is constructed and how it is used.

The FPX Indexes were designed to meet all of those criteria.

Components of the FPX Indexes

There are three FPX Indexes, each based on conventional strategic or long-term asset allocation models, as mentioned above. The three indexes are a conservative Income Index, a Balanced Index, and the most aggressive, the Growth Index. The three indexes and their components are as follows:

FPX INDEX COMPONENTS

INDEX	ASSET ALLOCATION PERCENTAGE		
	Cash and Equivalent	Fixed Income	Equity
FPX Income	20%	50%	30%
FPX Balanced	10	40	50
FPX Growth	5	25	70

The FPX Income Portfolio is the most conservative of the three benchmarks and consists of 20 percent in a 91-day T-bill, 50 percent evenly split among three Government of Canada bonds spanning the maturity structure, and 30 percent in equities allocated between i60s (based on the S&P/TSE 60 Index) and SPDRs (based on the S&P 500).

The FPX Balanced Portfolio is a classic 50/50 portfolio and consists of 10 percent in a 91-day T-bill, 40 percent evenly split among the three Government of Canada bonds described above, and 50 percent in equities allocated among i60s, SPDRs, and the five iShares (based on five separate international indexes) that met our criteria. You will recall that iShares were described in chapter 16.

The FPX Growth Portfolio is the most aggressive portfolio of the three and consists of 5 percent in a 91-day T-bill, 25 percent allocated strictly to the medium-term bond, and 70 percent in equities allocated among i60s, SPDRs, and the five iShares.

To select the country percentage composition in the portfolios, Croft and Kirzner attempted to replicate what Canadian investors are doing with the equity components of the portfolios and used equity mutual funds as their proxies. They calculated the respective aggregate asset values of broadly diversified Canadian equity mutual funds (excluding dividend income funds, small-cap funds, and other specialized funds), U.S. equity mutual funds, and international equity mutual funds, and used the values as the weights for the portfolios.

The Cash Component

The cash component is designed to provide nominal capital preservation and liquidity for the portfolios. Given the overriding goal of objectivity for the FPX portfolio, they selected Government of Canada 91-day Treasury bills. (Although money market mutual funds would have been suitable alternatives, they said at the time that they didn't want to violate the prime directive—"keeping their grubby hands out of the cookie jar!")

Treasury bills are pure discount securities (i.e., they are purchased at a discount to mature at par value). The yields quoted in the financial press are bond-equivalent yields based on simple interest and do not reflect true effective yields.

Normally, Treasury bills are issued and traded in $100,000 minimum denominations, although smaller units are available from some brokerage firms. Treasury bills are generally good interest rate hedges since they keep pace with short-term interest rate changes. They are highly liquid and have little or no interest rate risk exposure.

The Fixed-Income Component

The income-oriented portion of the portfolios was designed to provide nominal capital preservation and to generate periodic income cash flow for spending or reinvestment. To get a cross-section of maturities, they chose the "on-the-run" (or bellwether) Government of Canada bonds maturing in 3, 10, and 30 years. Government of Canada bonds were selected as they are free of default risk, thus avoiding active selection of credit risk levels with provincials or high-quality corporates. Although Government of Canada bonds are issued in par values or maturity values of $1,000 and multiples thereof, they are typically quoted in the financial press in terms of $100 par value. A quote of 108.30 means $1,083 per $1,000 par value.

The Equity Component

The third category in the FPX portfolios is equity. This category is designed primarily for capital growth and secondarily for dividend income. They used exchange-traded index funds (ETIFs) for a number of reasons, the most important of which are the following:

- They are strictly passive products.

- Their unique design allows them to track the underlying index very closely.

- They are relatively low-cost products. (For example, the bid/ask spreads on i60s and SPDRs are usually at the minimum. Maintenance expenses are extremely low for i60s and SPDRs, although they can run as high as 98 basis points for iShares.)

The Canadian equity product is the i60, the U.S. component is Standard & Poor's Depositary Receipts (SPDRs), and the international component they selected is iShares Morgan Stanley Capital International (MSCI) Index Funds.

They made their allocation to the non-North American countries by using an optimization program that was designed to replicate the MSCI Europe, Australasia, and Far East (EAFE) index as inexpensively and with as few countries as possible. Accordingly, the allocations in the indexes are to five different iShares country series, which are tied to MSCI country indexes. The countries are France, Germany, Japan, Mexico, and the United Kingdom.

For over three decades now, the MSCI indexes have been the most widely followed measures of market performance. MSCI publishes a number of broad and sub indexes. The MSCI All Countries Index is comprised of 50 countries, consisting of 22 developed countries and 28 emerging-markets countries. Each country sub-index is designed to replicate the performance of the broad equity market for the country on the basis of significant coverage of market capitalization. (At present, the target is 85 percent.) The largest components of the index are the U.S. (49.1 percent), Japan (10.7 percent), and the United Kingdom (9.3 percent).

The MSCI group also published two broad subsets of the All Countries Index, namely the 23-country developed market index (all 22 of the countries in All Countries plus Luxembourg) as well as a 28-country emerging-markets index. Each of these is further available in country, region, and value/growth forms. The best known of the sub-indexes is EAFE, which is comprised of 21 developed equity markets. Specifically excluded from EAFE are North American markets. The world market covered by MSCI has an estimated market capitalization of $18.6 trillion.

How the FPX Indexes Are Constructed

The overall objective was to create a passive yet investable and user-friendly set of indexes. The intention was to make the portfolio as neutral and objective as possible (i.e., the asset allocations and composition should be forward-looking and should not reflect the bias or views of the designers).

In order to fulfill the mandate of making the indexes investable, reportable, and transparent, a number of decisions had to be made. Here are the technical aspects of the three indexes and how they are maintained and revised.

- *Base year and index level:* The base period for all three indexes is April 1, 1996. Each of the indexes was initially set at a value of 1,000 as at the base period.

- *A representative and realistic portfolio size:* Each of the three indexes is based on an assumed portfolio size of $100,000. Their research indicates that this portfolio size is relatively representative of the average investment portfolios held by *National Post* readers.

- *Denominated in the Canadian dollar:* The indexes are denominated and expressed in Canadian dollars. Although each portfolio/index is marked-to-market daily in Canadian dollars, the U.S. investments are held in U.S. dollars within the portfolio.

- *Treatment of interest income:* Interest accrues daily on Government of Canada Treasury bills and Government of Canada bonds. The interest is calculated as earned in a daily mark-to-market; as a result, the closing index level includes the interest income accrued that day. However, interest is not earned on the accrued interest. The actual interest is deemed to be received when paid on the specific payment dates, and is then reinvested in Treasury bills.

- *Treatment of dividend income:* ETIFs generally pay dividends quarterly (i60s and SPDRs) or annually (iShares). No accrual of dividends is assumed. The actual dividend income is deemed to be received on the payment date and is immediately reinvested in the Treasury bills, subject to rebalancing on April 1.

- *Whole numbers only:* No fractional bonds, shares, or units are purchased. Instead, purchases are rounded down to whole numbers and the remainder is allocated to the cash account.

- *Index reporting:* Each index is marked-to-market in Canadian dollars at the close of markets each day. The indexes are reported in the *National Post* daily and reflect any surplus cash, accrued interest, and closing bond, share, and units values.

- *Commissions and other transaction costs:* Commissions and other transaction costs (other than the bid/ask spreads that are implicit in market pricing) are not included in the index calculations. Croft and Kirzner estimated the initial commissions associated with purchasing a $100,000 version of each of the three portfolios as follows: $325 for FPX Income; $700 for FPX Balanced; and $975 for FPX Growth. No taxes, personal or otherwise, are included in the calculations.

- *Annual rebalancing:* As security prices change and yields fluctuate, the indexes will deviate from their target weights. Accordingly, the indexes are adjusted back to these target weights annually on April 1. Rebalancing is the process of bringing a portfolio back in line with a target structure when the deviation is caused by fluctuations in market values.

For example, in the year ending April 2001, the Canadian government bonds had gained value, Canadian stocks had gained as well, while U.S. stocks and the Germany, France, Japan, U.K., and Mexico iShares were lower. To rebalance the Growth Portfolio, a small amount of T-bills and bonds were sold (although subject as well to a change in composition), SPDRs and iShares were purchased, and minor adjustments were made to the share holdings. These steps were taken to restore the desired target of 10 percent cash and equivalents, 20 percent fixed-income, and 70 percent growth (consisting of 35 percent i60s, 15 percent SPDRs, and 20 percent iShares in the proportion of 1 percent in Germany, 2 percent in Mexico, 4 percent in Britain, 5 percent in France, and 8 percent in Japan). Similar action was taken on the other portfolios.

The rebalancing activity was not conducted precisely to the target weights because the portfolios don't buy or sell fractional bonds, shares, or units. Instead, purchases are rounded down to whole numbers and the remainder is allocated to cash.

Why Indexing Is Important

Investors follow indexes because they recognize that the market itself has a systematic pull on a portfolio. If you own common shares, it is likely that up to as much as half of the daily returns on those shares are affected by how markets are performing. If you have a well-diversified portfolio, most of the returns—possibly in the order of about 90 percent—will be affected by the systematic pull of a proper market index.

Some investors also use market indexes to gauge the momentum and sentiment of the market. This approach is called "technical analysis" and indexes factor heavily in its use.

Most importantly, investors use indexes for performance measurement. Investors structure investment portfolios with specific objectives in mind. For some, it's to provide for a specific purchase at a future date—a house, for example. For others, it's to earn a nest egg for retirement. Whatever the objective, investors like to know how they are doing. Indexes are supposed to give you a measure of how a market (stock or bond) performed that day or over a period of time, serving as a benchmark for the performance of your own investment portfolio.

For example, if you have an actively managed stock portfolio, it is useful to compare its performance to a simple passive index portfolio. The difference between the performance of your portfolio and a passive index may reflect the value added by active management. If, for example, your portfolio earned 12 percent while a suitable or appropriate benchmark earned 9 percent, then you would assume that your active selection added three percentage points in value. (The difference could also be attributable to sheer chance!) The key is the word "appropriate"—in order to benchmark your portfolio properly, you need to use an appropriate index.

An index is simply a proxy for some underlying basket of securities. The basket can be large (TSE 300 Composite Index) or small (Toronto 35 Index), broad-based (Value Line Index of over 1,700 companies) or narrow (Montreal Exchange Banking Index). It is important to recognize strengths and weaknesses of indexes so their specific applications can be properly assessed. Some indexes are unrepresentative of a recognizable sector. Many aren't investable, meaning you cannot buy them. And others lack transparency—you don't know precisely how they are calculated and how revisions take place.

Here are some questions to ask yourself when assessing an index:

- *Is the index managed?* The problem with most pure indexes is that they are unmanaged since they do not charge management, administration, and transaction costs, or the other expenses typically associated with actually maintaining the underlying basket.

- *Is the index representative?* An index should be representative of a particular market segment. However, if it is a narrow-based index such as the TSE 35 or the Dow Jones, it represents a select segment of the stock population—the bluest of the blue chips, for example—and may not fairly reflect a more broadly based portfolio. A sector index like one based on oil and gas may be representative of oil and gas investments but clearly not so for the broad market. On the other hand, if the benchmark is very broad it has the merit of being representative, but it may not be investable. The S&P 500 Composite

Index is broad-based, but actual ownership of the underlying stocks is out of reach for most investors.

- *Is the index measurable?* In other words, can you calculate it? An index should be calculated and published periodically, and be subject to precise measurement and calculations.

- *Is the index unambiguous?* The question here is, Can you see it? The index composition should be published and investors should know exactly what comprises it and how its value is determined. Most important of all, users should know how and when the index's composition may be revised or altered and the conditions under which it may be rebalanced.

- *Is the index appropriate?* The index selected should match the investment or portfolio. A balanced mutual fund or balanced portfolio should be measured against a balanced index.

- *Is the index investable?* Can you use it? An ideal index represents a passive alternative. You should be able to actually trade it or find a useful proxy for it. Investors who have diversified portfolios face the task of putting together a benchmark or bogey to measure performance. For example, if they are holding a 20/30/50 mix, comparing the portfolio return to a stock or bond index is clearly inappropriate. The investor has to construct a benchmark index, instead.

Wrapping Up

The FPX Indexes were designed to meet all of the criteria for indexes: they are managed, representative, measurable, unambiguous, appropriate, and investable. Ultimately we recommend that you use the FPX Indexes as the litmus test—if your portfolio is actively managed and cannot beat the FPX passive portfolios it may be time to switch!

To close out the chapter, here are some numbers to confirm that the FPX Indexes have performed well since their inception.

In October 2001, the FPX Growth Index stood at 1,568.77, representing a gain of 56.88 percent (1,568.77 – 1,000/1,000 = 56.88 percent), achieved over a 66-month period. Expressed on an annual compounded basis, this translates into a return of 8.5 percent a year. All components of the portfolio have contributed to this return, although the fixed-income component has made the largest contribution.

The Balanced and Income Indexes, with proportionately lower growth and income components, have gained 58.27 percent and 58.93 percent respectively since April 1, 1996. These numbers translate into annualized returns of 8.7 percent and 8.8 percent, respectively.

The 2000–2001 bear market severely trimmed the gains on the indexes; however, the resulting index numbers are relatively consistent with historic returns for well-balanced portfolios.

Until the bear market struck, the FPX Growth Index, with its emphasis on equities, was the strongest performer of the three. The market meltdown understandably hit this index the hardest—so hard that it's longer-term performance actually fell below that of the balanced and income indexes. Looking forward, we expect over the longer term that the indexes will revert to the more logical ranking of Growth, Balanced, and Income, reflecting the long-term equity risk premium over fixed income.

18

KEEPING MORE OF
YOUR PROFITS

Canadian tax rates have eased in recent years, but they are still very high by international standards. So one of the most important criteria in building a securities portfolio continues to be the amount of money you'll end up with in your pocket at the end of the day. Surprisingly, many investors give little or no consideration to the tax consequences of their actions until it's too late to do much about it.

Investment Taxes

You're liable for taxes on any profits you make from your investments, whether it's a capital gain, an interest payment, a dividend cheque, or reinvested distributions in mutual fund units. But there are several ways to reduce the tax burden—if you know how.

The easiest way to cut taxes is to hold your investments in some sort of tax shelter, such as a registered retirement savings plan (RRSP) or a registered retirement income fund (RRIF). Most Canadian securities are eligible for such treatment, either without restriction or under the foreign content rules (no more than 30 percent of the book value of your RRSP or RRIF can consist of foreign investments, but there are lots of ways around that as we'll explain in the next chapter).

How Mutual Funds Are Taxed

If you can't tax-shelter your investments, there are other ways to reduce the Canada Customs and Revenue Agency's (CCRA) bite by selecting your securities wisely. If you're using mutual funds, the corporate structure of the fund will have an effect on the taxes you pay so you should be aware of what it is (most investors never bother to check). There are two types of mutual fund structures: mutual fund trusts and mutual fund corporations.

Mutual Fund Trusts

The most common structure, a mutual fund trust will distribute all the income it makes to unitholders in the same form that it received the money, so that the fund itself does not have to pay any taxes. This means any capital gains earned by the fund come to you as such, as do dividends, interest, rental income, etc. You'll receive a T3 supplementary form from the fund each year, showing the origin of all income distributed to you. For example, you may have received $1,000 from a fund last year, of which $500 represented your share of its total realized capital gains, $300 your share of dividends from taxable Canadian companies, and $200 your share of interest earned by the fund. Each of these individual amounts will be shown in a box on the T3 supplementary form and each must be declared separately on your tax return at the appropriate line.

Mutual Fund Corporations

In the case of mutual fund corporations, the fund itself pays taxes on the income it receives from all sources. Once all taxes have been paid, the fund declares a dividend for distribution to shareholders. This means any income you receive from the fund (except for capital gains, which are treated separately) is in the form of a dividend from a taxable Canadian corporation, and is therefore eligible for the dividend tax credit. It doesn't matter whether the fund originally received the income in the form of interest, foreign dividends, etc.—in your hands, it's all the same. The net result probably won't be any tax saving, since the fund has already paid appropriate taxes on the income before distributing the profits to shareholders. But it greatly simplifies the tax reporting of your income.

Now let's run down of the types of profits your securities may generate and the tax implications of each. As you'll see, in the case of mutual funds, the treatment will be different depending on whether the fund is structured as a trust or a corporation. Remember that fund units held inside a registered plan are not taxable.

Capital Gains

Whenever you sell shares, mutual fund units, or any other security for a higher price than you originally paid, you've made a capital gain. However, the amount subject to tax will be affected by several factors: load charges, disposition costs, reinvested distributions, and capital gains distributions.

Load Charges

If you paid a commission to purchase the security, this amount can be added to your purchase price for tax purposes, producing a higher "adjusted cost base."

Disposition Costs

Any expenses associated with the sale, such as a brokerage commission or a redemption fee, can be subtracted from the proceeds of the sale before calculating the tax owed.

Reinvested Distributions

In the case of mutual funds, if you have directed that distributions be used to purchase additional units, these amounts can be added to the adjusted cost base.

Here's how some of these costs can affect your tax payable. Suppose, for example, you buy 100 shares in a no-load mutual fund for $10 each (total: $1,000) and later sell them for $15 each (total: $1,500). You would have a capital gain of $500. However, if you paid a front-end load of 5 percent, you would add $50 to the amount of your original investment, producing an adjusted cost base of $1,050 and reducing the capital gain to $450. If you were charged a $25 fee for closing your account, you would subtract this from the gross proceeds of the sale, reducing the net amount to $1,475 and the capital gain to $425. Of this amount, 50 percent will be taxable.

Note that you must sell or otherwise dispose of your units (such as by contributing them to a self-directed RRSP or exchanging them for units in another fund) to trigger the tax liability. Unrealized capital gains are not taxed. The first 50 percent of any capital gain is free; the balance is added to your income and taxed accordingly.

One way to avoid a big tax bite when you eventually sell mutual fund units is by crystallizing capital gains when circumstances are right. Here's one way to do it, using as an example 500 units of XYZ Fund originally purchased at $10, now worth $4 (funds can take that kind of beating occasionally, as we saw when the high-tech sector crashed in 2000–2001). We'll assume the portfolio also holds 1,000 units of DEF Fund, which were purchased at $60. We'll say the current value of the DEF units is $65 each, and that the taxpayer sells 600 of them.

Purchase price of XYZ units	$5,000
Revenue from sale at current market	2,000
Loss	(3,000)
Amount eligible for capital loss (50%)	1,500
Purchase price of DEF units	36,000
Revenue from sale of 600 shares of DEF Fund	39,000
Capital gain from sale of fund units	3,000
Taxable capital gain (50%)	1,500
Net capital gain for tax purposes	0
Tax payable	0

In this case, the taxpayer crystallized the capital gain on 600 DEF Fund units, but the profit was offset by the loss on the sale of the units in XYZ Fund. The taxpayer can now repurchase the 600 DEF units at the new cost base of $65, thereby reducing future tax liability by $5 a share. The other 400 DEF shares retain their original cost base.

Capital Gains Distributions

Even if you don't sell any mutual fund units, you may be credited with capital gains for tax purposes if the fund distributes some of the profits it makes from the sale of securities to unitholders. These will be indicated in Box 21 of the T3 supplementary slip. These capital gains are treated the same way for tax purposes as those explained above.

Capital gains distributions can sometimes leave mutual fund investors confused and angry. For example, we know of an investor who owned 1,000 units in Templeton Growth Fund in his regular brokerage account. Early in 1999, he received a T3 slip from the company, advising him he had to pay taxes on $1,330, which was his share of the money that Templeton Growth distributed to its unitholders at the end of their fiscal year in June 1998.

This investor couldn't believe it. Templeton Growth gained only a fractional 0.65 percent in 1998—effectively, it broke even. He hadn't sold any of his units. So how could be possibly be on the hook for taxes on such a large amount of money?

Unfortunately, that's the way the system works. If Templeton Growth had gained 15 percent over the year, he probably wouldn't have thought twice about the tax. But in this situation, he actually ended up out of pocket for the year on this investment.

Here's how. The investor was a resident of British Columbia, in the highest tax bracket. Since the distribution consisted entirely of capital gains payments, he had to pay at a rate of 40.62 percent, the rate that applied to capital gains for the 1998 tax year. That added $540.25 to his tax bill. He was furious.

He would have been even angrier had he owned units of the Trimark Canadian Fund. During 1998, the total return on the fund was –4.11 percent. However, investors received a distribution that totalled $2.3179 per unit. Of that, $0.1653 was received in the form of dividends, with the rest treated as capital gains. For a top-bracket B.C. resident with 1,000 units, that translated into a tax liability of $934.86 for that year. And this for a fund that *lost* money during the year!

These are not isolated occurrences. They happen all the time but most people only notice in years when the fund in question loses money or shows only a marginal gain. We saw a repeat of the situation in 2000, when many fund managers sold stocks to lock in capital gains as the market was retreating. The net result was that in many cases the total return for the fund that year was down, but investors who held units outside registered plans received taxable distributions.

The way to deal with this problem is to contact your broker or the mutual fund company before the actual distribution date and ask what payments are expected. Many fund companies release preliminary estimates of their year-end distributions in late November and early December. If you find that a fund you own is expected to make a large payment, you may wish to temporarily switch your assets into a money market fund within the same company. This will avoid the taxable event, and you can switch back once the distribution has been made.

You won't lose any money this way. The net asset value per unit will be reduced by the amount of the distribution. So suppose your units are worth $10 each and you switch to a money market fund the day before a $1 distribution is made. You will avoid the taxable payment. When you switch back, you'll acquire the units again at $9. You should end up just about where you started in terms of total value because you'll own more units, and you'll have avoided a tax bill.

Just be sure that the switches are done without incurring any sales commissions or switching fees.

Canadian Dividends

Any dividends from taxable Canadian corporations that you receive from mutual funds, stocks, or preferred shares must be declared for tax purposes. However, you're allowed to claim the dividend tax credit in connection with these payments, thus reducing the tax impact. You should receive a T3 slip that shows the actual amount of dividends credited to you, the taxable amount of dividends eligible for the dividend tax credit (which will be higher because of a technical process called the "gross-up"), and the amount of dividend tax credit you can claim.

Foreign Dividends

Any dividends from foreign sources will be shown separately on your T3 supplementary, as will any tax withheld at source. Taxes withheld by another country may be eligible for a foreign tax credit on your Canadian return. This won't be the case, however, if the dividend is received in a RRIF or RRSP. Any foreign withholding tax paid in that situation is lost—you have no recourse under current tax regulations. However, recent amendments to the Canada-U.S. Tax Treaty have ended the requirement that tax be withheld on dividends paid to registered plans from U.S. companies, the main source of this problem in the past. Note that dividends from foreign corporations received outside a registered plan are not eligible for the dividend tax credit.

Interest

Any interest income credited to you will be shown on a T3 supplementary, headed "Other Income." This may be interest earned from a bond, GIC, mutual fund, bank account, or other source. Any such income will be subject to tax at your marginal rate (the rate you pay on the last dollar you earn) and is not eligible for any special tax treatment.

Note that tax is payable on interest income even though you have not actually received any money. If you have any compounding investments, such as GICs or Canada Savings Bonds, you are required to report the interest earned during each "investment year." This is the latest 12-month period that ends in the tax year for which you are filing a return. For example, suppose you invested in a five-year GIC on July 1, 2001. You do not have to report any accrued interest on your 2001 return. But on your 2002 return, you must report the total amount credited to you for the year ending June 30, 2001.

Rental Income

If you own units in a real estate mutual fund or real estate investment trust (REIT), some of the income you receive may be from rents. This income is eligible for special treatment because capital cost allowance (CCA) may be used to shelter part or all of it from tax. The REIT or mutual fund company will normally make the necessary calculations on your behalf. However, you should be aware that any tax advantages gained in this way may be partially offset when you sell your units in the fund through the application of an "adjusted cost base." This is a calculation that subtracts the value of tax-sheltered distributions from the price you originally paid for your shares or units to determine liability for capital gains tax.

For example, let's say you purchase shares in the Riocan REIT for $10 and receive $1 worth of tax-deferred distributions. Your new adjusted cost base will be $9 ($10 − $1 = $9). If you sell your shares for $12, you will have to pay tax at the capital gains rate on $1.50 per unit ($12 − $9 = $3 × 50% = $1.50).

If you receive income from a rental property that you own, a different set of rules apply and you are allowed to claim a range of deductions. See the CCRA guide titled *Rental Income* for details.

Royalty Trust Income

Many royalty income trusts and the mutual funds that invest in them pay cash distributions that are tax deferred in whole or in part. Such payments are technically known as "return of capital" and do not have to be declared on your return in the year they are received. However, the adjusted cost base rules described above will apply in this situation, affecting your capital gains tax liability when you sell.

Year 2001 Tax Rates

You'll pay tax at different rates depending on the type of distribution you receive from the mutual fund company. The applicable tax rates in all brackets for dividends, interest, and capital gains are below. They were prepared by Gena Katz, Principal, Ernst & Young Tax Practice and are reproduced here with permission. The dollar amounts are taxable income (not gross income). The tax rates are combined 2001 federal and provincial rates on employment income, incorporating all budget changes to September 2001. They include surtaxes and provincial tax reductions, where applicable. The basic personal tax credit has also been taken into account. All rates assume the investment income is being earned on top of a base salary. Tax on capital gains, when applicable, is only paid on half of the total gain. The rates shown below take that into account and represent the effective rate for the full capital gain. Dividend rates apply to the actual amount of dividends received from taxable Canadian corporations, not the grossed-up amount.

Special Tip: If you'd like a precise analysis of your tax situation and have access to the Internet, log on to the Ernst & Young Web site (**www.eycan.com**) and go to the tax page. There you'll find a special Personal Tax Calculator. Enter your estimated taxable income and your province of residence and it will determine your approximate tax liability and tell you your marginal tax rate for regular income, dividends, and capital gains. The section also offers an RRSP Tax Calculator and a weekly column, "EY Tax Mailbag." It's a free service.

2001 MARGINAL TAX RATES

TAXABLE INCOME	INTEREST	CAPITAL GAINS	DIVIDENDS
British Columbia			
$7,412 to $8,000	16.00%	3.33%	8.00%
$8,000 to $30,484	23.30%	5.08%	11.65%
$30,484 to $30,754	26.50%	9.08%	13.25%
$30,754 to $60,969	32.50%	16.58%	16.25%
$60,969 to $61,509	35.70%	20.58%	17.85%
$61,509 to $70,000	39.70%	25.58%	19.85%
$70,000 to $85,000	41.70%	28.08%	20.85%
$85,000 to $100,000	42.70%	29.33%	21.35%
$100,000 and up	45.70%	33.08%	22.85%
Alberta			
$7,412 to $12,900	16.00%	3.33%	8.00%
$12,900 to $30,754	26.00%	7.83%	13.00%
$30,754 to $61,509	32.00%	15.33%	16.00%
$61,509 to $100,000	36.00%	20.33%	18.00%
$100,000 and up	39.00%	24.08%	19.50%
Saskatchewan			
$7,412 to $8,000	16.00%	3.33%	8.00%
$8,000 to $30,000	27.50%	7.71%	13.75%
$30,000 to $30,754	29.50%	10.21%	14.75%
$30,754 to $60,000	35.50%	17.71%	17.75%
$60,000 to $61,509	38.00%	20.83%	19.00%
$61,509 to $100,000	42.00%	25.83%	21.00%
$100,000 and up	45.00%	29.58%	22.50%
Manitoba			
$7,412 to $8,680	16.00%	3.33%	8.00%
$8,680 to $22,500*	27.90%	10.71%	13.95%
$22,500 to $30,544	26.90%	9.46%	13.45%
$30,544 to $30,754	32.20%	16.08%	16.10%
$30,754 to $61,089	38.20%	23.58%	19.10%
$61,089 to $61,509	39.40%	25.08%	19.70%

TAXABLE INCOME	INTEREST	CAPITAL GAINS	DIVIDENDS
$61,509 to $100,000	43.40%	30.08%	21.70%
$100,000 to and up	46.40%	33.83%	23.20%
Ontario			
$7,412 to $9,878	16.00%	3.33%	8.00%
$9,878 to $12,329*	28.40%	6.00%	14.20%
$12,329 to $30,754	22.20%	4.67%	11.10%
$30,754 to $30,814	28.20%	12.17%	14.10%
$30,814 to $53,650	31.24%	15.97%	15.62%
$53,650 to $61,509	33.09%	16.99%	16.54%
$61,509 to $61,629	37.09%	21.99%	18.54%
$61,629 to $63,365	39.39%	24.87%	19.70%
$63,365 to $100,000	43.41%	27.58%	21.70%
$100,000 and up	46.41%	31.33%	23.20%
Quebec			
$7,201 to $7,412	17.00%	7.71%	8.50%
$7,412 to $26,000	30.36%	10.50%	15.18%
$26,000 to $30,754	34.61%	15.81%	17.31%
$30,754 to $52,000	39.62%	22.07%	19.81%
$52,000 to $61,509	42.87%	26.13%	21.44%
$61,509 to $100,000	46.21%	30.31%	23.11%
$100,000 and up	48.72%	33.44%	24.36%
New Brunswick			
$7,412 to $30,754	25.68%	12.36%	12.84%
$30,754 to $60,509	36.82%	19.86%	18.41%
$60,509 to $100,000	42.52%	26.98%	21.26%
$100,000 and up	46.84%	32.38%	23.42%
Prince Edward Island			
$7,412 to $30,754	25.80%	5.96%	12.90%
$30,754 to $51,855	35.80%	18.46%	17.90%
$51,855 to $61,509	37.18%	23.21%	18.59%
$61,509 to $100,000	44.37%	28.21%	22.19%
$100,000 and up	47.37%	31.96%	23.69%
Nova Scotia			
$7,412 to $10,302	16.00%	3.33%	8.00%
$10,302 to $15,000	25.77%	5.92%	12.89%

TAXABLE INCOME	INTEREST	CAPITAL GAINS	DIVIDENDS
$15,000 to $21,000*	30.77%	12.17%	15.39%
$21,000 to $29,590	25.77%	5.92%	12.89%
$29,590 to $30,754	30.95%	12.40%	15.48%
$30,754 to $59,180	36.95%	19.90%	18.48%
$59,180 to $61,509	38.67%	22.05%	19.34%
$61,509 to $79,525	42.67%	27.05%	21.34%
$79,525 to $100,000	44.34%	28.17%	22.17%
$100,000 and up	47.34%	31.92%	23.67%

Newfoundland

TAXABLE INCOME	INTEREST	CAPITAL GAINS	DIVIDENDS
$7,412 to $29,590	26.57%	5.30%	13.29%
$29,590 to $30,754	32.16%	12.28%	16.08%
$30,754 to $58,598	38.16%	19.78%	19.08%
$58,598 to $59,180	39.61%	20.59%	19.81%
$59,180 to $61,509	41.64%	23.12%	20.82%
$61,509 to $100,000	45.64%	28.12%	22.82%
$100,000 and up	48.64%	31.87%	24.32%

Northwest Territories

TAXABLE INCOME	INTEREST	CAPITAL GAINS	DIVIDENDS
$7,412 to $30,754	23.20%	4.83%	11.60%
$30,754 to $61,509	31.90%	15.71%	15.95%
$61,509 to $100,000	37.70%	22.96%	18.85%
$100,000 and up	42.05%	28.40%	21.03%

Yukon

TAXABLE INCOME	INTEREST	CAPITAL GAINS	DIVIDENDS
$7,412 to $30,754	23.36%	4.87%	11.68%
$30,754 to $61,509	32.12%	15.82%	16.06%
$61,509 to $71,288	37.96%	23.12%	18.98%
$71,288 to $100,000	38.56%	23.48%	19.28%
$100,000 and up	43.01%	29.04%	21.50%

Nunavut

TAXABLE INCOME	INTEREST	CAPITAL GAINS	DIVIDENDS
$7,412 to $30,754	23.20%	4.83%	11.60%
$30,754 to $ 61,509	31.90%	15.71%	15.95%
$61,509 to $100,000	37.70%	22.96%	18.85%
$100,000 and up	42.05%	28.40%	21.03%

Higher marginal income tax bracket results from the recapture of provincial tax reductions allowed at lower levels of income and from the selective elimination of the federal surtax.

Other Tax Considerations

There are a few other important tax considerations to remember when buying securities of any kind:

1. *Make sure your registered and non-registered portfolios are structured so you pay the least possible tax.* As a general rule, you should hold interest-bearing securities inside a registered plan, such as an RRSP or RRIF. That's because interest income is taxed at the highest rate, as you can see from the above tables. Keep securities that produce capital gains, dividends, rental income, or return of capital outside the registered plan, since these profits are taxed more favourably. If your money is being professionally managed, check to ensure these basic tax guidelines are being observed. We have seen at least one case where an investment house replicated exactly the same portfolio in a client's registered and non-registered accounts. As a result, the customer was paying several thousand dollars a year in unnecessary taxes.

2. *Switching from one mutual fund to another may trigger a tax liability.* CCRA takes the position that a fund switch is the same as a sale. If you've made a capital gain on the fund you're leaving, that profit will be subject to tax at the capital gains rate when you file your next return. Obviously, this won't apply if the switch takes place within an RRSP or RRIF. Some companies offer "umbrella" funds, which allow you to switch from one "section" of the fund to another without triggering a capital gain. AGF, CI, Synergy, Clarington, Mackenzie, and AIM are among the companies that use this approach. However, the tax-deferral is only temporary. When you eventually sell your units in the umbrella fund, taxes will have to be paid.

3. *Buying funds at year-end may cause tax problems.* Many funds make an annual profit distribution at year-end to unitholders of record on December 31, or sometimes earlier (December 15 record dates are becoming increasingly common). If you buy into the fund a few days before, you'll receive the same payment as someone who has owned it all year. Sound great? It's not. The net result is that you end up paying tax on what amounts to your own capital. For example, suppose you buy 1,000 fund units in December at $10 each, for a $10,000 investment. The fund manager declares a $0.50 distribution. You receive a cheque for $500. Because this is an open-end fund, the net asset value of the units is adjusted to $9.50, reflecting the distribution payment. You still have $10,000 in assets—only now you have

to pay tax on $500 of that amount. You're out of pocket by as much as $250 just because you bought in at the wrong time. The solution? Buy new units after the first of the year or choose funds that make distributions more frequently, thereby minimizing this effect.

Finally, to close this chapter, here are some tax-wise mutual fund investing strategies for income and growth investors with money outside a registered plan.

For Income Investors

Select securities with distributions that attract minimal tax, such as dividends or rental income.

Interest income gets no tax break, so you should avoid securities that pay mainly interest if you are investing outside a registered plan. Dividend and capital gains attract much lower tax rates. See the tax tables for examples.

Consider adding securities with tax-deferred distributions, like royalty trusts.

For Growth Investors

If you're investing in mutual funds, choose those with a history of low distributions.

If you don't need to generate steady income from your investments, select securities with a track record of good capital growth and small distributions.

Crystallize gains periodically.

Manage your portfolio so that you control the timing of any tax liabilities, rather than being at the mercy of fund managers and/or markets. Look back at the example of the XYZ and DEF Funds that we used to illustrate this point earlier in the chapter, in the section on capital gains.

Don't buy into mutual funds just before their fiscal year-end. And don't assume all funds have a December 31 year-end. Many do, but some, like Templeton Growth, have other fiscal year-ends (Templeton Growth's is June 30).

Wrapping Up

Canada Customs and Revenue Agency is going to take some of your investing profits no matter what you do. But there are several ways to minimize the tax bite. These are some key points:

- Understand how different forms of investment income are taxed, and which offer the best advantages for investors.

- In all non-registered portfolios, choose securities that maximize after-tax returns.

- Don't sell or switch any securities in non-registered portfolios without looking first at the tax implications.

- Be careful about buying new units of equity mutual funds at year-end in non-registered portfolios. You could end up with an unexpected tax bite.

- Manage non-registered portfolios in such a way that you control the timing of taxable events. Don't leave that decision in the hands of someone who is not aware of your tax status.

19

THE VANISHING FOREIGN
CONTENT RULE

The foreign content rule has long been a bane for investors in registered plans, such as RRSPs, RRIFs, pension plans, and the like. Although the limit has been raised to 30 percent, there are many financial experts who believe that it should be removed entirely because the net result is to depress returns over a long period of time, thereby leaving Canadians with less retirement capital than they might otherwise have.

While we're in favour of doing away with the rule, the reality is that the foreign content limit has become a sham. Knowledgeable investors can fill their RRSPs and RRIFs with U.S. and international securities if they want, and have been able to do so for some time. It's simply a matter of knowing how it's done and then selecting the investment products that best meet your specific needs. So any restrictions imposed by the federal government are nothing more than a legal fiction.

In this chapter we'll discuss the choices currently available for increasing your foreign content beyond 30 percent in registered plans should you so desire, and provide our assessment of their effectiveness.

Maximize Foreign Content with Canadian Mutual Funds

A Canadian fund may be fully RRSP-eligible and still have 30 percent of its portfolio in foreign securities. If you hold such a fund in your registered plan, the foreign content in its portfolio does *not* count towards your personal limit. If you want to increase a registered plan's foreign content in this way, seek out Canadian funds that maximize their allowable international holdings. Using only this approach, you could effectively increase the foreign content in your RRSP to 51 percent in 2001. This would be achieved by investing 30 percent of your plan in international securities and the balance in Canadian mutual funds that maximize foreign content in their own portfolios.

Effectiveness rating: Excellent.

Pseudo-Canadian Mutual Funds (Passive)

When the foreign content rule first began to emerge as a serious problem back in the early 1990s, a few Canadian companies introduced a radical new concept. They would load up a mutual fund's portfolio with Treasury bills to 80 percent of the assets, thus giving the fund full RRSP eligibility. They would then use the T-bills as security to invest in stock index futures on a foreign exchange. Initially, most of the funds focused on S&P 500 futures in the U.S., but today you can invest in pseudo-Canadian index funds that have positions in all parts of the world. The range and variety of these funds is now extremely impressive. Index (passive) investing is still the basic approach used by this group, although a few of these funds include some active stock selection.

All these funds use derivatives to some degree. But don't let that scare you off. These funds don't use leveraging, which could result in an unacceptably high degree of risk in an RRSP. The fund's returns will normally reflect the performance of the underlying index or indexes.

That said, there can be significant variations in the rate of return. For example, the CIBC U.S. Index RRSP Fund generated an average annual gain of 14.5 percent over the five years to August 31, 2001, while the Scotia

CanAm Stock Index Fund added just 10.3 percent a year over the same period. Both are based on the S&P 500 Index. In this particular case, fees and expenses (MER) accounts for some of the return differential—the CIBC fund has an MER of 0.96 percent, while the Scotia fund comes in at 1.34 percent. The higher the MER on an index fund, the greater the negative impact on the bottom line.

However, that's not enough to explain the difference in this case. Other factors may include the market timing for investing new cash, currency fluctuations (some funds are more active than others in terms of currency management), and the expiration date of the futures contracts they hold. (If the market has fallen between the time a contract was purchased and the time it expires, it has no value. Contracts on the S&P 500 mature in March, June, September, and December of each year.)

All this makes the management of these funds more complex than it may appear at first glance. It isn't a case of all of them being cut from the same cloth—some are indeed better than others.

Effectiveness rating: Poor. There are much better ways to beat the foreign content limits.

Clone Funds

Until 1999, all pseudo-Canadian funds were passively managed for the most part. But all that changed with the advent of the clone funds. These replicate existing foreign content funds, the difference being that the clones are fully RRSP- and RRIF-eligible. That means you can buy the same U.S., global, country-specific, or regional fund either in an RRSP version or a non-RRSP version, something we had not seen prior to 1999.

It may well have been the decision by the Canada Customs and Revenue Agency in August 1999 that the clones are indeed legal and the subsequent proliferation of these replica funds that forced Paul Martin's hand in the 2000 budget, in which he announced the raising of the foreign content limit to 30 percent. Certainly, the clones have made the whole idea of a foreign content restriction academic.

Here's how they work. You, the investor, put cash into one of these funds. That money is used to buy a portfolio of money market securities: T-bills, bankers' acceptances, corporate short-term notes, and the like. A third party (called a counterparty), likely a bank, then invests a comparable amount of money in units of the underlying foreign fund. Through a forward contract arrangement with the counterparty, the returns on the units held by the bank are "swapped" back to the unitholders in the clone fund. The bank receives the equivalent of the return on the money market assets plus a fee for its trouble.

Complicated? You bet! Legal? Absolutely!

This new innovation significantly broadens the range of RRSP-eligible foreign funds. All the big companies and many of the smaller ones are now on the bandwagon. However, we have found that not all the clones track their parent funds as precisely as you might expect. In some cases, there are significant variations in the returns, even though in theory they should be almost exactly the same except for a difference in MERs.

For example, over the 12-month period to August 31, 2001, the AGF International Value Fund gained 12.9 percent. However, its RRSP-eligible clone added only 9.6 percent, a difference of more than three percentage points. That's not the kind of close tracking that investors in these funds expect.

So our advice is to buy the parent fund if you have adequate foreign content room available. If you don't, check to see how closely the clone is emulating the underlying parent fund before you invest.

Effectiveness rating: Generally good.

Index-Linked GICs

When interest rates fell to their lowest levels since the early 1960s, the bottom fell out of the lucrative GIC market. Financial institutions, in a scramble to revive investor interest and keep at least some of the money from flowing into mutual funds, resurrected a concept that had first been tried with limited success in the 1980s–the index-linked GIC.

The idea is simple. Instead of receiving a specific rate of return on your invested money, your interest payment is calculated on the performance of an underlying stock index such as the TSE 300. The formulas used for the calculation vary according to the issuer of the certificate, but the bottom line is that if the index scores a big gain during the term of your GIC, you'll do quite well. If the index goes down, you at least get your capital back.

The relevance of this to RRSP/RRIF investors is that many of these GICs are based on foreign indexes. The S&P 500 is the one most commonly used, but you can also buy index-linked GICs that are tied to a combination of overseas markets. Because these certificates are issued by Canadian financial institutions, they are fully RRSP-eligible. Even though the return is tied to the performance of a foreign stock exchange, you do not actually own any foreign content. So you can fill your registered plans with these things, if you wish.

However, you need to be very aware of the risk involved here. Investors who put money into index-linked GICs just before the stock market tumble of 2000–2001 will probably end up with no profit at all when the time comes to cash in. They will get their capital back, but they will have lost as much as five years' worth of earning power.

The best time to invest in this type of security is when markets are at or near their lows. But that is very difficult for many people because of the prevailing negative psychology during such periods. As well, the banks tend to put these securities on the back burner at such times.

Effectiveness rating: Fair.

Index-Linked Notes

A variation of the index-linked GICs, index-linked notes are issued by Canadian financial institutions and government agencies that base their return on a foreign market. They are RRSP- and RRIF-eligible for the same reasons as the index-linked GICs. In some cases, these notes are publicly traded, which means they can be easily bought and sold on a stock exchange. They have never caught on with investors, however, and carry the same kind of risk as index-linked GICs.

Effectiveness rating: Fair.

U.S. Dollar GICs and Term Deposits

If you buy foreign currency GICs and term deposits issued by a Canadian financial institution, they're considered to be domestic content in your registered plan. U.S. dollar certificates are by far the most common. So if you're worried about the future direction of the loonie, you can hedge your bets by adding more U.S. dollar strength to your retirement plan at virtually no risk.

Effectiveness rating: Excellent, if you don't mind the low return.

Foreign Currency Bonds

Canadian governments and corporations frequently issue bonds denominated in other currencies, such as euros, Swiss francs, and U.S. dollars. They do so because many foreign investors don't like the currency risk associated with holding securities denominated in Canadian dollars, so they are accommodated with bonds in their home currencies. All these bonds are 100 percent eligible for registered plans. That's because the foreign content rules don't focus on the currency in which a security is denominated, but rather on the country of origin. Since all these bonds were issued by Canadian entities, they're RRSP-eligible. This means you can, if you wish, fill a self-directed plan with foreign currency holdings.

Bonds issued by organizations that have received a seal of approval from the Department of Finance, such as the World Bank, can also be held without restriction in a registered plan. These bonds are usually denominated in major international currencies. Just be careful about adding a lot of foreign currency exposure at a time when the Canadian dollar is on the rise—you'll get whipsawed.

Effectiveness rating: Fair.

Labour-Sponsored Venture Capital Funds

In the fall of 1998, the federal government did a U-turn in its policy on labour-sponsored funds and the foreign content rule. There has been a provision on the books for many years that people who own shares in a qualifying small business within an RRSP can increase their foreign content above the allowed limit on a three-for-one basis—three dollars' worth of extra foreign content for each one dollar's worth of small business shares.

Labour-sponsored venture capital funds had lobbied for years to be classified as "small businesses" for purposes of this rule, knowing it would help to generate sales. Revenue Canada always said no. But in 1998, with the labour funds in serious trouble, the federal Department of Finance took another look at the whole situation and decided that a policy change was needed. As a result, these funds now come under the small business rule and you can use any holdings in them to increase your foreign content. The change applies both to new purchases and to units you already have in your registered plan.

So if you buy $5,000 worth of a labour-sponsored venture capital fund for an RRSP, you can add another $15,000 worth of foreign content. The maximum you can increase your foreign content allowance to in this way is 50 percent.

Of course, you should not buy labour-sponsored funds simply as a means to raise your foreign content allocation. These funds carry more risk than broadly based equity funds and there is an eight-year holding period once you've made the purchase. That makes them inappropriate for people close to retirement who are likely to need access to the cash. Note that these funds are not eligible for direct purchase by a RRIF, although they may be transferred in from an RRSP.

Effectiveness rating: Excellent.

Wrapping Up

The foreign content rule for registered plans is effectively a joke, and the federal budget of February 2000 seemed to recognize that, without officially admitting it. The restriction no longer needs to inhibit anyone from creating a geographically diversified portfolio with as much, or as little, domestic content as they wish. If you wish to stick with mutual funds, you can now choose from among a wide range of index offerings or from a growing selection of RRSP-eligible clones of popular actively managed U.S. and international funds. You can also add a selection of U.S. or other foreign stocks to your portfolio by using the additional foreign content made available when you invest in labour-sponsored venture capital funds.

In fact, there are so many loopholes in this archaic rule that we have only scratched the surface here. If you go at it the right way, you can have 100 percent foreign content in your registered plans and no one can do a thing about it. We don't suggest you do that, but it is certainly feasible.

20

THE ADVANTAGES AND
DISADVANTAGES OF
LABOUR-SPONSORED FUNDS

There was a time when investors regarded labour-sponsored venture capital funds with about the same degree of suspicion as pie-in-the-sky tax shelter deals. Caribbean yachts, Arabian stallions, flow-through mining shares, movie syndications, software deals—all were lumped into the same category. Yes, the tax breaks were attractive; but you could end up losing a dollar for every 50 cents you cut from your tax payable.

But that was back when these funds were new. Some of them have now been around for more than a decade and those years of experience have allowed us to draw a number of conclusions about these investment options:

1. The tax breaks are genuine and attractive, and governments are making them even more so with special incentives.

2. Returns for some funds can be extremely volatile on a year-to-year basis. However, the better funds are able to produce respectable average annual returns over the long haul.

3. Some funds are set up in such a way as to minimize risk, and more such options are being offered to investors.

The bottom line is that labour-sponsored funds can play a role in a successful portfolio on a number of counts. But you have to understand how they work, and how best to take advantage of the potential benefits they offer.

The Tax Breaks

The number-one attraction of labour funds is the tax advantages they offer. Ironically, that's one of the main reasons they have come under fire. These funds require a trade union to sponsor them, which may have seemed like a neat bit of political window dressing at the time the legislation was passed. However, the powerful Canadian Autoworkers Union, for one, has sharply criticized the entire concept because it claims the tax advantages reward the rich rather than the ordinary working person.

In fact, the tax breaks can be used by anyone. You don't need to be a millionaire. All you need is a few hundred dollars (which may be your RRSP contribution) and you can get in on the tax action.

All Canadians qualify for a 15 percent federal tax credit annually on investments in these funds up to $5,000, or a maximum of $750 a year. That credit is deducted directly from your tax payable. Several provinces match that tax credit, including Ontario, New Brunswick, Manitoba, and Quebec, although the latter two provinces only allow their deduction to be used for a few specific funds. Other provinces, including Saskatchewan and Nova Scotia, have a $3,500 limit for their provincial credits.

Broadly, there are four levels of provincial tax credits for these funds across Canada, as follows:

1. 15 percent of $5,000, to a maximum of $750 a year (Ontario, New Brunswick, Manitoba, Quebec)

2. 15 percent of $3,500, to a maximum of $525 a year (Nova Scotia, Saskatchewan)

3. 15 percent of $13,333 to a maximum tax credit of $2,000 a year (B.C.)

4. No provincial credits (Alberta, Newfoundland, P.E.I.)

Some provinces offer added incentives in certain situations. For example, Saskatchewan makes an exception for the local Golden Opportunities Fund, which gets a provincial credit of 20 percent on investments up to $5,000. So a Saskatchewan resident who invests $5,000 in that particular fund qualifies for a federal tax credit of $750 and a provincial credit of $1,000. That's a combined total of $1,750 that comes directly off the tax payable.

In 2000, the Ontario government added an extra sweetener of its own by creating a special category of labour funds, known as research-oriented investment funds (ROIFs). To qualify, the fund has to invest a portion of its assets directly in projects being carried out by a university, college, research institute, or hospital. Investors in qualifying funds receive an extra 5 percent provincial credit, which is not to exceed $250 in any year (based on a maximum investment of $5,000). For qualifying funds, that brings the total tax credit in Ontario to 35 percent (20 percent provincial, 15 percent federal). Only two funds qualified for the 2001 RRSP period: the New Generation Biotech Equity Fund from Triax and the Canadian Medical Discoveries Fund. However, eligibility is determined on a yearly basis, so if you live in Ontario check which funds get this bonus before making your investment decision.

Of course, if labour fund units are bought for an RRSP (they are not eligible for direct purchase by a RRIF), an additional tax break is available because of the RRSP deduction. However, don't be misled by promotional material for these funds, which shows that the combined effect of the tax credit and the RRSP deduction can cover more than 80 percent of the actual cost of your investment. The RRSP deduction is available no matter where you put your money. The only tax incentives that specifically relate to the labour funds are the federal tax credit and any applicable provincial credits.

Other Tax-Related Advantages

There are some other tactical tax advantages relating to owning labour fund units of which you should be aware.

The "Quick Flip"

Once you have completed the mandatory holding period (now eight years, but five years in the case of investments made prior to March 1996), you can exercise a "quick flip" and enjoy another tax credit. You do this by cashing in your existing units and then reinvesting the money in new units of the same fund or another labour fund of your choice. In some provinces, including Ontario, this can even be done inside an RRSP. Thus you can use "old" RRSP money to generate a new tax break.

For example, suppose you live in Ontario and you own units in Working Ventures Canadian Fund in your RRSP that you acquired in 1995. You instruct the administrator of the RRSP to redeem the units. There may be a small residual deferred sales charge, but it won't amount to much. You then have two options. You can place an order for new units in Working Ventures or you can decide to invest the money in one or more alternative funds. Either way, you'll generate new federal and provincial tax credits that can be deducted when you file your return. However, you won't get a new RRSP deduction, since the money is already in your plan.

The "Old Lamps For New" Tactic

Even if you don't own any labour fund units already, you can still generate a tax deduction from inside your RRSP in some provinces. You'll need a self-directed plan to do this. You simply use cash already in the RRSP to buy labour fund units. They'll be eligible for the applicable tax credits when you file your return although not, of course, for an RRSP deduction. This is a good strategy to use if you have no available RRSP contribution room.

The Foreign Content Bonus

Shares in labour-sponsored funds that are held in RRSPs are classified as "qualifying small business assets" for purposes of calculating allowable foreign content. That means you can increase the foreign content in your RRSP to above the allowable limit if you hold any labour fund units, as we outlined in chapter 19. The additional allowable foreign content is three times the value of the labour fund assets. However, your total foreign content may not exceed 50 percent of the value of your plan.

For example, suppose you buy $5,000 worth of labour fund units for your RRSP. That will entitle you to an additional $15,000 in foreign content, over and above the limit. For those who have been buying labour funds for some years and have large RRSPs, this change could open up many thousands of dollars of foreign content room.

When this rule change was originally instituted, there was to be a three-month phasing-in period before it fully applied. That period has now been eliminated and you can take advantage of the foreign content bonus immediately.

To illustrate the point, consider this scenario. A $350,000 (book value) RRSP would normally be limited to $105,000 in foreign content under the 30 percent rule. But if you've bought $22,000 worth of labour funds over the past five years, you will be able to add another $66,000 to that, bringing your total foreign content maximum to $171,000, or 48.9 percent of your plan.

Investment Performance

Labour-sponsored funds are, by nature, high risk. That's because they invest in fledgling companies, which have a higher-than-normal failure rate. The funds were created as a source of capital for such companies, which is why governments offer tax incentives to encourage people to use them. If you wonder why the performance numbers are so erratic, that's the answer in a nutshell.

To illustrate, take a look at the annual returns for some selected labour funds. The 2001 numbers are to October 1 of that year.

FUND	1995	1996	1997	1998	1999	2000	2001
B.E.S.T. Discoveries	N/A	N/A	−1.9%	−2.0%	+34.7%	+18.6%	−26.6%
Canadian Medical Discoveries	+5.1%	+3.7%	+1.2%	−9.6%	+0.4%	+25.1%	−14.8%
Centerfire Growth	N/A	N/A	N/A	−10.4%	+42.9%	+30.0%	−32.5%
Dynamic Venture Opportunities	−18.8%	−10.3%	+6.4%	−19.6%	+99.1%	+11.7%	−10.1%
Triax Growth	N/A	N/A	+2.9%	−0.9%	+58.9%	−20.5%	−39.9%

As you can see, the swings can be wild. At the most extreme, the Dynamic fund went from a loss of almost 20 percent in 1998 to a gain of just under 100 percent in 1999. That's a one-year swing of about 119 percentage points!

Part of the reason for that volatility is the nature of the investments many of these funds made. Not only were they putting money into start-up companies but, since this was the 1990s, their main focus was on technology. The big gains realized by many funds in 1999 came because high-tech companies in which they had a stake went public at premium valuations or were taken over by bigger competing firms at very attractive prices.

Some of the funds continued to enjoy profits from these sources in 2000, but by 2001 the tech industry was in retreat everywhere and the returns showed it. Funds like Triax Growth were hit especially hard because they held a large percentage of publicly traded shares. This was because of share-swap takeover deals for private companies in which they had positions, or because some of the firms in their portfolio went public. Triax held shares in Nortel, Descartes Systems, and Research in Motion, among others. All were clobbered in the market collapse of 2000–2001.

However, not all labour funds are subject to this kind of volatility. Check the following performance numbers:

FUND	1995	1996	1997	1998	1999	2000	2001
Crocus Investment	+3.8%	+4.9%	+12.9%	+10.6%	+1.2%	–0.5%	–8.4%
First Ontario	N/A	+2.9%	+3.0%	+5.6%	+0.6%	–1.4%	–3.4%
Retrocomm Growth	N/A	+1.4%	+5.2%	+4.1%	+1.9%	+1.4%	–1.1%

These numbers are in sharp contrast to those we looked at previously. There are no elephant gains here (the largest one-year advance is the 12.9 percent scored by Crocus in 1997). But neither are there any huge losses. The net result may seem rather dull, but when you take the tax credits into account, these funds are actually do quite well for their investors. Certainly, they are not giving anyone a heart attack!

Each of these funds takes a different route to stability. In the case of Crocus, it's broad diversification. First Ontario invests 25 percent of the money placed into their A units in bonds and cash to reduce risk (for the B units, they invest that money in index-linked securities, so don't go there if you are risk-averse). Retrocomm Growth keeps its risk low by investing primarily in convertible debentures.

So there are labour-fund investment options for low-risk investors if you want to take advantage of them. But remember, when markets are soaring, these funds will continue to fly low.

If you want to go for bigger returns, remember that being in the right fund is something akin to winning the lottery. There is no way of predicting in advance where lightning is going to strike. That's why diversification is a good idea here. By spreading your money among the most promising funds, you improve your chances of being in on a big score.

The key point is that there are lower-risk and higher-risk labour-sponsored funds—they're not all cut from the same cloth. This makes the selection process even more important. Decide in advance which style of fund you prefer—aggressive or conservative. That becomes your first cull. From there, you can select the specific fund(s) for your needs.

Investing Tips

If you are considering investing in these funds, here are some of the issues to look at:

- *See what tax credits the fund qualifies for.* All funds get the federal credit but all won't necessarily get a provincial tax credit. Some provinces offer no provincial tax credits at all. Others restrict them to just one or two provincially sponsored funds. Ask before you invest.

- *Ask if the fund is eligible for direct RRSP purchase.* This allows use of our "Old Lamps For New" tactic, which can be done with no problem in provinces such as Ontario. But the rules are different across the country. If you're interested in this approach, ask a sales rep if it is allowed where you live.

- *Remember that the credits can only reduce your tax to zero.* The tax credits generated by labour-sponsored funds aren't refundable. If you don't owe enough tax to make full use of them, you won't get the maximum benefit from this strategy.

- *Recognize that the units are above-average risk.* The mandate of all these funds is to invest in small- to medium-sized companies that are not usually traded publicly. Such companies may have above-average growth potential, but they're also higher risk than more established firms. There are funds that invest in such a way as to minimize risk, but they also tend to produce minimal profits in good times.

- *Don't forget that you can't get your money out.* All labour-sponsored funds have a minimum holding period of eight years. If you take your money out before then, you'll have to repay your tax credits— up to 30 percent of the value of your total investment! There are no exceptions to the eight-year rule. So these funds are not suitable for RRSPs that are about to be converted to RRIFs or for people who are likely to need access to their cash within eight years.

- *Look at the track record.* These funds have now been around long enough to establish an investment record. Focus on those funds that have shown the ability to produce above-average gains consistently, with minimal risk. If you live in a province where several funds are available, a good strategy is to diversify. Ontario residents are especially blessed in this regard, as they have the widest range of funds available to them. There's no way of knowing which funds will perform best over the long term. So instead of putting all your money in just one, spread it among three or four.

- *Reinvest the tax savings.* If you put money into one of these funds and hold the units in an RRSP, calculate your tax savings and reinvest that amount outside your registered plan. A good U.S. or international mutual fund with strong capital gains potential is a sound choice. This will provide a cushion in the event the labour-sponsored fund underperforms.

Wrapping Up

Labour-sponsored funds should be given serious consideration, especially if you're on the younger side (under 55) and live in a province where you'll receive both federal and provincial tax credits. These funds are not suitable for anyone who may need to use the invested money before the expiration of the eight-year holding period.

Since we can't predict which funds will do best, make sure to diversify your labour-sponsored venture capital fund portfolio. Select carefully since some funds adopt a conservative investing style while others are quite aggressive.

For maximum potential return, reinvest the tax savings in a high-quality equity fund to be held in your non-registered portfolio.

21

INSURING YOUR FUTURE: THE ROLE OF SEGREGATED FUNDS

For a brief period in the 1990s, segregated funds lit up the investment sky like Roman candles. At one point, the president of a highly successful mutual fund company predicted that seg funds would account for 25 percent of his new business going forward.

Everybody wanted to get in on the seg fund act. Investors clamoured for them and companies obliged by making more product available. Well-known mutual funds were packaged in seg fund wrappers by companies like Manulife, and units flew off the shelves like umbrellas in a thunderstorm. Suddenly, everyone seemed to want to own this "new" investment—one that had actually been around, virtually unnoticed, for years.

Then, also like a Roman candle, the flame fizzled and died, mainly as a result of intervention by nervous financial regulators. Several seg fund lines closed down entirely. Others were withdrawn from sale. Some were replaced by new, less generous versions. Confused investors fled the seg fund marketplace.

What exactly happened to cause this dramatic reversal? And what happens now? Are seg funds still a serious option to consider?

The short answer to the last question is yes. But you need to be very selective and understand exactly what you're buying.

The Background

Segregated funds are insurance-based products. The odd name derives from the fact that the assets are held separately or "segregated" from those of the insurance company. They've been offered by the insurance industry for many years, mainly in registered plans or as a form of deferred annuity investment, but not many people paid much attention. Included in that group were the insurance companies themselves. A decade ago, it was extremely difficult to get any information on these funds from some of the big organizations. They were nowhere on the radar screen in terms of product interest.

Governments and securities regulators didn't pay a lot of attention either. Seg funds tended to be very conservatively managed, so regulators weren't concerned about the guarantees they offered in terms of their potential drain on a company's assets. As for the federal government, they were so disinterested in seg funds that the Department of Finance didn't even bother to include them under the foreign content regulations for registered plans like RRSPs. There wasn't enough money in them to worry about.

All that changed in a single stroke when Manulife launched its Guaranteed Investment Funds (GIFs) in the mid-1990s. The formula was incredibly simple and amazingly powerful. Manulife entered into arrangements with several leading mutual fund companies such as AGF, CI, Fidelity, and Trimark (which was independent at the time) to create seg fund versions of some of their most popular products. Investors were able to buy funds with familiar names like Fidelity International Portfolio, but with a whole new range of features, including the following:

- *Guarantees:* With an ordinary mutual fund, your investment is totally at risk. Mutual funds are not protected by deposit insurance, and fund managers take pains to point out that a strong past performance record is no guarantee of future results. If a fund makes poor investments, the value of the assets it holds will decline, and so will the value of your units. But with segregated funds, you have a degree of protection. Some insurance companies guarantee that, at the maturity of the investment contract (normally 10 years) or at death, you or your estate will receive not less than 75 percent of the total amount you invested in the fund over the years. Other companies, looking for a competitive edge, offered a guarantee equal to 100 percent of your invested cash—in effect, a no-loss guarantee, even if the stock market collapsed. (As we'll explain in a moment, that guarantee has become one of the casualties of the rapidly changing seg fund climate.)

• *Creditor protection:* If a close family member is named as beneficiary, segregated funds offer a degree of protection for your investments in the event you run into financial problems and have to declare bankruptcy. This protection is not absolute and may not apply in some cases, but recent court rulings have tended to uphold and strengthen it. If creditor protection is important to you, get legal advice.

• *Estate planning:* Assets in a segregated fund pass directly to the beneficiary if you die. That means they avoid probate fees, which are on the rise in some provinces. Also, assets in segregated funds may receive favourable tax treatment if the investment is being made as part of a life insurance contract. In such a case, when you die, no capital gains tax is payable on the profits. Your beneficiary inherits the money tax-free, as part of the life insurance proceeds.

• *Unlimited foreign content:* The rules that applied to mutual funds held in an RRSP, RRIF, LIF, or pension plan did not extend to seg funds. Manulife exploited this loophole as a major selling point. (The loophole has now been closed by Ottawa.)

All these goodies came with a price tag, in the form of a higher management fee. The management expense ratio (MER) of the Manulife GIF funds was (and is) significantly higher than that of the underlying mutual fund on which they are based. For example, the Fidelity Growth America Fund carries an MER of 2.51 percent. The Manulife segregated version has an MER of 3.20 percent or 3.70 percent, depending on which units you choose. The difference comes straight off the bottom line of your net return. In effect, it is the price you pay for the extra features the seg version offers.

Despite the higher costs, investors poured money into the Manulife GIFs— some $700 million in the first year alone. The surprising success of the product pushed several mutual fund companies into launching their own line of segregated products in joint ventures with insurance firms. The lengthy list included TD, Trimark, Templeton, BPI, CI, Mackenzie, AIC, and more.

Seg funds were perceived as the wave of the future and everyone wanted to be in on the action.

The Problems Emerge

As the seg fund phenomenon took hold, many investors and financial advisors saw it as a way to play volatile stock markets with impunity—speculation without risk, as it were. Remember, these were the late 1990s. The high-tech sector was flying high and Nasdaq set a new record almost weekly. There were those who said it couldn't last, but their voices were lost in the cacophony of buy orders that flooded the stock markets.

Aggressive financial planners advised clients to go into high-risk seg funds, using the rationale that there was only upside potential—zero downside risk. If the bubble burst, the worst that would happen was that they would get their money back at the end of the day. Some insurance companies responded to the growing demand by creating super-aggressive seg funds that tracked the Nasdaq index or employed high-risk stock selection techniques. Many seg funds also introduced "reset" options that allowed investors to lock in stock market gains at any time. The result was a product that was heavily weighted in favour of the investor, with all the risk borne by the insurance companies that were underwriting the guarantees.

It worked just fine for a while. But behind the scenes, the faceless bureaucrats who regulate Canada's financial institutions were becoming increasingly nervous. They saw a situation developing that was increasingly fraught with danger. Insurance companies had already shown they were not immune to financial collapse, with the failure of Confederation Life in 1994 the most shocking example. What would happen, they wondered, if stock markets went into reverse and investors suffered huge losses for which the insurance companies would be liable? Could they meet their obligations, or would there be more Confederations down the road?

The regulators decided to err on the side of caution. Insurance companies were told to significantly increase their contingency reserves against the possibility of big payouts at some future time. The effect of that decision was to tie up capital that might otherwise be deployed elsewhere, thereby reducing the profit potential of the insurers.

While this was happening, the great bull market of the 1990s came to a screeching end. The first signal of real trouble came in the early spring of 2000 when stock markets around the world went into retreat. Nasdaq dropped 25 percent in the week after Easter, but that turned out to be small potatoes compared to what was to come. After a summer rally that caused everyone to breathe a sigh of relief, the real rout began around Labour Day and continued on for more than a year, further exacerbated by the terrorist attacks of September 2001. By October of that year, Nasdaq was down more than 70 percent from the all-time high it had set in early 2000—a stunning decline of the magnitude suffered by stock markets in the Great Depression.

The potential liability of the insurance companies soared, especially those that had taken a more aggressive route with their seg funds. The only thing that saved them was the fact that the maturity guarantees on their seg funds don't come into play until 10 years have passed. By 2007–2010, when the first maturity claims from the seg fund sales spike come due, the stock markets may have recovered from their devastating losses and be back in positive territory. At least, that's the hope.

Death benefits are another matter, however. Anyone who put money into seg funds at the height of the market and dies is assured that the estate will receive partial or (usually) full restitution of the principal. The potential cost of that protection at this point isn't known, but it could be significant.

What Has Been Done

The new regulations governing seg funds have thrown the entire industry into turmoil. Several seg funds have closed their doors to new business and some have shut down entirely. Other funds have raised their management fees. However, in most cases the reaction of insurance companies has been to withdraw their existing line of seg funds from sale and replace them with a new series that carries lower (and therefore less costly) guarantees.

For example, in January 2001 Manulife launched its GIF Series 2 and GIF Encore Series 2 funds. These are basically the same products as the original GIFs, except the maturity guarantee has been reduced to 75 percent after 10 years, instead of 100 percent. Since their guarantees are less valuable, their MERs are less than for the original funds. From Manulife's perspective, the change means the company faces much less exposure if stock markets founder over a long period of time. That is certainly not impossible, as we've seen most recently in Japan.

Predictably, all this has taken a lot of the glow off what had been a booming market. Investors, rightly, feel the guarantees are no longer as attractive as they were and that, as a result, the risk they are running is significantly increased. It's one thing to be told that if markets perform poorly, you'll at least get your capital back after a decade. It's quite another to face the prospect of a 25 percent loss—and to have to pay what amounts to a healthy premium even for that. As a result, we believe that in the coming years the seg fund market will contract as investors and insurance companies adjust to the new reality. Don't be surprised if there are many more mergers and closings to come.

What You Should Do

The changes that have rocked the industry don't mean that segregated funds have suddenly become products to avoid. It's a matter of understanding the new rules and using the funds in the most intelligent way.

Seg funds still offer some important benefits. The death guarantee is useful for older people who want some degree of certainty in their estate planning. It allows them to invest in the potential growth of the stock market without exposing their heirs to financial loss. However, it should be noted that while more insurance companies are maintaining the 100 percent death guarantee, some are phasing it in over several years. Make inquiries before you invest.

Creditor protection continues to be a useful feature, especially for those in professions and businesses that may be prone to lawsuits and/or bankruptcy, such as doctors and owners of small businesses. In the event the worst happens, the assets of seg funds held in registered plans will usually be protected from seizure.

The foreign content waiver is a thing of the past, however, phased out effective January 2002. This means seg funds in registered plans are now subject to the same rules as all other securities.

Investors have to decide whether the new, reduced benefits are worth the extra price attached to seg funds, especially those that use a "wrapper" approach like the Manulife GIFs. If you're still interested in these products, this suggests some careful shopping. Many stand-alone seg funds offered by insurance companies (those that aren't based on an underlying mutual fund) carry much lower MERs. Example: the Great-West Life Equity Fund (M), which is managed by Mackenzie Financial's Ivy team, has a 2.55 percent MER on its back-end load version. That's only slightly higher than the 2.47 percent MER of the Mackenzie Ivy Canadian Fund, which has a similar performance record and is run by the same people. By comparison, Manulife's CI Harbour GIF 2, a similar type of fund, carries an MER of 3.25 percent.

Here are some other tips that may be useful.

- *Don't spend money on a guarantee that has little value.* The chance of a well-diversified, conservatively managed equity fund losing money over a 10-year period is small, especially now that stock markets have gone through a major correction. The chance of a bond or balanced fund losing money is even less. We don't believe maturity guarantees are needed at all except for the most speculative funds, and few investors are likely to be interested in those these days. Certainly we cannot recommend paying high fees to insure a bond or balanced fund.

- *Consider the importance of the death guarantee.* For older investors or those in uncertain health, the death guarantee could be the most attractive feature of a seg fund, especially if it offers 100 percent protection for your capital. This guarantee enables you to remain fully invested throughout your life, without having to retreat into low-paying, ultra-conservative securities for fear of jeopardizing the value of your estate.

- *Review the reset feature.* As we have explained, this feature allows you to reset the maturity and death benefit guarantees. Not all companies offer it, so you may have to shop around. The reset option kicks in if the fund increases in value. For example, suppose you invest $100,000 and six months later your fund is up 10 percent. Your investment is now worth $110,000, but your guarantee is only for $100,000. The reset privilege allows you to reset your maturity guarantee and death benefit to the new, higher value. You lock in your profit and, in the worst-case scenario, at maturity you—or your estate in the case of death—will receive a minimum of $110,000 if there is a 100 percent guarantee on the fund. (A 75 percent guarantee in this example would mean the return of at least $82,500 at death or maturity if the reset is invoked).

However, every time you use this option, you restart the clock. That means the maturity date is reset as well, to 10 years from the time of the new date. If you made your investment on January 1, 2002, your original maturity date would be January 1, 2012. But if you exercised your reset option on January 1, 2003, your new maturity date would be January 1, 2013.

Wrapping Up

Segregated funds are sponsored by life insurance companies, although some major mutual fund companies now offer them as well, in partnership with an insurance firm. For years seg funds received little attention from investors; however, that changed in the mid-1990s with the launch of the Manulife GIF products. These took well-known mutual funds, such as those from companies like Fidelity, and put them into a seg fund "wrapper" that included such popular features as death and maturity guarantees and creditor protection. However, many seg funds charge higher management fees to cover the cost of these extras, and that practice has escalated in the past few years.

Recent changes in the regulatory standards for segregated funds has led to the closing of some funds and changes in the guarantees offered for others. All this turmoil suggests investors should be very careful about investing in seg funds. Make sure you understand exactly what the terms are. This isn't always easy. We note with dismay that the information folders supplied by companies offering segregated funds are often very dense and difficult to understand. The mutual fund industry has made great strides in recent years to improve the quality and clarity of its prospectuses. The insurance industry would be wise to emulate this. As things stand now, we don't feel investors are receiving the required information in a form that can be easily comprehended and compared with alternatives.

22

CLOSED-END FUNDS: UNEXPLORED TERRITORY

There are two types of investment company funds: open-end and closed-end. We've already discussed the better-known open-end variety in detail—they're the regular mutual funds that everyone is familiar with.

Closed-end funds (CEFs) are another matter. Like mutual funds, they represent a portfolio of securities. But unlike mutual funds, investors cannot purchase shares from the fund treasury after the initial public offering—the fund is then "closed." However, in most cases CEFs are publicly listed, so shares can be bought and sold on a stock exchange.

Closed-end funds are not well publicized in Canada and are generally misunderstood. Frankly, we like them. We have been following them for years; there are some real good ones out there. You just have to know how to go about choosing the right ones.

Open-End versus Closed-End Funds

Open-end funds sell units to the public on a continuous basis and invest the proceeds in a portfolio of securities. The term *open-end* refers to the continuous distribution of new units (subject to a limit only on the number of authorized units outstanding) and to the fact that the issuing fund will always redeem units at the current net asset value (NAV) per unit (assets minus liabilities divided by the number of units outstanding). Units of open-end funds are sold to the public at the current NAV plus, in some cases, a load or commission. They are sold back to the fund by the unitholder at the prevailing NAV at the time of redemption.

Closed-end funds, on the other hand, do not sell shares continuously to the public. Like the open-end fund, the CEF invests its assets in a portfolio of securities according to an investment strategy. CEF units are traded on stock exchanges and over-the-counter markets; prices are determined by the usual auction process applicable to stock trading. Prices at any time may be above or below net asset value, with the latter case (or discount to net asset value) more usual in recent years.

CEFs are often specialty funds. They concentrate on areas such as precious metals (BGR Precious Metals Inc.), foreign securities (BPI Global Opportunities II or the Canadian World Fund), individual countries (the Korea Fund), and foreign currencies (First Mercantile Fund). Some, however, hold diversified portfolios of primarily Canadian securities (Canadian General Investments or United Corporations Ltd.).

In general, CEFs have lower MERs than mutual funds since they do not have sales forces, they engage in limited marketing, and they have lower administration fees. CEFs are generally more transparent than mutual funds because there are no trailer fees paid to salespeople.

Although they may have similar investment objectives, mutual funds and CEFs are subject to different evaluation techniques and performance measures. CEF valuation requires an evaluation of the discount to NAV as well as all other factors pertinent to open-end funds.

The CEF is not a new idea. The first ones were introduced over 170 years ago in Belgium, and they grew rapidly in popularity in other parts of Europe. Ironically, a financial crisis in 1890 involving the House of Baring and some South American loans interrupted the rapid growth of closed-end funds. Their image was further tarnished when CEFs performed poorly in the Great Crash, and investor interest waned. However, they have regained popularity in the past two decades and their growth has proliferated everywhere. Over the past five years, they have been catching on in Canada as well.

We like the CEF vehicle. It has some valuable and interesting aspects. The pricing method offers chances to buy at opportune times such as when the discount is large (although the importance of the discount factor is often overrated). CEFs never suffer from the "new money/old money" syndromes associated with mutual funds. The "new money" syndrome refers to the fact that fund managers may have to invest the proceeds of new investor purchases at inopportune times (such as when there is a lack of good products or when there is an overheated market). The "old money" syndrome refers to cases in which the fund manager is forced to liquidate portfolio holdings (again, often at an inconvenient time, such as in a depressed market) in order to meet redemption requests from investors.

The Discount Dilemma

CEFs trade at discounts or premiums to NAV—usually the former. Since CEF units are traded rather than redeemed, the market determines the price, reflecting supply and investor demand. This price is rarely equal to the actual net asset value per unit. In Canada, the discount for the typical fund has ranged between 5 and 20 percent in recent years, although the discount (or premium) varies depending on the specific CEF and the fund type. In fall 2001, the average discount for income-oriented CEFs was around 7 percent, as compared to 18 percent for equity-oriented closed-end funds.

The discount has become a technical measure of contrarian sentiment. The notion is that as small investors become increasingly pessimistic, they bid down the shares relative to the NAV, thus increasing the discount. Contrarian analysis says that the small investor is usually wrong at important turning points, and the increasing discount is therefore deemed bullish for the stock market.

Other explanations for the discount include imbedded tax liabilities on previously realized profits in the portfolio; accrued fees, salaries, and bonuses; the potential price impact of liquidating stocks within the portfolio; the maintenance costs of the portfolio; the degree of optimism and pessimism in the marketplace; the comparative advantage (skill) of the manager; and the opportunity to invest in restricted markets.

People sometimes buy CEFs for the wrong reasons. For example, some people are attracted by large discounts. Although buying at a discount may be useful, keep in mind that it could—and often does—stay just where it is. In our over 20 years of following CEFs, we have *never* seen a sudden change in the level of a discount or a premium.

The CEF World

Although CEFs are traded all over the world, Canadian investors typically focus on Canadian and U.S.-based issues. There are about 50 CEFs traded in Canada, primarily in the form of fixed-income and Canadian equity classes. Net asset values for many of the Canadian funds are published on Saturdays in the *Globe and Mail Report on Business*.

In the U.S. there are over 400 CEFs, ranging from pure income funds to specialty country and regional funds. There are no restrictions preventing Canadians from trading these U.S. financial products. The funds listed in the U.S. are, of course, traded in U.S. dollars, so there is some foreign currency risk exposure involved. Net asset values, discounts and premiums, and one-year returns are quoted on Mondays in the *Wall Street Journal* under the heading "publicly traded funds" or "closed-end funds."

CEFs and Rights Offerings

CEFs make extensive use of rights offerings. Unsure of what this means? Then let's go over some rights mechanics.

In a typical rights offering, the company announces that shareholders of record as of a specific future date (the record date) will receive a specified number of rights per share (usually one right per share), which they can then use to buy additional shares on the basis of a specified number of rights (often three) for one new share at a specified price (the subscription price) up to a final date (the expiration date). If the rights are transferable they will trade on the same exchange as the common shares and be temporarily listed with a stock symbol. The shares will trade at a minimum value calculated as $[(P - S)/N]$ where P is the current price of the common share, S is the subscription price, and N is the number of rights required to buy a new share. In the early stage the rights will usually trade at a premium to this minimum value.

For example, the China Fund (NYSE: GC) issued rights to shareholders on the following terms: Each shareholder received one transferable right per share. Shareholders were then entitled to buy one common share by surrendering three rights plus $13 per share at any time up to May 13, 2000. So if you owned 300 shares you received 300 rights, which entitled you to buy 100 shares at $13 per share. The shares were trading at about $19 per share at the time the rights began trading. The minimum value of a right was initially calculated as follows:

$$[(P - S)/N] = [(19 - 13)/3] = \$2 \text{ each}$$

That is how rights offerings work. Now, what do you do if you receive rights in an offering? Here are our three "Rules for Rightsholders":

1. Always take action! Either sell your rights or exercise them! On the day that the shares begin trading without the rights (this is called the ex-rights date), the shares will drop by an amount approximately equal to a right (this is called the dilution effect). If you don't exercise or sell, you lose the amount of the dilution.

2. If you don't want to commit additional capital to your investment, sell the rights in the market. If you go that route, sell the shares early in the period when the premium over intrinsic value is, everything else being equal, likely to be the highest.

3. The usual choice is to exercise your rights. Since the rights represent a call option, always wait until the final date before exercising–just in case the common stock falls below the subscription price during the period.

Types of CEFs

Now that you have a clear idea of how CEFs work, let's take a look at the various types of closed-end funds that are available. We'll focus on CEFs that trade in Toronto or New York.

Income-Oriented CEFs

Income-oriented CEFs hold "portfolios" of high-yield fixed-income or equity securities and earn cash flow on these investments. The net cash flow (cash flow minus management fees and administration costs) is passed on to the unitholders in the form of distributions. They make periodic (typically monthly or quarterly) distributions to unitholders and in fact have characteristics similar to Absolute Return Funds, in that their strategy generally is to earn positive returns regardless of market conditions.

An example of a closed-end income fund is the Citadel Diversified Investment Trust (TSE: CTD.UN) .The fund's primary objective is to generate high income for unitholders. CTD holds a diversified portfolio of oil and gas royalty trusts (recently approximately 20 percent of portfolio), real estate investment trusts (27 percent), income funds (35 percent), and utility and infrastructure funds (12 percent).

There were 31 names in the portfolio at the time of writing. The fund's largest holdings were in North West Company Fund, Atlas Cold Storage Income Trust, ARC Energy Trust, Enerplus Resource Fund, Morguard REIT, Cominar REIT, Riocan REIT, Algonquin Power Income Fund, Koch Pipelines Canada L.P., and Superior Propane Income Fund.

CTD has a mandatory repurchase program, which requires it to buy back shares when the discount to net asset value exceeds 5 percent. The program is subject to a maximum of 1.25 percent of the total number of units outstanding at the beginning of each calendar quarter.

Another such CEF is the DDJ Canadian High Yield Fund (TSE: HYB.UN). The fund's primary objectives are to provide an 8.5 to 9.0 percent annual return, while maintaining the market value of the investment. The underlying strategy for achieving the objectives is to invest primarily in high-yield U.S.-dollar denominated fixed-income securities issued by Canadian corporations. HYB is a closed-end investment trust with a fixed life to August 15, 2007.

The high-yield market is generally considered to include that of bonds rated BB by Standard & Poors or BA or lower by Moody's Investor Services.

The major risk associated with any high-yield bond or high-yield bond portfolio is default risk. There are two types of default risk with a portfolio: unique and systematic. Unique risk is that associated with a default by individual companies. The limitations placed on individual positions, plus the diversification strategy, pretty well eliminate the risk associated with any single default—the unique risk is diversified away. However, the systematic or economy-wide risk is not. In the event of rising interest rates or an erosion of investor confidence in a weakening economy, the risk premiums for lower-yield bonds will increase and the portfolio will weaken. The opposite, of course, is also true. Nevertheless, given the return history and relatively low correlations with traditional investments, some portfolio exposure to the high-yield market is warranted.

As of fall 2001, this fund had about 75 percent of the portfolio in high-yield securities. The allocation was about 71 percent to Canadian issuers and 29 percent to U.S. issuers. The heaviest allocations were to consumer products and services (22 percent), paper and forest products (19 percent), oil and gas (19 percent), and communications and media (17 percent, well down from 30 percent earlier in the year). There are about 60 names in the portfolio. The top 10 holdings, which comprise about 40 percent of the portfolio, include some well-known and some not-so-well-known names, such as Ainsworth Lumber, Marsulex, Doman Industries, Black Hawk Brewery Casino, Acetax, Canadian Forest Oil, Microcell Communications, Paperboard Industries, Derlan Manufacturing, and Intrawest.

Global and International Bond CEFs

Global fixed-income funds have virtually all of their assets in fixed-income securities, primarily bonds issued by foreign governments and foreign corporations. The primary objective is stable and regular income.

Global and International Balanced CEFs

The fund manager of a global or international balanced CEF maintains a balanced portfolio of stocks and bonds, normally within a pre-specified range. The primary objective is stability of returns. Balanced funds are either formalized (the portfolio is fixed in some proportion, such as 40 percent bonds and 60 percent equities) or semi-discretionary (proportions can be changed when the advisor deems it wise).

Canadian Equity CEFs

The portfolio of a Canadian equity CEF is invested in Canadian common shares subject to diversification and style constraints. There are only a few CEFs in this category, and they tend to have a long-term, value-based orientation.

Global Equity Growth CEFs

The portfolio of a global equity growth CEF is invested in a global portfolio of common shares (including Canada), subject to diversification and style constraints. An example is the BPI Global Opportunities II Fund (TSE: BOI.UN). It was originally created as a Canadian equity closed-end fund under the name BPI Canadian Opportunities II Fund. But it performed poorly in that incarnation and the name was changed on November 5, 1998, to reflect a new set of worldwide investment objectives. BOI is a globally diversified investment fund. It is subject to a wide range of trading and investment targets including (1) companies with dominance in their industry, (2) companies at discounts to earnings and assets relative to global peers, (3) short-term trading opportunities, and (4) short selling of overvalued companies. The fund, which is now part of the CI organization, is scheduled to be liquidated on June 30, 2007.

Management has instituted redemption rights that allow unitholders to redeem units at the end of each quarter, at the net asset value per unit less 6.75 percent, with this redemption penalty reducing at a rate of 0.75 percent to 2.25 percent in September 2006.

International Equity Growth CEFs

The portfolio of international equity growth CEFs is invested in a portfolio of foreign common shares (not including Canada), subject to diversification and style constraints.

Global Aggressive Equity Growth CEFs

Global equity growth CEFs pursue a strategy of investing in a portfolio of very aggressive global common shares (including Canada) and look for unusually high growth.

Single-Country CEFs

Single-country CEFs invest all of their assets in one nation. These funds have become popular in recent years, reflecting the increased investor interest in emerging and smaller equity markets, such as Chile, the Philippines, and South Korea. Single-country investment funds often represent the only investment vehicle available to a Canadian investor interested in specific countries with emerging markets.

A typical single-country CEF is Japan Equity Fund (NYSE: JEQ). It invests in first-tier stocks traded on the Tokyo Stock Exchange and is an actively managed, well-diversified Japanese equity fund. The portfolio concentration is on non-financial Japanese companies and the fund is as direct an investment route as you can find for Japanese securities.

The fund manager, Daiwa SB Investments, uses a fundamentals-based approach to stock selection. The objective is to outperform the 1300-company Tokyo Stock Price Index (TOPIX). The recent major allocations were 17.4 percent to electrical appliances, 7.6 percent to communications, 7.5 percent to banks (prior to April 2000 the fund was prohibited from investing in the financial sector), and 6.9 percent to transportation equipment.

The Japan Fund has transparent goals, as it doesn't try to predict the benchmark's direction and stays fully invested, typically holding less than 1.5 percent of portfolio in cash. So it represents a true investment in Japanese stocks. When the Japanese market makes a comeback, a fund like this will provide investors with maximum participation.

An example of a U.S. single-country CEF is the Royce Value Trust (NYSE: RVT), which trades on the New York Stock Exchange. Charles Royce has been the portfolio manager since the fund's inception in 1986. He employs bargain-hunting investing in its classic form. Royce is a proponent of both small-cap and value style investing and has a particular penchant for both "Fallen Angels" (previously successful companies with recent financial difficulties) and "Neglected" companies that have escaped the attention of analysts and the financial press.

As we discussed in chapter 11, value investors are bargain hunters. They search for stocks trading at bargain levels, employing various value yardsticks. Investors employing a value approach will look for stocks trading at low price to book and low price to earnings multiples, and often focus on small-cap companies as well. Some of these small-capitalization companies have little public exposure and, being ignored, are undervalued and trade at a low P/Es. Benjamin

Graham defined "value" as the lowest third of the Dow Jones Industrial Average, while managers focusing on growth will pick high-P/E stocks.

Another approach using two major benchmark indexes of the S&P, Barra and the Russell 1000 index, is to designate stocks below the mid-point as value stocks and those above it as growth stocks. Generally about 75 to 85 percent of the portfolio is in small-cap companies, with only about 5 percent at most in large caps. The range of sizes of companies in the portfolio is about $400 million, up to a maximum cap of $1 billion. Recently the median market capitalization was about $470 million.

The portfolio is well dispersed and very stable. The largest positions at the time of writing were in "old economy" companies, including White Mountains Insurance Group, Charming Shoppes, Proassurance, Arnold Industries, Florida Rock Industries, Ash Grove Cement, Arrow International, Simpson Manufacturing, Covance, and Thor Industries. The turnover among the largest holdings is relatively light—this not only means increased transparency but also means lower trading costs. The largest allocations in fall 2001 were 16 percent to technology (which it had underweighted for years), 12 percent to industrial products, 12 percent to industrial services, 12 percent to financial intermediaries, and 8 percent to health services.

The weighted average ratios for its portfolio reflect RVT's value orientation. In fall 2001, the price/book ratio was 1.2X and the weighted average P/E was 13.5X. These are very low numbers and are consistent with a value approach. The weighted average dividend yield was a relatively high 1.3 percent. A high dividend yield means high dividends relative to price—also consistent with a value approach. The fund is one of the few closed-end funds using leverage—RVT has a convertible note outstanding as well as a preferred shares issue outstanding.

The fund has a long and healthy track record. From November 1986 to September 2001, it realized an annual compounded rate of return of 13.1 percent. The latest five-year average annual return was 11.8 percent. The fund has had two losing years since 1986, a 26.5 percent loss in 1987 and a 10.4 percent loss in 1990. The units were trading at a 10.1 percent discount to net asset value in fall 2001, slightly below the fund's five-year average discount.

The fund's MER is set at a base of 1 percent. If the fund outperforms (underperforms) its S&P 600 benchmark over a rolling 60-month period, the fee is increased (decreased) by up to half a percent, according to a specific formula. Furthermore, no fee is paid for any month in which the fund's performance over the trailing 36-month period is negative.

The fund's target distribution is $0.35 a quarter, although it has managed to improve on that at times. It's eligible as foreign property for an RRSP or RRIF.

Regional CEFs

Regional CEFs invest all of their assets in specific regions. There are now funds specializing in regions as diverse as the Far East, Latin America, Western Europe, Eastern Europe, North America, the Pacific Rim, and Africa.

An example is the Europe Fund (NYSE: EF). It uses a bottom-up stock picking style, which means the managers focus on searching for undervalued European companies. Despite the bottom-up bias, the portfolio is generally well diversified across Europe. Recently, the major portfolio allocation was to the United Kingdom (around 25 percent of portfolio), France (21 percent), Germany (15 percent), Switzerland (11 percent), and Italy (8 percent). Compared to MSCI Europe, the portfolio at the time was overweighted in France, Germany, and Italy and underweighted in the United Kingdom.

The portfolio is widely dispersed—the top 10 holdings at the time of writing represented only 29 percent of the total portfolio and included Vodafone Group, Siemens, BP Amoco, Shell Transport & Trading, GlaxoSmithKline, HSBC Holdings, ING Groep, Telecom Italia Mobile, Total Fina, and Nokia.

The Golden Rules of Selecting CEFs

CEFs certainly have a place in a well-designed portfolio. But as with the mutual funds, you have to shop carefully. Here are some guidelines:

1. Select CEFs whose managers build portfolios that really match the stated objectives. At least 80 percent of the portfolio should be exclusively allocated to the primary target, whether that is a specific country or a market segment.

2. Select CEFs whose performance generally remains within a specific risk category.

3. Hold some CEFs denominated in foreign currency.

4. Select management styles (active versus passive or value versus growth, for example) that match your tastes.

5. Do not select CEFs based on the size of the discount or the level of MERs. These are important, but by no means are they critical factors.

6. CEFs with portfolio strategies that aren't available in mutual fund forms are particularly useful. For example, the Newcastle Market Neutral Trust is a "fund of funds" hedge fund. There just aren't any retail-based mutual fund counterparts to this CEF. (See more details on this CEF in chapter 10). You will also find that if you want to invest in a specific country, the only available route may be a CEF. (Examples are the First Philippines Fund and the Singapore Fund, both of which are traded on the New York Stock Exchange.)

7. As a general rule, don't buy CEFs on the initial purchase offering (IPO). Often the units will be available at a discounted price once public trading begins.

Wrapping Up

Closed-end funds, like their mutual fund cousins, represent a portfolio of securities. But unlike mutual funds, you buy them from other investors on an exchange rather than from a mutual fund dealer.

The CEF world is large and complex. If you are going to venture into it, be sure that you understand exactly what you're buying and how the fund fits into your investment strategy. As we pointed out in this chapter, make sure that you are getting what you need. To do so, look for CEFs in which the portfolio matches the stated objectives, and where the management style is what you are looking for.

One of the most valuable application features of CEFs is that some have portfolio strategies or a country focus that aren't available in mutual fund forms. The next chapter provides more examples of Canadian-based closed-end funds.

23

MUTUAL FUND COUSINS: ROYALTY, INCOME, AND GROWTH TRUSTS

Just about everyone knows what a mutual fund is. More of a mystery to many investors are the securities we call "mutual fund cousins"—the various types of trusts that have appeared on the scene in recent years, offering what sometimes seem to be too-good-to-be-true prospects.

This chapter is devoted to an in-depth examination of these trusts—the good, the bad, and the terrible. By the time you're finished, you'll have a better understanding of what these securities can do for you, and how to avoid the many potential pitfalls involved in these investments.

Royalty Income Trusts

In the mid-1990s, what seemed to be a new investing phenomenon appeared: the royalty income trust. Actually, the concept had been around for years but had never received a great deal of attention. But times change and so do investors' needs. The flood of royalty trusts that came to market during this period is a classic example.

From the late 1960s to the early 1990s, interest rates were unusually high by historic standards. The inflationary trend that began with a series of high wage settlements in the '60s, and was exacerbated as governments continued to build deficits through the '70s and '80s, pushed rates into double-digit territory. The peak occurred in August 1981, when the yield on six-month Government of Canada Treasury bills soared to an astounding 20.76 percent.

Although rates trended down after that through much of the '80s, by April 1990 the yield on six-month T-bills was back up to 13.76 percent as the Bank of Canada tried to cool what was perceived as an overheated economy. The result of the Bank's efforts was a deep recession that sent rates into a downward spiral. By November 1996, T-bill yields had fallen below 3 percent and rates on everything from GICs to home mortgages had followed the trend.

The result was to leave conservative investors in a quandary. For years, they had been able to tuck their money into such low-risk securities as Canada Savings Bonds and guaranteed investment certificates and enjoy a decent return. Suddenly, that rug was pulled away. Five-year GICs that were rolled over in December 1996 paid only 4.5 percent at major banks—about half of what investors had received in 1991.

The reaction was predictable. People began to cast around for income alternatives that would provide better cash flow. The stage was set for the entry of the royalty trusts.

What Royalty Trusts Are

Royalty trusts are classic flow-through investment vehicles. The trust, like a mutual fund, holds a "portfolio" of assets, in this case operating businesses. These assets can be anything from producing oil and gas wells to power generating stations to factories. The net cash flow (cash flow minus management fees and administration costs) is passed on to the unitholders as distributions.

Most royalty trust units trade on the Toronto Stock Exchange, but not necessarily at their current net asset value (NAV). The market price of a trust at any given time will reflect the long-term expected value of its cash flows. For example, when oil and gas prices are strong, the trading price of energy-based trusts will tend to rise because higher prices translate into greater profits, thus increasing the expected payout to investors. That's exactly what happened in 2000 and the early part of 2001. Conversely, when energy prices drop, so does the market price of the trusts that specialize in that sector, as we saw in the latter part of 2001.

Other factors that can influence the market price of a trust are interest rates, the exchange rate of the Canadian dollar, general economic conditions, and the price of other commodities. For example, the market value of the Rogers Sugar Income Fund is directly affected by the world price of sugar. The price investors are willing to pay for the Westshore Terminals Income Fund is driven in large part by the international demand for Canadian coal (the trust owns a coal-shipping terminal south of Vancouver).

Royalty trusts, then, are simply pools of capital invested in a specific business. Because they are industry-specific, when you invest in one you are exposing yourself to the risks inherent in that particular business.

How Royalty Trusts Work

In chapter 4 we discussed Harry Markowitz and the work that won him a Nobel Prize and led to what is now called Modern Portfolio Theory (MPT). One of the lessons we learn from MPT is that efficient diversification means holding securities that normally react differently to market and economic events. One key diversification principle is purchasing power protection—holding assets that guard against unfavourable inflation rate movements. Although subject to sometimes severe short-term swings, real estate and commodities have been inflation hedges over the long run.

There are different types of royalty trusts, each geared to different investor income, investment and tax needs, and circumstances. The most popular are trusts based on commodities such as oil and gas, coal, and iron, although many other innovative versions exist, including mattress factories and hotels. Most of these trusts distribute income monthly or quarterly. If there are a million units of the trust outstanding and you own 10,000 units, then you own 1 percent of the pool and are entitled to 1 percent of the distributions.

There are two key valuation and investment considerations. First is the cash-on-cash yield, which is the current one-year expected payout on the unit, divided by the current unit price. As of September 2001, yields ranged from about 7 percent to as much as 26 percent—much higher than those available on bonds and other conventional fixed-income securities.

The problem is that the cash-on-cash yield is highly misleading on its own, because it ignores the life of the underlying assets or pool of assets. The cash-on-cash yield has to be measured against the actual yield on the portfolio. If cash-on-cash yields remain steady or rise when the market value of the assets in the portfolio is falling, the fund will essentially be repaying capital to unit holders.

Accordingly, in royalty trusts based on non-renewable resources, the cash-on-cash yield has to be measured against the expected life of the property or the Reserve Life Index (RLI). This is calculated by dividing the proven and probable reserves (normally only one-half of the probable reserves are used) by the annual rate of production. Obviously, the shorter the Reserve Life Index, the faster the reserves and portfolio assets will be depleted and the sooner the investment will cease to pay off.

Take the case of a representative oil and gas trust. The fund's annual distributions were recently $1.44 a unit, or 16.1 percent based on its $8.90 price. But with an estimated reserve life of only about eight years, this translates into an internal rate of return (IRR) of about 6.1 percent a year if the reserves are not extended. The projected annual return is highly sensitive to this estimate. For example, if the reserve life is extended to 10 years, the yield will be 9.89 percent a year. Obviously, if management is successful in acquiring or finding and developing new products, it will extend the estimated life of the property, and values will rise. The best royalty trusts have been successful in doing exactly that.

A further problem is how any growth will be financed. If it is continuously done through the sale of new units, the existing unitholders suffer dilution unless the rate of return on the new projects at least equals the rate of return on the old ones relative to the cost of capital. So royalty trusts that have short lives are a bit of a "shell game." Management must keep selling new units and investing in new projects or expanding existing ones, or face rapid deterioration in unit values.

However, it is important to note that not all royalty trusts are subject to this problem. Some are based on renewable resources, such as power generating stations. The TransCanada Power LP is an example. Others are based on continuing businesses that should spin cash in perpetuity. The North West Company Fund is an illustration of this type of royalty trust. We'll give you more information on each of these in a moment.

How Royalty Trusts Have Fared

You must realize one thing about royalty trusts from the outset: they can be highly volatile. These are not government bonds. Their income is not guaranteed. They are businesses and their returns are subject to the same vagaries as any other corporation. That means the value of their shares can rise or fall sharply, depending on what's happening in the world in general and in their specific sector in particular.

Investors who rushed to buy units in these trusts when billions of dollars in new issues came to market in the mid-1990s were stunned to discover just how volatile they could be. For example, units in the Luscar Coal Income Fund, which went public in 1997 at $10 a share, reached a high of $12.65 that year. Two years later they were trading at $2.15 as the Asian economic collapse shrank international demand for metallurgical coal.

Freehold Royalty Trust, which is an oil and gas fund, went public in late 1996, also at $10 and the units traded as high as $12.70. Then the bottom fell out of the oil market and crude prices plunged. By 1999, you could buy them for as little as $4.15. Then oil prices rebounded and by mid-2001 the units were trading at close to the original issue price again.

Not all royalty trusts are subject to such violent price swings, however. The TransCanada Power LP, which came out in 1997 at $25, has traded within a relatively narrow price range ever since, never falling below $21.40 or going higher than $31.65 (to October 2001). If you want to reduce the risk in royalty trust investing, seek out the funds that display that kind of stability. You will find, however, that their yields are lower.

The Tax Advantages

Some royalty trusts offer special tax breaks to investors, which makes them better suited for non-registered portfolios. These benefits are usually found in the commodity-based funds, especially those that specialize in the energy sector.

Because these are trusts, the tax deductions that a corporation would be entitled to can be flowed through to investors. So, where applicable, unitholders are allocated the depletion allowance, royalty tax credits, or capital cost allowance on the underlying properties. Accordingly, a portion of the distributions may be "tax-deferred," depending on whether there is still a depletion or capital cost allowance pool. (Every trust is at a different stage, and some don't qualify for this kind of tax treatment.)

Income received on a tax-deferred basis is technically known as "return of capital." You don't have to pay tax on the money in the year that it is received. However, you have to subtract the total amount of the "return of capital" from the price you paid for your units. This produces what is called an "adjusted cost base," which becomes the new basis for calculating your taxable capital gain when the time comes to sell.

Here's how it all works. Let's say an investor buys 1,000 units of XYZ Trust at $24 per unit, and receives $3,500 ($3.50 per share) in aggregate tax-deferred distributions over time and $4,000 ($4 per share) in taxable dividends. He then sells the shares for $21.50 per share. Here are the tax consequences (ignoring commissions):

ROYALTY TRUSTS AND TAXES

	PER SHARE	TOTAL
Proceeds of disposition	$21.50	$21,500
Adjusted cost base:		
Original cost	$24.00	$24,000
Less: Tax-deferred return of capital	$3.50	$3,500
Adjusted cost base	$20.50	$20,500
Capital gain	$1.00	$1,000
Taxable capital gain (50%)	$0.50	$500

Even though the investor sold the units for less than he originally paid, the application of the adjusted cost base calculation resulted in a capital gain of $1 per unit, or $1,000 on the total transaction. The amount actually subject to tax is $500, since only half of the gain is included in income.

The $4,000 in taxable dividends does not affect the adjusted cost base. That money is included in income in the year received and is eligible for the dividend tax credit.

Although most royalty trusts are RRSP-eligible, holding them inside a registered plan eliminates any tax advantages. Therefore, if you want to use these trusts to boost cash flows in a retirement plan, such as a RRIF, we suggest you focus on the trusts that do not offer any special tax breaks. Income from those will be considered as interest.

A Look at Some Royalty Trusts

To help you understand royalty trusts better, here are profiles of five different funds of varying types.

Canadian Oil Sands Trust (COS.UN)

Originally, two royalty trusts owned a piece of the Athabasca Oil Sands: Canadian Oil Sands Trust and the Athabasca Oil Sands Trust. However, in 2001 they merged into one mega-trust with total assets in excess of $1.2 billion. Payments to unitholders are largely determined by three factors: total production, cost per barrel of oil produced, and the world price of crude oil. Therefore, the amount of the distributions and the market price of the shares, which trade on the TSE under the symbol COS.UN, will fluctuate significantly. In this case, reserve life is not a major consideration since the Athabasca Oil Sands are estimated to have a life of about 30 years or more.

A look at the cash flow for this trust from 1997 to 2000 shows how important the price of oil is in the equation. In 1997, shareholders received $1.58 per unit. In 1998, when oil prices slumped, the payout dropped to $1.15. In 1999, as oil prices started to move back up, the distributions began to rise again, to $1.25. In 2000, as oil prices rebounded to a 10-year high, the distribution rose to $2.25 a share, almost double what it had been in 1999. The final amount for 2001 was expected to be in excess of $3.00.

The market price of the shares followed the same pattern. From a 1997 high of $28.80, the price tumbled all the way to $15 in 1998. In 1999, the shares rallied to close the year at $25.75. By the end of 2000, they stood at $28.90, just above the 1997 high. In October 2001, the units were trading at $39.

This gives you a good idea of the volatility that can be associated with royalty trusts. The cash-on-cash yield may appear attractive, but you have to look beyond that and consider the risk involved before making a decision.

Pengrowth Energy Trust (PGF.UN)

Pengrowth Energy Trust is also an oil and gas trust but, unlike Canadian Oil Sands Trust, reserve life is an important consideration here. Petro Panarites, who analyzes royalty trusts for RBC Dominion Securities, sets the Reserve Life Index of this trust at 14.1 years (as of September 2001). That means the trust's properties would be exhausted and the fund would generate zero income after that time, if nothing were done.

That's one of the main questions when you consider investing in a trust of this type: Is anything being done to extend the reserve life? In this case, the answer is a strong yes. Pengrowth's management has steadily added new reserves over the years to ensure that the trust continues to remain viable. In fact, the RLI is longer today than it was a couple of years ago—proof of management's success in making needed acquisitions.

The pattern for distributions and share price movement is the same as that displayed by the Canadian Oil Sands Trust, with payouts running at record levels in mid-2000. That's no surprise, because the two are involved in the same business, with the same basic variables. The difference here is reserve life and how it is managed. Because reserve life in this case is only about half of that projected for Canadian Oil Sands, investors demand a higher return. In September 2001, the cash-on-cash yield of this trust for 2001 was estimated at 20.7 percent. Canadian Oil Sands, by contrast, traded at a price that generated a cash-on-cash yield of only 8.2 percent. Longer reserve life makes a big difference!

Luscar Coal Income Fund (LUS.UN)

Oil prices went into a slump in 1998 but rapidly recovered. Coal prices went into a slump and didn't recover. World demand dropped, and as a result, investors in this trust ended up licking their wounds.

This is a textbook example of how the bottom can fall out of a commodity-based royalty trust. In 1997, shareholders received $1.10 a unit, which had an original price of $10. The next year wasn't quite as good, but the $1.02 distribution was quite acceptable. Then came the collapse. The Asian flu of 1997 hit Luscar's Far East markets hard. Distributions slumped to $0.54 per unit in 1999. At year-end, the trust announced it was suspending all distributions for 2000. The share price reacted accordingly. By late 1999, the original $10 units were trading as low as $2.15. In early 2000, they fell all the way to $0.65 before rallying somewhat.

Finally, in early 2001, investors were put out of their misery by a takeover bid from Sherritt International and the Ontario Teachers' Pension Plan. They grabbed the troubled trust for the bargain price of $4 a unit.

Net result for investors: no income for more than a year and a huge capital loss. It can happen that way with certain types of royalty trusts.

TransCanada Power LP (TPL.UN)

As we have already noted, not all royalty trusts are vulnerable to the winds of commodity pricing. This one isn't. TransCanada Power LP owns six operating power plants in Canada and the United States and is building a seventh plant near Hearst, Ontario. So in this case, you're investing in the electricity-generating business (mainly hydro power), a renewable resource with a steady cash flow.

The cash-on-cash yield here won't be anywhere near as high as you'll receive from an energy trust like Pengrowth. But you aren't assuming anything like the same degree of risk, either. Distributions from this trust have been steady and gradually increasing. In 1998, shareholders received $2.13 a unit. In 1999, distributions rose modestly to $2.28. In 2000, distributions totalled $2.40, and the final payment for 2001 was expected to be $2.49. Solid, steady stuff.

Predictably, the market price has been fairly stable as well. However, the shares traded at record highs in the fall of 2001, driven by interest rate decline. With a cash-on-cash yield in the 8 percent range, investors saw these units as a good alternative to bonds and other fixed-income securities and the money flowed in.

Compared to the high action of the oil and coal trusts, this fund may seem rather dull. But if you're looking for above-average cash flow at relatively low risk, it may be right up your alley.

North West Company Fund (NWF.UN)

Finally, here's a royalty trust that has nothing to do with resources of any kind. This is the old North West Company—yes, the one you read about in your history books. It operates general stores across the Canadian north and Alaska and has reconstituted itself as a royalty trust.

Commodity price movements have no impact here. Neither do economic cycles—people still have to eat and buy clothes, whatever the conditions. So in this case you are investing in a specialized retail operation with steady cash flow, gradual increases in distributions, and not much risk. Shareholders received $1.00 a unit in the 12 months to the end of January 1999, and $1.44 a unit in the year to January 29, 2000. The total distribution for the year to the end of January 2001 was $1.44, and the payment for the year to January 2002 was expected to be $1.46.

The trading price has been more volatile than you might expect, given these steady payments, with interest rates a driving factor. Units dropped as low as $9.80 in 2000 as interest rates rose, but by the autumn of 2001 they were trading at over $16, as central banks aggressively lowered rates in an effort to restart the sagging economy.

Real Estate Investment Trusts (REITs)

Real estate investment trusts (REITs) are a special type of royalty trust. They specialize in real property, anything from office buildings to long-term care facilities.

For illiquid assets such as real estate, a closed-end fund like this makes the good sense. Open-ended or "mutual" real estate funds are subject to new money and redemption problems that these closed-end trusts avoid. In fact, the birth of REITs in Canada can be traced directly to the liquidity crisis encountered by open-end real estate mutual funds in the 1991–92 real estate collapse. Faced with redemption demands from unitholders, the funds were presented with the unpalatable option of selling valuable properties into a distressed market to raise cash. Instead, they chose to close off redemptions and most of them eventually converted into REITs. Only a few open-end real estate mutual funds continue to own real property; most now invest in shares of real estate–related companies.

The typical Canadian REIT usually distributes about 85 to 95 percent of its income (rental income from properties) to its shareholders, usually on a quarterly basis. This income gets a special tax break because the REIT shareholder is entitled to a deduction for the pro rata share of capital cost allowance (depreciation on the properties). As a result, a high percentage of the distributions are normally tax-deferred; however, the amount will vary from year to year and will differ depending on the REIT you select.

As with royalty trusts, the value of your tax-deferred income will reduce the adjusted cost base of your shares. If you buy 1,000 units of, for example, Riocan at $15.50 per unit, receive $3,000 ($3 per share) in aggregate tax-deferred distributions over time, and then sell the shares for $17.50 per share, you will have a capital gain of $5,000 [1,000 × ($17.50 – $15.50 + $3.00)] before adjustments for commissions. The gain will be subject to capital gain treatment, so 50 percent of the gain, or $2,500, is included in income and taxed at your normal rate.

REITs are RRSP-eligible and are not considered foreign property as long as the real estate portfolio doesn't contain non-Canadian property in excess of the allowable limit.

REIT yields and the market price of units tend to be strongly influenced by interest rate movements. As rates drop, REIT prices rise, and vice versa. When interest rates were pushed up in 2000 by the Bank of Canada and the U.S. Federal Reserve Board, the market price of the bellwether Riocan REIT fell to as low as $7.50. At that level, they were yielding more than 14 percent. But by the autumn of 2001, with short-term rates dropping rapidly, the same units were trading in the $11 range, with a yield of less than 10 percent. Keep that relationship in mind if you're considering investing in these trusts. If interest rates appear poised to rise, you may want to defer any purchases. If you own units, you may wish to consider reducing your exposure and taking some profit.

Because REIT yields are much higher than the rates on preferred shares and other fixed-income securities, they may seem too good to be true. But remember, as the "no free lunch" theorem of investment finance tells us, anything that seems too good to be true probably is.

There are two catches with REITs. Since you are a unitholder rather than a shareholder, you are potentially jointly and severally liable with all other unitholders (plus the trust itself) in the case of insolvency. Instead of limited liability, you are relying on the REIT management to have property, casualty, and liability insurance, prudent lending policies, and other safeguards in place. Nevertheless, there is the possibility of a problem—say, a catastrophic fire or a building collapse—that isn't covered by insurance. This may have seemed like a very small risk prior to the attack on the World Trade Center in September 2001; now it is something that has to be taken seriously.

The second problem is less transparent. Real estate properties depreciate in value unless significant amounts of money are earmarked for maintenance and renewal of facilities. Since most or all of the REIT's income is being distributed and the capital cost allowance is being allocated to you, you are in a sense getting your own capital back. The book value of the real estate properties will be steadily depleting. Of course, if the properties are appreciating in value, this could offset the depreciation factor. The point is that the long-term income stream is quite variable, certainly more variable than some advisors would have you believe.

REITs have their place in a long-term investment portfolio, particularly for tax-advantaged income. But you need to understand their strengths and shortcomings. And don't buy them for capital gains purposes unless you have a clear strategy for doing so—buying at an interest rate peak and selling at the next interest rate low.

Income Trusts

Royalty trusts and REITs hold assets in operating businesses. That's the key point that distinguishes them from income trusts and growth trusts, both of which invest in portfolios of securities. The difference is in their ultimate objective. The purpose of income trusts is to generate above-average cash flow while preserving principal. The goal of the growth trust is to achieve capital gains. Let's examine each in turn.

Income trusts (ITs) hold portfolios of securities that may include shares in royalty trusts, REITs, high-yield bonds, and common stock. Income trusts are structured to earn cash flow on these investments through dividends, interest, rental income, capital gains, and covered call writing, depending on the composition of the portfolio. The net cash flow (income minus management fees and administration costs) is passed on to the unitholders in the form of distributions. Most of these trusts distribute income monthly or quarterly.

The cash-on-cash yield of an income trust is usually what attracts investors' attention because returns are always projected to be higher than prevailing interest rates (an 8 to 9 percent annual return is the typical goal). But cash flow is only part of the equation for assessing a trust's effectiveness. The cash return has to be measured against the net asset value (NAV) of the portfolio. If yields remain steady or rise at a time when the value of the assets in the portfolio is falling, the market price of the trust units themselves will decline and the fund will essentially be repaying capital to unitholders. For a poorly designed or badly performing fund, investors could be looking at the worst of all tax worlds—one in which they have high taxable interest income coupled with declining unit prices, for which there is little or no offsetting tax benefit.

For example, take the case of Triax Diversified Income Trust, whose primary objective is to provide a high portfolio return while maintaining the market value of the investment. If you focused strictly on the cash-on-cash yield, you'd see that in October 2001 the fund's $1.20 in distributions over the latest 12-month period translated into a yield of almost 15 percent based on the unit price at that time. The problem is that over that same 12-month period, Triax actually lost value for unitholders on a total return basis, with the unit price falling from over $12 to the $8 range. So investors ended up with a taxable distribution but with a capital loss that could not be claimed unless they actually sold their units. This is not a good situation to be in.

Some of the newer income trusts offer unitholders a continuous right to redeem units. For example, one fund allows unitholders a privilege as follows: "Units tendered within five business days of the last day of the month are redeemed as at that final date with payment on or before the eighth business date following the redemption date. Units tendered after that date are redeemed on the last business day of the next month. The redemption price is the NAVPU less the lesser of: (1) 4 percent of the NAVPU and (2) $1.00 per unit. In February each year the redemption price is the NAVPU without adjustment." The effect of this feature should be to substantially limit the discount to net asset value that often plagues income trust units.

A Look at Some Income Trusts

Here is a capsule look at some of the leading income trusts available in Canada.

EnerVest Diversified Income Trust (EIT.UN)

The objective of EnerVest Diversified Income Trust is to distribute a high, stable, partially tax-deferred monthly income to unitholders. It invests most of its portfolio in royalty trust units, with a focus on gas and oil. However, in October 1999, the restriction that required a minimum of 65 percent allocation to energy-related royalty trusts was lifted. The fund has maintained a monthly distribution thus far, although its original target of $0.09 per month has turned out to be overly optimistic. The distribution in fall 2001 was $0.07 per month, an increase from the $0.065 per unit that prevailed up to April 2000.

Because this is actually a fund of funds, investing primarily in other energy trusts, its fortunes will be largely governed by changes in oil and gas prices.

Mulvihill Premium Canadian Fund (FPI. UN)

Mulvihill Premium Canadian Fund holds a diversified portfolio of Canadian common shares spanning the major industry sectors. The objective is to make quarterly distributions of at least $0.50 per unit, and so far it has succeeded in maintaining that. Cash flow is generated from a combination of dividends and covered call option writing.

Despite the plunging stock markets of 2000–2001, this trust managed to hold its market value at close to the original $25 issue price, which means the managers have been very skillful at fulfilling their mandate without having to resort to repayment of capital.

This fund is one of the flagships of the Mulvihill Capital Management Group of income trusts. John Mulvihill, the CEO, is one of Canada's top practitioners of covered option writing and he has taught his team of managers how to properly employ this craft. Mulvihill's basic investment policy is to hold a high-quality targeted portfolio and to write call and put options against all or most of the holdings.

The company offers several other trusts that are structured in a similar way. They include the following:

- *Mulvihill Premium U.S. Fund (FPU.UN):* A diversified portfolio of common shares issued by corporations that rank in the top 50 of the Standard & Poor's 100 Index.

- *Mulvihill Premium Oil and Gas Fund (FPG.UN):* A portfolio of common shares that are included in the TSE 300 Oil & Gas Sub-Index. May include up to 20 percent of the cost amount of its assets in common shares from the Standard & Poor's 500 Energy Sub-Index. This trust had to reduce payments when energy prices slumped and traded well below its issue price for several years.

- *Mulvihill Premium 60 Plus Fund (SIX.UN):* A portfolio of common shares selected from the S&P/TSE 60 Index. May invest up to 20 percent of the cost amount of its assets in the top 60 corporations of the S&P 100 Index or in ADRs (American Depository Receipts) of the top 60 corporations on the New York Stock Exchange or Nasdaq, as well as covered call options.

- *Mulvihill Global Plus Fund (GIP.UN):* A portfolio of common shares selected from the S&P 100 Index and ADRs of the top 100 corporations trading on the New York Stock Exchange or Nasdaq. May invest up to 25 percent of the net asset value in iShares, as well as covered call options.

- *Mulvihill Premium Canadian Bank Fund (PIC.A):* Invests in common shares issued by Bank of Montreal, The Bank of Nova Scotia, Canadian Imperial Bank of Commerce, Royal Bank of Canada, and The Toronto Dominion Bank, and will write covered call options.

- *Mulvihill Premium Split Share Fund (MUH.A):* This is a diversified portfolio consisting of common shares selected from the TSE 300 Index, from time to time investing up to 20 percent of the cost amount of its assets in shares selected from Standard & Poor's 100 Index, and covered call options. It is one of the older Mulvihill products so it is worth additional comment. This trust debuted in February 1998 at an issue price of $15. The fund's objectives are to pay a quarterly dividend (the target is $0.30 per quarter) to unitholders while preserving or enhancing capital and to return the original issue price to investors at the fund's termination date of February 1, 2008. The trust has actually improved on its distribution targets in recent years, paying out $2.95 a unit for the year ending in January 2000 and $2.75 a unit for the 12 months to January 2001. However, it has suffered some erosion in its share price; in October 2001 units were trading in the $14 range.

- *Mulvihill Premium Global Telecom Fund (GT.A):* A portfolio of common shares of telecom companies. May also include covered call options in respect of all or part of the portfolio.

- *Mulvihill Pro-AMS U.S. Fund (PAM.UN):* One of the newest additions to the Mulvihill line-up, it offers a diversified, managed portfolio consisting of common shares issued by corporations with a market capitalization in excess of $5 billion, selected from the S&P 500 Index. May include covered call options in respect of all or part of the portfolio.

- *Mulvihill Pro-AMS RSP Fund (PR.UN):* Portfolio consists of common shares issued by corporations selected from the S&P/TSE 60 Index and from the S&P 500 Index, with a market capitalization in excess of $5 billion. So this is the Canadian/U.S. version of Pro-AMS U.S. Trust.

- *Mulvihill Summit Digital World Fund (DWT.UN):* This portfolio is made up of common shares issued by leading digitally based companies selected from the Digital World Universe, and may also include covered call options in respect of all or part of the portfolio.

Obviously, some of these portfolios represent higher risk than others in terms of market volatility. The Digital World Fund is the most obvious example of this. Originally issued in February 2000 at $15 a share, the units traded as low as $5 in 2001, a loss of two-thirds of their value. The fact that the trust had distributed $3 per unit (taxable) up to that time didn't help to ease the pain.

Split Yield Corporation Capital Shares (YLD)

The objective of Split Yield Corporation Capital Shares is to pay a high quarterly dividend ($0.45 is the target) to unitholders while preserving or enhancing capital. That is equivalent to a yield of 12 percent based on the fund's original issue price of $15. The fund's strategy, which is similar to that of the Mulvihill offerings, is to hold a portfolio of Canadian common shares listed on the Toronto 100 Index and U.S. common shares listed on the S&P 100 Index, and to write call options against all or part of the portfolio to enhance returns. Management is by Quadravest Inc.

The $0.45 per quarter goal was extremely aggressive and, although the trust has maintained it, there has been a loss of unit value in the process. As of October 2001, the shares were trading at $12.50, down 16.7 percent from the issue price.

Income Financial Trust (INC.UN)

Income Financial debuted in February 1999. The fund's objectives are to provide a monthly cash distribution of $0.17708 per unit or $2.12496 a year, which translates into an 8.5 percent nominal annual yield based on the original price. Because of tax advantages, the targeted return is equivalent to a 10.40 percent pre-tax interest return on a nominal basis (assuming the units are held outside a registered plan). To date, the trust has been able to meet its stated distribution goals.

The fund has a termination date of January 1, 2009, at which time unitholders may redeem their units at a redemption price equal to the net asset value per unit. Quadravest Inc., the same company that manages Split Yield Corporation Capital Shares, manages the fund.

The portfolio is concentrated primarily (at least 75 percent according to the by-laws) in financial services companies listed on the Toronto Stock Exchange Financial Services Index, the S&P Financials Index, and the S&P MidCap Financials Index. Dividends form part of the income stream and the manager will also write call options against all or part of the portfolio from time to time to enhance returns.

Unitholders have a continuous right to redeem units. Units tendered within five business days of the last day of the month are redeemed as at that final date, with payment on or before the eighth business date following the redemption date. Units tendered after that date are redeemed on the last business day of the next month. The redemption price is the NAVPU minus either (1) 4 percent of the NAVPU or (2) $1.00 per unit, whichever is less. In February each year the redemption price is the NAVPU without adjustment.

Income Trust Investment Strategy

The bottom line is that most income trusts have succeeded in maintaining the cash flow that was originally promised to investors. But in many cases, there has been a price to pay in the form of a declining unit value, which has translated into a falling share price. The message to investors is obvious. Even though income trusts are supposed to be lower risk by nature than royalty trusts, that isn't always the case. Before making an investment in this type of security, carefully consider what type of securities will be included in the portfolio and the degree of risk they are likely to carry.

If you are considering investing in an income trust for enhanced cash flow, we therefore recommend the following precautions:

- *Select a trust that has a track record.* There are several of them available.

- *Review the trust's NAV history to determine stability.* Remember, an important part of the overall objective of these trusts is capital preservation. A trust that shows a record of NAV volatility should be viewed with suspicion. One that has consistently lost value should be avoided.

- *As a general rule, avoid new issues, even those from reputable organizations.* There have been several innovative approaches to income trusts in the past few years, but great ideas on paper don't always translate into profitability. Let someone else take the initial risk.

- *Avoid income trusts that focus on a single sector of the market.* As a general rule, they have been poor performers. As with all other parts of your portfolio, good diversification is the key to steady returns and capital preservation.

Growth Trusts

Growth trusts, like income trusts, also invest in a portfolio of securities, usually common stocks. The difference is in the objective. Growth trusts do not throw off any cash flow as a rule. You buy and hold them in the expectation of eventually realizing a capital gain.

The biggest marketer of growth trusts in Canada at this time is a company called First Trust Portfolios. It's a subsidiary of a U.S. firm, Niké Securities of Chicago, which has been creating similar products for American investors for years.

The First Trust Portfolios are somewhat different from the typical income trust. Think of them as the financial equivalent of the dog you'd expect to bring home from an animal shelter. Mutts. Crossbreeds, with no clearly defined lineage, but a lot of similarities to other securities in your portfolio. They aren't mutual funds, but they share some of the same characteristics. They aren't closed-end funds, although in certain stages of their relatively brief life they act something like them. They definitely aren't royalty trusts, for which many people mistake them. And they operate differently from most income trusts, which are usually structured along the same lines as closed-end funds. No, they're quite different; a breed unto themselves. But if you select carefully, they're worth owning. Here's a little history and some background on these "mutts."

Growth trusts, at least those of the type offered by First Trust, are similar to mutual funds in that you buy a portfolio of securities, usually stocks, often built around a specific investment theme. However, they differ in these ways:

1. *The purchase period is limited.* Sales are usually closed about a year after the units are first offered. Open-end mutual fund units are always available for purchase. Closed-end funds cut off the sale of new units at the time the issue comes out. These growth trusts fall somewhere in the middle.

2. *The life of the trust is limited.* Typically, they run for about five years. At the end of that time, the assets are liquidated and the proceeds distributed to unitholders.

3. *Trading is limited.* Usually, the portfolios are buy-and-hold (although there are exceptions). This keeps MERs low and makes most growth trusts very tax efficient.

   Unlike closed-end funds and most income trusts, the growth trusts from First Trust don't trade on stock exchanges. However, like regular mutual funds, you can redeem units any time from the treasury at the current NAV if you wish to get your money out before maturity. So they offer good liquidity, but you are at the mercy of the vagaries of the market if you need capital or want to take profits. This is an important investment consideration.

Generally, these trusts are eligible for registered plans, although most are considered foreign content for that purpose.

The First Trust Portfolio products typically focus on a specific investment theme, which makes them similar to sector mutual funds. For example, in 1996 co-author Gordon Pape recommended the company's Pharmaceutical Trust 1996 to readers of *The MoneyLetter*. It offered a portfolio of about 20 of the world's top drug companies–firms like Merck, Pfizer, Warner-Lambert, and the like. The trust would buy the shares and hold them until maturity. There would be no trading unless it was forced by acquisition, merger, or some similar event. Pape suggested that readers should buy the units when they were issued, at $15. When the trust was wound up at the end of December 2000, investors received a payout of $44.58 per unit for a gain of 197 percent on a plain buy-and-hold portfolio.

Other themed equity trusts coming from the company have been based on financial institutions, technology, communications, biotechnology, New Economy companies, the Dow Internet Index, and the world's leading brand names. In 2000, First Trust unveiled a new product based on the Lehman Brothers 10 Uncommon Value stocks, the top picks of each year from the world-famous brokerage house.

Not all the offerings have been profitable, however. In fact, some have produced terrible results. The Communications Trust 2000, which came out at an issue price of $15, had an NAV of $6.39 in early October 2001. If you think that's bad, the Dow Jones Internet Index 1999 portfolio, which also was issued at $15, was down to $2.61 in October 2001. The strongest performers have been those that focus on the lowest-risk industries, such as financial services and pharmaceuticals. Portfolios that are diversified across several sectors have also held up reasonably well. These include the Target 10 portfolios, which use the "Dogs of the Dow" theory, buying shares in the 10 companies in the Dow Jones Industrial Average that have the highest dividend payout.

Earlier in this book, we expressed our concern over investing in sector mutual funds. The same caveats apply to growth trusts. The narrower the focus of the trust, the higher the potential risk. If you feel this type of security is appropriate for your needs, we recommend you choose well-diversified portfolios.

Wrapping Up

There is a wide range of trust products available, designed to meet both income and growth objectives. However, performance has been uneven and in many cases the risk is above average. That is not to say that one or more of these mutual fund cousins won't have a role to play in your portfolio-building process. However, the decision on which type of trust to use and the specific security to select must be made with great care. This is a potential minefield for the unwary investor. Tread cautiously.

24

PUTTING IT ALL TOGETHER

You've read through a lot of information to this point. But now you've come to the end, and it's time to put it all together. What follows is a summary of our dozen Secrets of Successful Investing.

Secret #1: Investing Is a Marathon, Not a Sprint

How well—or badly—your securities perform over one, two, or three years is not important in the grand scheme of things. What matters is how well they do over 10, 20, and 30 years. Sometimes it's difficult to keep that in perspective, especially when a particular mutual fund is tanking. Every investor has to be prepared to accept both good and bad times. What's important is to maximize returns when conditions are good and to minimize the losses when the bad times come. A well-designed portfolio with carefully selected securities that meet your specific needs is the best way to achieve that.

What kind of returns should you expect? Over the long haul, an average of about 8 percent for a balanced portfolio is good. An aggressive growth portfolio that averages better than 10 percent annually is doing extremely well. If you're able to generate an average annual return in the 12-percent range over a decade, consider yourself a super-investor. Even the best of the pros would have difficulty matching that.

Secret #2: Safety Is Expensive

The less risk you're willing to accept in your portfolio, the lower your probable return. Those who opt for a very low-risk portfolio should expect to do no better than about 6 percent annually over time, and less than that when interest rates are very low, as they were in 2001. When interest rates are high, a low-risk portfolio will perform much better. However, that kind of economic environment does not show up on our radar scope at this time.

So it's important that you maintain realistic performance expectations. If you give safety a high priority, don't then turn around and expect your portfolio to generate annual returns of 8 to 10 percent. That may seem like an obvious statement. However, we receive dozens of questions every year from people asking exactly that: "Where can I invest my money to get 10 percent a year with no risk?" The answer is: Nowhere.

Secret #3: You Don't Need Big Scores to Become Wealthy

You don't have to have 10 percent annual returns to build a sizeable nest egg. An investment of $3,000 a year that earns 6 percent annually over 30 years will grow to more than $235,000 at the end of that time. Of course, we don't recommend that anyone with that long a time horizon invest in such a conservative manner. But if that's your decision, you can still achieve some respectable results.

Secret #4: Asset Mix Is Critical

We have said many times in this book that getting the right asset mix is the single most important investment decision you can make. Specific security selection is a distant second. The right asset allocation can account for over 90 percent of a portfolio's returns over time, yet many investors don't even think about it. They just add stocks or bonds or mutual funds as the spirit moves them to do so, and their portfolio grows like Topsy. Then, when they get hammered in a falling stock market, they wonder what went wrong.

Secret #5: You Must Have a Plan

If you don't know where you want to go, you can't get there. It's as simple as that. Before you even begin the investing process, you must establish clear objectives, set risk parameters, and put realistic benchmarks into place. If you already have money invested and don't have a comprehensive plan, put everything on hold until you have time to think through what you're trying to do.

Secret #6: Be Disciplined

Once you have a plan in place, you must have the self-discipline to see it through. This is where many people come up short. They lay the foundation but then fail to build the house. Being a successful investor isn't easy. Along the way, you'll come up against numerous temptations to deviate from the game plan. A hot tip at a dinner party. A call from a broker with a great IPO. A stock that looks like a genuine bargain, even though it doesn't fit comfortably in your portfolio. You'll have lots of chances to go wandering in the desert. Do your best to turn your back on them. If they don't fit, don't buy. Whenever you have new money to invest (and you should do so on a regular basis), examine the portfolio carefully and see what weaknesses you perceive. Then act to shore them up.

Secret #7: Remain Patient

Every value-oriented money manager will repeat the same mantra: patience, patience, patience. But it can be tough, especially if you see others making big gains. If you've taken the kind of balanced approach that we advise, the results may seem to be slow in coming at the outset. But it's like a snowball rolling downhill—as it gathers momentum, it grows larger and larger, and by the time it reaches the bottom it is 10 times or more its original size. That's what will happen to your investments if you choose them with care and look after them properly.

Secret #8: Value Will Prevail

The high-tech collapse of 2000–2001 left many investors shaking their heads ruefully and muttering to themselves: "Never again." They had ventured way out on a limb and, predictably, it had been sawed off behind them. This has happened many times before in history, and it will happen again. People were left skittish and afraid after the terrible bear market that began in the early spring of 2000. But the time will come when the markets will turn around and greed will again regain the ascendancy over fear in that never-ending tussle for investors' psyches.

If you find the temptation to succumb to that "irrational exuberance" creeping into your mind at some future time, remember this lesson. And remember that true value will always emerge triumphant in the end. Benjamin Graham, Sir John Templeton, Warren Buffett, and the other great value investors of our era didn't become wealthy because they were lucky. They got rich because they understood the difference between value and speculation. It's a lesson every investor should take to heart.

Secret #9: Be Cautious with Other People's Money

Borrowing to invest, or leveraging as it's called, can be a very powerful tool for increasing profits. When markets are booming, many investors are tempted to use leveraging to increase their potential gains, often with the encouragement of financial advisors who stand to benefit from the increased account activity. But leveraging can magnify losses as well as gains. And many people are not psychologically prepared to deal with the stress that can be created when things turn against them. So be very careful here. Don't increase your stake by using other people's money unless you're betting on a virtual sure thing (such as an RRSP loan) or you can deal with the impact of a heavy loss if the markets turn sour.

Secret #10: Be Tax Smart

No matter how successful you are as an investor, what counts in the end is how much you keep after the tax people get through with you. There are many ways of improving after-tax returns and/or getting tax deductions, ranging from the humble RRSP to tax-deferred cash flow from certain types of securities. Make yourself aware of all the options. However, don't get too cute—you don't want to attract the attention of the Canada Customs and Revenue Agency. And never, never make an investment on the basis of a tax advantage alone. We have seen more tax shelters than we can count go down the tubes, leaving investors holding worthless paper. If they were lucky, they at least got to make a deduction (although sometimes even those have been disallowed). But what's the point of saving 50 cents in tax if you lose a dollar in your investment?

Secret #11: Be Prepared for Change

Nothing stays the same—not in investing, not in life. For better or worse, we live in a dynamic world in which events can move us in completely different directions, sometimes within a few hours (consider what happened to the investment climate after September 11, 2001). No one who employs an invest-it-and-forget-it philosophy is likely to prosper. There are always new dangers, and new opportunities. You most be prepared to make changes in your portfolio as conditions dictate. This does not mean you should panic and attempt a complete overhaul every time something happens. If you have a well-balanced, carefully thought out portfolio, that won't be necessary. But it does mean you should review your situation periodically (at least quarterly), do some asset mix fine-tuning and rebalancing, replace underperforming securities, and take advantage of opportunities. The aware investor is likely to be the successful investor.

Secret #12: Keep Your Perspective

This book is about successful investing strategies. But making money isn't what life is all about, only a means to an end. So never put yourself in a position where investing concerns overwhelm you or where profit becomes an obsession. If you achieve the kind of success we believe is possible by employing our principles, enjoy the fruits of your earnings and share them with others—family, friends, those less fortunate. Our run here on Earth is short enough. Make the very best of it!

INDEX